OPRAH GIRL
MEMOIRS OF A FALLING FACADE

KAYLAH PANTALEÓN

THE TMG FIRM

New York

The TMG Firm, LLC
112 W. 34th Street
17th and 18th Floors
New York, NY 10120
www.thetmgfirm.com

For Nana

ACKNOWLEDGEMENTS

When I was fifteen years old, I started telling myself I'd publish a book by the time I was thirty. I didn't know what kind of book I would write, and I for sure never imagined it would be this one. But if I've learned anything in the past thirteen years, it's that things don't always turn out as we plan. In fact, I had no idea that after my senior year of high school in 2007, I wouldn't pick up the pen for another ten years. I lost the dream I had at fifteen and any hope of creating something that made me nearly as proud as my Oprah essay. Then one day, the opportunity to publish my story literally felt like it had dropped out of the sky and God said, "Hey, remember this?" And I did remember. I especially remember the day I found out I was a finalist in *Oprah's National High School Essay Contest*, and Oprah Winfrey not only recognized my love for writing, but the potential to do something great in this world. Thank you, Oprah, for giving me the opportunity to change my life forever and for helping me see my ability to inspire and change the lives of others. Your love for the world is relentless and unconditional, and I pray to do God's work as effortlessly as you one day.

Thank you to my publisher SD Green and The TMG Firm for making dreams come true! Your patience and faith have been greatly appreciated. Thank you to my family for all of your endless love and support, even when I had some serious mood swings during the writing process. Thanks for the awesome foreword, Dad. I know that wasn't easy. Thank you, Yonkers and Riverdale Avenue, for raising me! No other place in the world could've kept me motivated like you. Thank you, Elie Wiesel, for living a long life dedicated to eliminating hate from our world. You spoke only truth and reminded us all that there is still so much work to be done, and I pray my generation will help manifest your vision one day. May you always rest in peace. Thank you, Yonkers High, for the best four years of my life. My interests evolved into passions in that school building, and you will forever have a big chunk of my heart. Thank you to my favorite teacher in the whole wide world, Mr. Christopher Vicari. You held me hostage after school until that Oprah essay was perfect, and I couldn't be more thankful for the way you believed in me. It was you who told me to, "write on, write on, write on," and I will always and forever love you for those words. I hope I've made you proud. Thank You, God, for every time You wiped my tears and confirmed I was exactly where I was supposed to be. Without You, there is nothing.

FOREWORD

I was nineteen years old when God blessed me with a beautiful baby girl at 2:19 a.m. on Saturday, January 28, 1989. Raysa and I named her Kaylah Ninoska Pantaleón, and found a whole new meaning of LOVE the first time she opened her eyes.

I had dropped out of high school my senior year to start a really good union job at the sugar refinery in Yonkers a few months before Kaylah was due to arrive. Raysa and I got married, and though we were young and not living in the best of neighborhoods, life was good after our daughter came into the world. I never wanted to put her little body down, which my wife didn't mind if it meant getting a few more hours of sleep. Kaylah and I were inseparable from the moment I first held her in my arms, so it was no surprise to anyone when her first word happened to be, "Dada." She was a Daddy's girl from that point forward.

It was amazing to watch my first child grow up and to witness her personality blossom. Kaylah was so curious, so full of energy, and so imaginative. She was the only child I had ever known to love TV commercials and walk around mimicking them all day (especially if Richard Simmons had anything to do with it). She loved Halloween and, unfortunately for Raysa and me, scary movies. She loved telling stories from the minute she was picked up from pre-school to the minute she sat in a warm bath.

I was excited to watch Kaylah grow up for the rest of my life, but I fell into a downward spiral before she even turned five. Since I was a kid, I always found the most dangerous things the most appealing. In my lifetime, I had broken nine out of ten fingers, my left arm, right leg, and taken over eighty stitches on my body, but there would be no greater adrenaline rush than the one in a shot of heroin. The drug was as accessible as going to the bodega to buy candy. If I didn't find it on Riverdale, I was getting it at the refinery, spending three-hundred to four-hundred dollars a day to feed my addiction. I could clearly see how I was jeopardizing my family and my job, and still could not bring myself to stop. I was sick and surrounded by enough people who loved me and wanted to help me, but no intervention or program could get through to me.

Eventually, I lost my job just when I found out we were expecting another baby. I was afraid that my addiction would affect my unborn child, and I wanted to stop more than ever. However, I had already lost sight of who I was and every moral and fundamental principle I was taught as a kid. I began committing crimes to support the habit and inevitably found myself behind bars for several counts of armed robbery and assault. I was arrested on November 17, 1993, two months after the birth of my second daughter, Janessa Marie Pantaleón.

Prison was difficult for everyone in my family to deal with, but for Kaylah especially. Her last memory before I left was of a heated argument between Raysa and me where I justifiably got kicked out of the apartment. Kaylah used that memory to blame her mother for my absence in the months immediately following my arrest. Raysa had no choice but to put our first born in child's therapy, hoping it would help her cope better. We thought visits at the prison would ease her pain, but they only seemed to make the situation more detrimental. The first few times she came to see me correctional officers had to assist in tearing her little arms from around my neck. The end of every visit was a sad and cruel scene that always sent me back to my cell in tears. I talked to her on the phone a lot and lied about how Daddy was in school or sick in the hospital and how I would feel better soon. Then, I told her to write me, write me anything and everything she wanted until I came home. Though unable to watch Kaylah grow up in person, I got to see my baby girl grow in letters. She accepted my absence easier when she found the power of the pen. Her creativity blossomed on loose-leaf paper, in birthday cards and Christmas cards, and of course, Halloween cards. She drew colorful pictures and wrote stories to go along with each one of her drawings. I received a beautiful storybook in the mail at least four times a month. As Kaylah got older, Raysa started to send me her report cards, and it was obvious that she definitely didn't take after me in academics. Raysa and I divorced shortly after my incarceration, but I always appreciated her for the way she instilled a strong sense of education in both our daughters who grew up to ignore what they saw on Riverdale Avenue and focused on what they saw at home or in class.

Despite her crime-filled environment, Kaylah's letters, poems, and short stories only progressed and evoked so many emotions that I knew for sure writing was going to be a part of her life forever. I got to witness her evolving gift first-hand for twelve years, so I was not surprised when we found out she was one of the finalists for *Oprah's National High School Essay Contest*. I came home December 7, 2005, and Kaylah gave me the most amazing homecoming present two months later when Oprah called in February, 2006. She continued to bless me with her talents in the summer of 2006 when I got to sit front and center at her first Shakespeare play and hear her recite an original poem at the Yonkers Puerto Rican/Hispanic gala. Maybe I'm a little bias, but there was no denying that my daughter had something special to offer the world. Today, she has published her first book. Today, I am just as proud to call

Kaylah Ninoska Pantaleón my daughter as I was the first moment I laid eyes on her. Today, I get to write in support of my baby girl's first book, and I promise she has a passionate and profound story that'll open your mind and keep you turning the pages. Enjoy!

—Marino Antonio Pantaleón

"You are braver than you believe, stronger than you seem, and smarter than you think," said Christopher Robin to Pooh.

CHAPTER ONE

An ocean of sickly gray clouds stretched out forever across the sky. The clouds were so defined I thought I could use my small thumb and index finger to pinch the corner of one and pluck it from its resting place. Would any sunlight beam through then?

Thousands of people as gray as the early morning sky were crowded in the field of dirt below. They held on tightly to their loved ones and winter coats, desperate for protection from the cruel weather or something else. They didn't know. I sat looking out my window a few yards away and could still make out the confusion on their faces.

"Women to the left! Men to the right!" A strange, pale man wearing a rifle and big boots commanded so loud I could make out every syllable from where I watched in the distance. Though his voice traveled far, the man had clones that joined in shouting the words with him to ensure all had heard.

"Women to the left! Men to the right!"

"Women to the left! Men to the right!"

Their booming voices together vibrated the dirt beneath my feet, making pebbles jump from the ground. Even the deaf and dead understood what to do, and masses of people began to slowly drift apart like the continents of Pangea.

If only I had money, I could save them all, is what I thought to myself. Surely, money would set my people free. These strange White men couldn't resist a briefcase with ten million dollars, could they? A shiny, black briefcase stuffed with bundles of one-hundred dollar bills just like that one Jim Carrey found in *Dumb and Dumber.* I squeezed my eyelids closed tight and tried to wish the briefcase into existence. It would be lying in plain sight on the ground, but only my eyes would spot it, and I would sprint toward it, swoop it from the mud and heroically shout to the top of my lungs, "Hey! I have what you want! Let them go!" The identical White men would smile, cock their heads back and laugh out loud in unison. They would happily take the briefcase stuffed with money, praise me for a job well done, and let everyone go home, but not before splitting the ten million with me so that I could share with my family and my people.

Inevitably, I opened my eyes, and there was no shiny briefcase in the mud, and I was still a useless Brown girl in the hood.

The hairs on the back of my neck suddenly straightened with the brush of hot, abrupt air. Someone was standing behind me. His breath crept up the back of my head, electrocuting my hair follicles. My ears pulsed hot blood as the sound of his exhales grew louder, and I could feel him creep closer. My neck was chilled stiff from slipping beads of sweat or the condensation of his exhales; I wasn't sure. But I was certain my body had fully succumbed to paralysis. I was as still as the icicles hanging from the corners of my abandoned brown building, too scared to turn around and face reality. I prayed for the biggest and sharpest icicle to break free and pierce through the lost one's chest, striking him dead, just like the monster met his fate in Alice Sebold's book, *The Lovely Bones*. But once again, my prayers went unanswered.

Then the touch of freezing steel on the small of my back reminded me of my own fate without having to turn around and accept it. I squeezed my eyelids closed tight as though blinding myself would make it hurt less. The sound of the safety clicking off traveled to my ears fast like the Express 4 train during rush hour. Only, there was no light at the end of this tunnel.

"Peanuts?" The gangster finally spoke when I thought I was dying from a heart attack before he pulled the trigger. The broken silence took me so much by surprise I was sure I had heard wrong.

"Peanuts?" He repeated, and I had no choice but to unclench my eyelids and turn to face him.

Grinning like a twinkle-eyed SpongeBob at his happiest, a polished flight attendant stood over my sleeping mother and me, holding out a small blue bag of airline peanuts. I wanted to smoosh his spongy face for waking me up. Nonetheless, I was grateful to escape the dream and be back on the flight to Chicago, so I took the damn peanuts.

"Thank you." My manners hadn't failed me, but my laser beam eyes said, *I'm gonna give you to the count of ten to get your ugly, yella, no good keester off my property before I pump your guts full of lead*, like that scene from *Home Alone*. And because I couldn't resist, I added, "Keep the change, ya filthy animal," under my breath so that the happy peanut man couldn't hear me.

The flight attendant's rubber-band grin stretched so wide I thought his lips might snap apart as he carried on to disturb the passengers behind us. "Peanuts?"

I lowered the window shade to help my eyes adjust to the brightly lit plane. I tried to open the plastic wrapper as quietly and skillfully as possible, careful not to wake my mother or ruin my freshly done French manicure. Mom and I had enjoyed a few hours pampering ourselves the day before leaving New York in preparation for our big TV debut. A professional manicure was definitely a treat for me, but I was annoyed with how much brain power was required to keep from scratching or chipping a nail Mom had just paid twenty-five dollars for (pedicure included). I moved as stiffly as one of those human robots in Times Square, and it was still very unlikely that I'd make it to the taping without doing some kind of damage.

Society's beauty standards were a hard concept for me to grasp, mainly because I grew up thinking that I would never be as pretty as other girls in school, so there was no point in trying. I was always the tallest and *healthiest* among the girls *and* boys throughout elementary, making me the center of much unwanted attention during recess where I anticipated hearing the latest Hungry Hippo and/or Godzilla joke. I got used to kids hurting my feelings in class and Mom trying her best to piece me back together at home. Despite her best efforts in damage control, I was never able to see myself completely whole; "The Humpty Dumpty Effect," I called it.

High school finally came around, spiking my self-esteem meter from non-existent to mediocre due to boys catching up to my height and some subtle blossoming here and there. I walked through the school halls with a bruised confidence, but overall, I was happy and just didn't care for all the glitz and glam that went into being a girl. Getting a mani/pedi, buying makeup and anything related to such "lady-like" adventures was certainly never scheduled in my planner unless I was due for a new pack of maxi pads. A good day for me started with extra sleep rather than spending an hour in the mirror trying to figure out the difference between the "honey beige" and the "light caramel" foundation. Makeup didn't look right on me, anyway. In fact, the first time I tried on red lipstick, Mom had provided her feedback in the nicest way possible—"You look like the Joker." I, personally, didn't take offense to the light-hearted comment, especially after checking my smile in the mirror and having no choice but to absolutely agree with her. I put the stick of Revlon Fire and Ice away and thought to save it for an awesome Halloween costume down the line. I was more concerned with wearing clothes that were too big for me and running free in grand open spaces. Softball and all other high-intensity activities that involved plenty of dirt and sweat were my idea of a fun-filled Friday night.

What also kept me from qualifying for a beauty pageant was my severe nail biting problem; a nervous habit with dire consequences that my mother reminded me of every chance she got. "I swear you're gonna chew your fingers right off one day and never be able to write again...or get married!" I heard my mother echo her own mother, my Nana. My sweet Nana. No one could force-feed me a plate of *arroz con pollo y plátanos maduros* and simultaneously advise me to get on a diet soon (because I was looking *más gordita* than usual) like she could.

No te vas a conseguir un buen hombre así, Nana always added innocently, making me flinch in my chair when she crouched over to pinch my love-handles and sweetly plant a kiss on my forehead as she cleared the plate and utensils I licked clean. So, in conclusion, I needed to stop eating food and my fingers in order to find a boyfriend who could tolerate me long enough to marry me. Not likely to happen before my 30th birthday. Though I definitely found boys interesting, it was usually natural for me to prioritize the more mandatory subjects at school.

The sound of soft snores escaping Mom's slightly open mouth took me away from my pinky nail that had just seen the end too soon. I silently planned to limit the use of my right hand as much as possible in hopes she wouldn't notice.

I was relieved SpongeBob hadn't woken my mother up because she never got much sleep at home. She was up at 5:30 every morning making my little sister and me scrambled eggs, toasted English muffins with butter and the best hot chocolate in the world (I know that hot chocolate today as Swiss Miss). The food was left covered in a pan until we were ready to drag our feet to the kitchen and eat it with eyes half open. Mom typically left our little brother, Nunu, sleeping for as long as she could to avoid dropping off a cranky toddler at the babysitter's.

Needless to say, my mother was always up first and ready to go last. But it never took her very long to get ready because she wore oversized scrubs for work and also never bothered applying makeup. I loved looking through old-school pictures of my mother in the early nineties when she could've easily been mistaken for that freestyle singer, Lil Suzy, who I only knew of because Mom blasted the song, "Take Me in Your Arms," every Sunday morning while she mopped the floor. The nineties evolution was noticeable in Mom's photo albums when she went from a bland face and high ponytail to dark brown lipstick and straight hair, a look inspired by Mary J. Blige and the ladies from En Vogue. Except, my mother was a fair-skinned Latina and in later years, I thought she started to look more like the singer Selena Quintanilla with her painted lips. I loved Selena, and I loved that Mom looked like her.

Despite the bit of drool making its way out the corner of her mouth, my mother was a sleeping beauty. I still found it hard to believe she was sitting next to me on a flight to Chicago that Oprah Winfrey had paid for. We were just watching *Murder in the Hamptons* on *Lifetime* the month before like a normal mother and daughter, but this was the quality time I had never dreamed of. My mother had, on the other hand. It wouldn't even be overly spiritual to say she spoke this moment into existence.

I was a sophomore in high school just the year before and attended community drama classes every Saturday. One particular Saturday when Mom came to pick me up after Mr. Arena dismissed the one-hour class, we ran into an old friend of hers outside of the school building.

"Wow! Is this baby Kaylah all grown up?" The stranger beamed my way.

"Yes, this is my Kaylita!" Mom excitedly nodded and squeezed my cheeks together like I had just stepped out of daycare.

"Unbelievable how time flies. What are you up to these days, young lady?"

The genuinely curious stranger directed his question to me, but before my lips could part, Mom answered, "She's acting and writing a lot. She's gonna be a star. You'll see her on *Oprah* one day."

Creepy. I know. But, that's just the kind of faith Mom had in me. She truly believed I was destined for greatness, and I never realized it until that moment. Her smile, her excitement, the energy in her voice, the way she clenched her purse while she spoke the words; it was like I was seeing my mother for the first time. I was seeing her as a little girl with big dreams.

As loving and nurturing as she was, Mom hesitated to clearly communicate her feelings about a lot of things while I was growing up. I was an above average student, and yet would never hear her say things like, "You're special" or, "I'm proud of you," like I watched the grown-ups often do with DJ, Steph, and Michelle throughout a season of *Full House*. However, I always guessed she was proud of me because I felt it in other ways. For example, she faithfully made it right on time to all my academic awards ceremonies to watch me collect tiny trophies for Most Outstanding in English and Most Outstanding in Math (this one always caught us both by surprise). She also bought me a new horror movie on VHS whenever I brought home an exceptional report card. I loved all kinds of movies, especially the ones with Freddy Krueger and Jason Voorhees as the main antagonists. And if I got straight As, I was looking forward to a scary movie *and* McDonald's that night. Success was my only option.

I assumed as I got older that a big reason Mom kept most of her feelings bottled up was because of my dad. Though he had gone to prison when I was four years old, and she had since moved on and remarried my stepfather, being a single mother of two while your husband is behind bars is a traumatic experience for any woman. She buried her feelings when he left, consistently making an effort to put on a strong front for her girls and the world.

With the help of Mom's old friend, I had also come to the bittersweet conclusion that my mother believed in me more than I believed in myself. How did I expect to ever leave the hood if my drive was left on autopilot? The person who knew me best saw everything I was capable of, and yet I couldn't see it for myself. I stepped my game up in school after catching an honest moment of Mom's pride, determined to see her light up the way she did that Saturday morning.

I finished the bag of stale peanuts in less than sixty seconds, and hunger pangs continued prodding at my unhappy stomach. My mouth watered at the thought of devouring my first Chicago deep-dish pizza when the pilot's raspy voice blared on the plane's intercom, interrupting a heavenly image of me biting into a "meat lovers" slice. We would be landing at the Chicago O'Hare International Airport in approximately thirty minutes.

"Thank you for choosing American Airlines," the pilot concluded and nearly coughed up a lung before disconnecting. Mom began to fidget to consciousness.

"Did I snore?"

"Yes."

"Oh, no."

"It's okay. Only a few people were staring," I snickered.

"Shut up."

My smile gave way as I turned to look out the window. I felt my eyes growing as big as Mia's did when she saw the land of Genovia for the first time from her window seat in *Princess Diaries*. The world was divided into symmetrical squares and rectangles, patches of dark brown and bright green surrounding a rainbow of miniature houses and buildings in organized perfection. I never felt so big.

Not being much of a world traveler, I stayed close by my mother's side for fear of getting lost among the bustle of people who actually knew what they were doing and where they were going. I was seventeen years old and had seen the inside of an airport twice before—once on a school trip to Spain and the other time for a family reunion in the

Dominican Republic three years prior. The D.R. trip was my least favorite since all I could remember was a merciless sun and countless old people forming more wrinkles by the second as they claimed to be related to me through a man or a woman whose name I had never heard of and forcing me to give them a kiss because, *¡Sí! ¡Soy tu tía!*

Fortunately, my first time in Chicago had the promise of being a little more memorable. However, if Oprah suddenly shocked the world by announcing she was my long-lost aunt on national television, then well, "memorable" would be a ridiculous understatement.

Scenarios of how the next twenty-four hours would play out rolled around in my head like dusty luggage riding around the conveyor belt in baggage claim. I was blessed with a big imagination that could keep me entertained with daydream after daydream, especially now that I had so much material to work with. I wrote an award-winning one-thousand-word essay and was on my way to meet *the* Oprah Winfrey because of it. What was she like? My first thought was that Ms. Winfrey, in all her glory, was something like my favorite English teacher.

Mr. Vicari was the creator of nervous whispers among freshmen and sophomores, their fears of the unknown filling the plain hallways at Yonkers High School with adventure. Like a prayer, he was someone you spoke of quietly and respectfully in a huddle of your closest friends. But, you never fully believed he existed until you finally reached junior year and a level of maturity strong enough to withstand the literary sorcerer.

Rumor had it that Christopher Vicari not only read *Dante's Inferno* aloud to the class as students under hypnosis followed along, but he used an ancient African gong to turn fiction into reality. The vibrations of the enchanted gong sent energy waves so ferocious throughout the classroom that every student was instantly teleported to the gates of hell where Mr. Vicari himself began the guided tour through all nine circles, thoroughly uncovering life's deepest secrets along the way. If you did well in class, you were guided back to Earth. If not, well...

As it turns out, Mr. Vicari knew so much about the life of Dante Alighieri because the two adolescent scholars had crossed each other's paths at a poetry festival in Florence in the year 1280. They grew to become the best of friends, joined together at the hip until the Florentine government exiled Dante for life in 1302. The news left Mr. Vicari alone and broken-hearted; but when he later learned of Dante's *The Divine Comedy*, the young scholar became a teacher, vowing to live out the rest of his life sharing his best friend's masterpiece and all symbolic literary works of art in hopes of changing the world for the better. (Okay, I may have had something to do with this rumor).

Mr. Vicari had kept his promise for over seven-hundred years, but flaunted the skin of a classically handsome man born just after 1970 with no grays in sight to interrupt the youthful growth of his thick, organic head of hair, the color and strength of tar. An immortal vampire? There was a hint of a sparkling Edward Cullen to him, no doubt. The Wizard of Words was a rare character you only found in a book dated back centuries. The second-coming of Jesus was perhaps the most popular of the theories.

The Teacher stood determined outside the temple every morning, impatiently waiting for his disciples to appear one by one, eager to share the good Word. There was always too much knowledge and not enough time. A beam of light radiated from his body and painted the halls gold. His presence reminded us all that God's work was in progress, and every soul in the building wanted to get saved in the experience. Each disciple that arrived on time was in store for a three-part initiation at the start of class; the *eye contact*, effectively communicating an appreciation for the student's presence; the *"Good morning,"* said in a tone miraculously eliminating all sense of self-doubt; and the *handshake*, confirming the Teacher's acceptance of the disciple into his sacred temple of knowledge. The morning greeting alone was a spiritual awakening, equipping each student with enough honor and confidence to excel beyond measure within the next forty-five minutes.

Believe it or not, exiting class was even more enlightening than entering. The school bell never confirmed the end of the lesson; only the Teacher's singing gong had the power to do so. The charmed instrument closed with a song of goodness, and the Prince of Peace positioned himself outside the door once more to make the final connection with every student before their return to the other side. For the second time, he initiated the eye contact, the sacred handshake and strategically added the words, "Good job," instead of, "Good bye." The words were simple, yet left us with a profound feeling of purification. All accomplishments were acknowledged, each soul cleansed of sin, and every heart and mind prepared to gift their newfound wisdom to the world. It was a baptism that took place every day, five days a week.

However, on some rare occasions when a student's work ethic had fallen below expectations and dubbed too unworthy of the "Good job," Mr. Vicari used only his eyes to say, "wait here." The student knew exactly what to do in this situation and stood on the side to wait for him to finish blessing all who exited the place of worship. The Teacher would then turn to the outcast and softly share his thoughts so that no one but themselves could hear. No one ever knew what was said. But getting pulled aside after English class was equivalent to being convicted of a heinous crime. You didn't want it on your record.

Nonetheless, every life that entered Mr. Vicari's room was changed forever. God's work was done on the inside of four walls, year after year. He was my favorite teacher even before our first official handshake. I imagined Oprah was something like that. She was an example of the goodness of God, creating Earth as it was in heaven. She was not exactly a figment of my imagination because I knew in order to have the highest-rated talk show in American television history, she kind of had to exist. But, she was certainly an untouchable idea, someone to admire and aspire to be like from afar. Really, really far.

The possibility that the sound of my name could even leave Oprah's mouth was no more than a frequent daydream. A mouth that always spoke such perfectly organized, distinguished sentences without hesitation, always so certain of the next word. A mouth that could command the attention of over a hundred crying toddlers at once and make them instantly forget ever being sad. A mouth, powerful enough to start a world war, but strictly used to bring World Peace. That same eloquent mouth that twenty million people tuned in to hear daily would probably say my name if she hadn't already. Had she already? The possibility manhandled my brain like a child retrieving change from his piggy bank. Oprah saw my name. Oprah read my name. Oprah said my name. Oprah heard my name. Oprah probably had a difficult time saying my last name at first glance, so Oprah butchered my name. After some practice, Oprah pronounced my name. Wow, could she have actually practiced saying my name? Oprah rehearsed my name. Oprah learned my name. Oprah knew my name. That was it. Along with the routine beat down our next-door neighbor gave his wife every night, the idea that Oprah knew my name now also kept me from a good night's sleep. Oprah knew that somewhere in the world a girl named Kaylah Pantaleón existed. What she didn't know was that Kaylah Pantaleón, one of fifty winners of her first-ever national high school essay contest, would grow up and fall deep in love with a man serving fifteen-years-to-life behind bars.

CHAPTER TWO

Mom made the executive decision to stuff all of our clothes and toiletries into one suitcase for our two-day vacation in Chicago. The large, lumpy suitcase bursting at the seams was decorated with a thousand little palm-trees and easy to spot among the mundane black and gray luggage lacking imagination. I helped Mom pull the festive, abnormally shaped object from the conveyor belt and cracked a smile when I realized how out of place it looked in the Windy City.

"What's so funny?" Mom asked, more concerned with hand-picking the lint from her black slacks than the answer.

"Nothing. Just excited."

"Me, too." She agreed unconsciously, now anxiously smoothing out the wrinkles in her pants before letting out a long, exaggerated breath, "Do I look fat?"

I rolled my eyes. Mom's constant focus on her body was one characteristic I wish I hadn't inherited. All the women on both my mother and father's side were prone to weight fluctuations, but it was very seldom to find one of them pleased with her reflection in the mirror. I was so used to hearing the question that I started to believe it was rhetorical after a while, never answering with more than a thoughtless "no" just in case it wasn't. But Mom's jitters were new to me, so I tried to provide a little more consolation with an even more honest and detailed reply.

"No, Mom. You look beautiful."

She returned the eye roll, grabbed the long-stemmed handle to the suitcase and started walking. My mother was clearly more nervous than I was. You'd think Oprah herself was waiting to greet us with a full-blown camera crew outside of baggage claim. Then the thought made me hesitate for a second. Was she? Did Mom know something I didn't? She had tuned into the *Oprah Winfrey Show* for half her life and knew very well how much this magician of a woman enjoyed surprising not only her guests, but her entire audience around the world. So, it was no wonder she half-expected to physically meet the enchanting Queen of Television in the next sixty seconds. Were we getting a new car? I was suddenly very grateful Mom made me wear the only (incredibly uncomfortable and incredibly cream-colored) pants suit I owned.

The airport buzzed with hasty people of all ages, shapes, sizes, colors, and stories. I paid close attention to my surroundings, focused on trying to spot teenagers with eyes as lost as mine, with uncertainty in every step they took, and the unmistakable glow of positive energy. These teens I searched for were most likely my co-finalists and future friends.

However, other than the haze of excited travelers rolling luggage around and charging for the sliding exit doors to look for a loved one or a taxi, all I noticed was a black sea of men wearing tuxedos. They all held signs, each one showcasing a different name written in a different style of child-like scrawl. The men looked like hungry penguins from a distance, eagerly making eye contact with anyone who might feed them, or be their client. Once the penguins came into clearer view, they suddenly transformed into the secret agents I had only seen in *Men in Black*. They were sharp and serious, ready to attack the extraterrestrial threats here on Earth. Maybe, I thought, the signs read the names of all their new agent recruits.

Then I saw mine, and my heart leaped into my throat, blocking my windpipe for a split second. I had a sign. I had a big, white sign and my name was written in clumsy, black letters, "Kaylah Pantaleón." I was a new recruit. I mean—I had a chauffeur. Oprah's team had sent a driver to pick Mom and me up from the airport and take us to the Omni Chicago Hotel. When my eyes met the eyes of the intimidating man in black holding my name, I gave a bashful wave that he instantly responded to with a lovable, Barney-like grin. I was ready to fight a war against the Earth's most dangerous aliens just two minutes before, and skipping through a field of tulips now seemed like the more appropriate thing to do with this oversized teddy bear of a man.

Our new friend escorted us outside to a black, shiny stretch limo and my mouth fell open at the sight of it. The strong April winds helped quickly close it back up for me. Even though the limo looked nothing like the one in *Pretty Woman*, I still thought it'd be cool if Oprah popped out from the sunroof to hand me a bouquet of red roses just like Richard Gere did for Julia Roberts. Now, that's what you call a surprise. Oprah was nowhere in sight, however, and I settled for the chivalry of our attentive chauffeur who opened the back door and waited for Mom and me to scoot all the way in before closing it and walking around to the driver's side.

My eyes scanned the inside of my first limo, almost forgetting how to blink. The interior was lined with black leather seats. It reminded me of Tío Edgard's fancy leather couch, minus the bird droppings from his illegal parrot. There was a sparkling clean bar across from where Mom and I sat filled with freshly topped ice buckets, miniature cans of pineapple and cranberry juice, room temperature bottles of Pellegrino and Fiji water, and drinking glasses polished so well I could see a tiny rainbow dancing in each one from three feet away. Mom and I both twisted open a bottle of Fiji and sat back to enjoy our thirty-minute ride to the hotel.

I didn't realize how dehydrated I was until the refreshing water met my lips, and I nearly swallowed the half liter in one gulp. With quenched thirst, I dropped my head back against the firm, leather seat, noticing the giant mirror on the ceiling for the first time. I stared into my mud brown eyes. They looked as tired as they felt. The brisk city winds had revealed my straight hair as an imposter, exposing my natural curls around the edges of my forehead. Despite my disheveled appearance and exhaustion aggressively taking hold of my body, I sat in awe. It was hard to believe this was all really happening. To me, out of all people.

I was a Dominican-American girl who lived on Riverdale Avenue in Downtown Yonkers, New York her whole life. I was born at St. John's hospital, just about two miles away from our low-income housing complex on January 28, 1989. Believe it or not, my mother and I shared the exact story...almost. Mom was first-generation Dominican, her immigrant parents arriving in New York during the early 1960s after the assassination of Dominican dictator, Rafael Trujillo. She too spent her entire thirty-six years of life on Riverdale Avenue and was born at St. John's hospital on April 29, 1969. Dr. Rahzman was the man who delivered us both, nearly twenty years apart.

Minus a lot of the romance, our government-assisted neighborhood resembled the crowded buildings, streets, and blatant race war that you found in *A Bronx Tale*. But our wars pinned Blacks against Latinos and Latinos against Blacks and Blacks against Blacks and Latinos against Latinos. If there was a White sprinkled in somewhere, his family most likely fell on some bad luck like a heroin addiction, leaving them broke, disadvantaged, and lost among the colors. But there was always a chance he'd grow up and try to save us like Tarzan did for his animal family in the jungle. That's probably why no one ever had a real problem with a White sprinkle.

However, when there was no money, there was always a reason to be at war, no matter the color of one's skin. This was the main idea I described in my "Oprah essay," comparing Elie Wiesel's oppression to that of our own. Poverty was the Nazi outside my door, sizing us up and driving the weakest ones to their deaths and the strongest ones to work until starvation. Poverty birthed fear and those controlled by it grew up too scared to offer a solution, resulting in the invasion of one struggle after another. So, there were multiple perpetual wars going on at once—race war, drug war, sex war, gang war, teen pregnancy war, high school drop-out war, public school system war, homeless people war, food stamps war, crooked cop war, mass incarceration war and any other battle that comes to mind when you picture your typical "hood;" where the motto, "it is what it is" originated and was inherited generation after generation.

In fact, according to statistics, I should have been riding the 4 bus to Planned Parenthood for my second abortion and centuries away from a limo ride on behalf of Oprah Winfrey. The odds of this limo ride taking place were one in a million, as a fellow classmate exaggerated nonchalantly after the news broke out across town.

Rebecca Wilson had taken unusual pleasure in ridiculing me for "actually wasting time with that stupid essay contest."

As if dissatisfied with my shoulder shrug and weak smile for a response, Rebecca continued coldly, "You have no chance," and stopped popping her dried bubblegum in-between her tongue and teeth to let out a condescending chuckle before walking away in the opposite direction.

Her words chewed at my self-esteem like a starving coyote on a helpless deer. She was one of the skinny cool girls with flawless ebony skin who prided herself on having no filter and always saying what everyone else was thinking. I wasn't exactly a nerd in the shadows, but certainly nowhere near as popular as she was. I felt like I had no other choice but to stay quiet throughout the entire verbal beat down and try my best to tune out her destructive voice. I knew what everybody else knew— I had a very small chance of winning. But it didn't hurt to try, and somewhere along my short life's journey I learned it didn't hurt to have hope either. I just didn't share my thoughts aloud.

Then the miraculous day came when the halls filled with excited and disbelieving chatter of, "Kaylah won the Oprah contest," and Rebecca pretended to be bored with the news.

I couldn't resist purposefully flashing a grandiose grin her way when she walked into the girl's locker room at the start of gym class.

"What are the odds? Like one in a million," she answered her own question and rolled her big, brown eyes in response to my gloating face, seriously trying to care less while she slipped sweatpants on over her skin-tight jeans because she had no intention of putting any real effort into tag football that day. She focused on tying the cotton strings of her sweatpants below a red pleather belt so that the color-coordination of her new Jordan sneakers and belt didn't go unnoticed while half-assing her way through class. Little did she know, I was on my way to finding a solution.

What are the odds? I asked myself, still staring up into my drowsy eyes, still trying to figure out how I got to this point despite the nonbelievers that criticized my dreams on a daily basis. Oprah and her team had received over fifty-thousand essay entries across the country and only selected fifty lucky students to fly to Chicago and appear on her show. There, we would have the honor of meeting Professor Elie Wiesel, the Nobel Prize winning author of *Night* and the motive behind Oprah's first-ever national high school essay contest.

Night was a graphic story about a young boy and his family's experience during the Holocaust in 1944. The small work of art was Professor Wiesel's primary description of a hopeless time at the Auschwitz and Buchenwald concentration camps in Nazi Germany. But Eliezer was the character who took the place of Elie Wiesel on the heartbreaking journey, keeping the book from officially being categorized as a memoir. I theorized that though Professor Wiesel had the desperate desire to tell the world his story and the story of millions, the reality of the event was still too difficult for him to accept. Using Eliezer helped lessen the blow of his truths, making it possible to write the book from beginning to end with relentless determination. I found myself doing something like that when I wrote in my journal at night. Sometimes it felt better detaching my spirit from Kaylah and the world she lived in.

Mr. Vicari introduced *Night* to the class curriculum in December 2005, not far from the start of the holiday break. He read each line out loud, giving us a one-man show experience every 4th period for a week. His captivating voice held everyone hostage at their desks, forcing us to see the protruding rib cages of the starved men and women, smell the bodies being burned alive inside the crematory, taste the hydrogen cyanide inside the gas chambers, hear the last breaths of those passing away in their sleep, and feel Eliezer lose faith in God and humanity all at once. Pleasant thoughts of decorating the Christmas tree and having snowball fights after school had been completely obliterated. The book was so gruesome I wanted to believe it was fiction just as much as Elie Wiesel did. But it was a real story that required real courage to tell.

In January 2006, Oprah started the New Year off the only way she knew how—by making history. The Queen celebrated Professor Wiesel's bravery by adding *Night* to her famous book club and announcing an essay prompt for the participation of every high school from New York to California.

"Why is the book *Night* by Elie Wiesel relevant today?"

The miracle worker who never stopped working was now giving students across the United States an opportunity to find the courage to speak their own truths.

Mr. Vicari jumped on the project as soon as it hit his desk, amazed by the timing of his curriculum and Oprah's announcement. He encouraged every student, inside and outside his class, to submit a one-thousand-word essay as soon as possible. His excitement and confidence in Yonkers High School's student body was enough to motivate the laziest of the under-achievers to attempt at least a sentence or two. As for me, I was a modest over-achiever with an agenda to find a solution and make a name for myself one day, and Mr. Vicari noticed.

The end of 4th period bell rang just as the Teacher was finishing up his announcement of the contest rules and instructions. An essay submission wasn't optional if you were his student. We were all expected to have a double-spaced-Times-New-Roman-12-point-font-one-thousand-word-essay drafted by the end of the week. He put the mallet to his gong and its tranquil notes vibrated throughout the temple, indicating the official end of class. One by one, the students took the Teacher's extended hand and proceeded with the handshake ritual before carrying on with the rest of their day. But when I joyfully went to reach for my handshake, the prophet denied me, giving me the "wait here" eyes instead. My smile and all joy I had ever known vanished. Wait here? Was I getting pulled to the side after class? Yes, I was. My chest tightened with fear and embarrassment and anxiety and disappointment and self-loathing and....It felt like a lifetime before my favorite teacher finished blessing the last student to trickle out of the classroom and finally turn to face me. No matter how hard I tried to focus, I couldn't read the expression on his face but was automatically convinced that I was off the honor roll list and had to attend summer school and possibly repeat junior year.

"Have something for me by tomorrow. Just write." The words were short and sharp like a dagger that sent a wave of chills from my clammy feet up to my chapped lips, but an overwhelming sense of relief warmed me back up once the letters came together and finally registered. All I could manage to do was nod my head in accordance, incredibly grateful that I wouldn't have to go to summer school. The tight-lipped look on his face was so intimidating that from afar everyone must have thought the Teacher was scolding me for plagiarizing last week's ten-page Siddhartha paper from SparkNotes. But only I knew that the discerning twinkle in his eyes and the distinct tone of his voice expressed nothing but faith, and faith was all I needed.

The limo door opened, inviting in a beam of light and a blast of Chicago springtime air, finally taking me away from my reflection in the mirror. We had arrived at the Chicago Omni hotel.

CHAPTER THREE

I paid thirty-five dollars for a roundtrip *Greyhound* ticket leaving at 7:30 p.m. the night of February 13, 2008. I preferred riding *Bolt* because it was ten dollars cheaper and provided efficient wi-fi, but tickets were sold out due to my impulsive, last-minute decision to cut two freshman seminar classes at Emerson College and head back home for Valentine's Day. The ride from Boston's South Station Bus Terminal to New York City's Port Authority took over four hours, leaving me in desperate need of a chiropractor and smelling like a mix of old cheese and Cucumber Melon body lotion. All I carried in my small Nike sackpack was a pink pleather wallet and a half-eaten Arby's chicken sandwich as I exited the *Greyhound* and snuck away into the underground subway tunnels like a Ninja Turtle.

The New York City Subway gave me the eerie feeling that someone was watching my every move. Lying about my whereabouts turned into a habit as regular as showering, so paranoia usually tagged along everywhere I went. I had to keep the stories I told people fresh in my head so not to forget which person knew what and end up ratting myself out later down the line. As of now, my professors and managers at P.F. Chang's believed I was sick in bed, my roommates believed I took an impromptu mini vacation to New York, and my mother believed I was in Boston working hard on my five-page English Composition paper.

I dazed out at the train tracks, trying to convince myself that Mom was much better off sinking into her soft pillows with one less worry at night. An emptiness fell on my chest as my eyes zoned out on the trash-filled tracks, following the excursion of a busy subway rat. I leaned against a steel pillar inches away from the yellow safety line and invited my guilty conscience to torture me. Was it really worth coming all this way? Was it worth lying to my mother over and over? Was it worth lying to everyone around me? How long could I keep this up?

Because she lived three-hundred miles away, I assumed Mom would be the easiest person to lie to, but it was no surprise to find out that assumption was completely false. This was my first time, sort of living on my own, so we spoke for at least thirty minutes each day talking about how risky it was to mix light colors with dark colors and exactly how much water was needed to boil one cup of rice. I dove into a fit of stutters when I attempted to report my weekend plans even though I had the whole story well-thought-out prior to our conversation. But the story, and any knowledge of how to form a complete sentence, evaporated from my brain at the sound of her voice.

She was my mom, and all my life I believed Mom knew everything because somehow she did. She was an all-knowing being with eyes and ears in every room. She carried a no-nonsense kind of attitude and a face that demanded respect with just one glare. My little sister and I always voluntarily threw ourselves under the bus when the chestnut in her eyes faded to black, and she impressively arched her right eyebrow for so long we thought it was stuck there permanently. The demonic Chuckie doll would instantly bow his head in shame at the sight of that terrifying face. I was thankful for the phone and the distance between us because I wasn't talented enough to perform the monologue in person. I barely had the mental capacity to carry out the conversation over my two-month-old Blackberry with a spider web crack down its screen. Lying to my mother always brought on a sudden fever, cold, sweaty palms and a loss of appetite so bad I couldn't imagine ever eating again. I was catching a worsening case of pneumonia with every sad stutter, desperate to end the call before the fever knocked me out cold in front of South Station and I missed the bus.

"Okay. I'm gonna watch a little TV before I go to bed. Good luck with your paper," Mom said, letting out a long yawn at the end.

"Thanks, Mom. Good night."

"Good night. Momma loves you," she playfully spoke in the third person before making the sound of a kiss and hanging up.

I knew my mother's daily routine had been interrupted by only one minor change since I left to college. She came home from work every day at 5:30 p.m.; changed out of her worn scrubs and into a comfy *bata* before starting dinner (which usually consisted of something easy like rice and beans with chicken cutlets or spaghetti with meat sauce) by 5:45 p.m.; had dinner ready by 6:45 p.m.; washed everyone's dishes and ironed my little brother's outfit for school the next day by 7:30 p.m.; and watched *Channel 12 News* and/or *Law & Order* reruns until she fell asleep by 8:30 p.m. Mom was always exhausted enough to stay faithful to her 8:30 p.m. bedtime.

Now that I wasn't around, however, our phone calls were added to my mother's tight schedule, and I had the audacity to waste her time with lies. I left her resting in bed three-hundred miles away, believing I was en route to spend an all-nighter at the Emerson library, because the truth promised to keep sleep from carrying her off to the white sand and clear blue waters she deserved to see that night. The lie was meant to protect her. Seeing my mother hurt was equivalent to watching my father turn around and head back to his cell at the end of a day's visit. I never wanted her to feel pain, and I never wanted him to leave. The sadness that came over me in both situations lit my organs on fire, my brain always certain that death was moments away.

I watched my father exit the crowded visiting room, listened to the sound of the massive steel security door slowly drag to a close and automatically lock behind him countless times over the duration of twelve years. Big, swollen tears poured from my eyes, fell from my chin and left the front of my shirt damp and cold. I cried hoping all the strange, White men wearing the same clothes would take notice and feel bad enough to set my father free right then and there. But they always looked the other way. More than once, a White man in uniform had to personally remove Mom and me from the visiting floor because my cries were too loud. I learned how to suppress my hysteria as I grew up, but the reaction always hit me the same. It was the same as my mother's the day we knew my father wasn't coming back home.

I remember a loud, agonizing howl that snatched me from the deep dream entertaining my four-year-old head at the time. I hesitated to leave my bed to investigate the noise out of fear of running into the leprechaun I strongly believed lived in my closet. But the volume of an injured cat's cry decreased to soft sobs in which I could recognize the sound of my mother's voice. I slid carefully off the bed until the tips of my tiny toes touched a furry pink rug and kept the closet in my peripheral view as I went to take a look outside. My bedroom door was left ajar, and I could peek out just enough without being seen by Mom whose room was directly across from mine. The door across the hall was left wide open, and my eyes immediately found her sitting on the corner of her bed crying hysterically. I turned away quickly, thinking that I was somehow invading my mother's privacy. This was wrong. It was something I wasn't supposed to see. It was a scene I certainly knew I couldn't talk about at school, but I promised the universe I wouldn't before turning back around to continue the investigation.

I could make out the puddle of water left on the front of my father's oversized, blue shirt she wore to bed. The unbearable sadness covered her body like a contagious rash, attacking me with an abrupt itch to want to know more. I had no idea that Mom could even cry until witnessing it for the first time that night. I was in awe and confused, wanting to know what could have possibly made her so upset in the middle of the night. I wanted to lift her spirits again but kept my feet planted in the long hairs of the rug because I didn't think I was strong enough to.

I watched her choke back wild sobs, failing to get them under control. My mother was drowning. She clung to the neck of her shirt with both hands and pulled on it violently like a mermaid trying to come up for air. The unrecognizable woman then dropped her head backward, and the ceiling vibrated when she remembered everything that ever made her sad since the day she was born.

Mom's heavy head dragged forward again with long strands of oily black hair covering her tear-stained face. But through the black hole, I could hear her voice.

"Why?"

She looked ready to collapse onto the cold, hard tiles and without any further hesitation, I ran barefooted down the short hallway to catch her before she did. Her body stiffened at the sound of my small, clammy feet sticking to the floor with every quick step. I opened my short arms wide in an effort to embrace her with the best hug my small body could possibly offer. Mom immediately responded with a terribly sorrowful noise I hadn't heard yet; a cry just as desperate as all the rest, except with a different tone and vibration. I jumped back instantly, thinking that maybe I really wasn't supposed to see her this way and it made her mad that I had. Or that my hands had done something wrong, that my hug was too rough, and that I may have broken her apart more instead of fixing her like I wanted to. This often happened with my favorite Barbie dolls, and I figured it was possible. She saw the fear in my eyes and attempted to make sense of the horrific scene for me.

"Daddy's gone," the raspy whisper came from Mom's shiny face as she used the backside of both hands to clean the falling drops from her swollen cheeks.

I didn't fully understand what she meant, but I still felt a sudden sense of loss and then frustration. Daddy was most likely gone because of the big fight they had the night before when Mommy kept screaming and screaming and screaming, "Get out!" He was gone because of her. I wanted to know more, but it was obviously an inappropriate time to ask questions. I just stayed quiet and stepped in closer to my mother, realizing it was safe to. I placed a sweaty hand on her boney, bare knee to signal my need now for attention. My father was gone, but I couldn't let my sorrow outdo hers. I just wanted to be comforted before it did.

She wiped her wet nose with the worn collar of my father's shirt and finally leaned over to return my hug. I could feel her chin trembling on top of my shoulder as she tried to catch her breath and hold back a new body of water from streaming down her face. I cried like my mother.

I don't remember Mom shedding as many tears on the visiting floor as she did that night. As days turned into months, I imagine she grew more resentful toward her husband for leaving us the way he did. Because of the multiple armed robberies he committed to feed his heroin addiction, my father and mother would only ever share gummy bears with their two daughters at a 3x3 foot table in the middle of a state penitentiary. My little sister slept the day away in her stroller most of the time while I put scraps of crayons to paper to draw Mommy, Daddy, Janessa, and me playing in a big, green park with a field of different colored flowers and a rainbow in the sky to match. I was drawing what the day would look like when Daddy felt better, and the doctors let him come back home.

Little did I know, every child in the "play room" was coloring in a dream of their daddies at home even though none of them would feel better for a really long time.

Mom stopped driving my sister and me up to various prisons fairly close to the start of my father's sentence in 1993, asking his family to take us along on their monthly drives up from Brooklyn instead. She wouldn't lay eyes on him again for ten more years. She filed for divorce in 1996 when a new relationship promised to save her from the inconvenience of loneliness. But there would be many more nights to come when I could hear Mom cry herself to sleep from across the hall where I stayed helplessly in bed, outlining the glow-in-the-dark stars on the wall with a tiny finger until I fell asleep. The sound of my mother's agony carved itself into my dreams, forever reminding me that I never wanted to be the cause of such pain. And yet, I inevitably would be. I would grow up to lie and make Mom cry, not once or twice, but too many times to count.

The clash of steel against steel shocked my ears like dynamite, and I looked up to find the approaching headlights of the Uptown 2 train. The train engaged me in a staring contest with its beaming eyes from a hundred feet away. It screamed against the tracks, daring me to tell myself the truth. How long did I plan to do this? I suddenly felt so lonely and quickly forfeited the contest because of the tears blurring my vision. I was in New York where my friends and family lived just a few train stops away, but I couldn't reunite with anyone without risking the mission. I couldn't risk everybody finding out my secret. Not now. Why? Because everybody would judge; that's all anybody knew how to do. Even the psychologist at Emerson couldn't help glancing up from her notepad to give me two big eyes filled with so much pity I thought for sure she was going to have me admitted to the local nut house, and then break the oath of confidentiality by sharing my life story with her girlfriends over Sunday brunch in the North End. I wanted to retaliate with witty comments like Matt Damon did effortlessly in all his therapy sessions in *Good Will Hunting*. But I wasn't nearly that smart, and instead decided therapy was pointless as I walked out of the room regretting ever saying a word.

The train taunted me more the louder its thunderous presence became, the number 2 growing bigger every half-second. It was like twelve of the menacing, big-mouthed boys in the fourth-grade reminding me all at once of the many reasons I'd never get a boyfriend. The train made me hate myself for making it this far, for skipping two classes and traveling all this way without a strategy, without a solid plan for the future, just my heart's obsession with the present. I looked down at my worn Converses, unconsciously fidgeting less than a foot away from the edge of the tracks. The train's horn roared through the station, sending me back on my heels as it flew past. There was no time to duck the gust of musty, piss-polluted subway air slapping me in the face; something I knew I deserved.

I boarded the Uptown 2 to the Bronx, quick to take an orange seat at the end of the car away from people so that I could catch my breath in peace. I wiped a stray teardrop from the corner of my eye and let my head rest back on a toothy grin of a girl graduating from DeVry University. She looked like me in a shiny cap and gown at Yonkers High School's graduation nearly a year before. I proudly graduated with the yearbook award for Best Smile; with a 7 out of 7 on my final World Lit paper; with honors; as Senior Class President; as the first-place winner in Yonkers High's Talent Show; as Editor and Chief of the school poetry magazine; but most notably, as "Oprah Girl." I was the really smart girl from Downtown Yonkers who went to public school and won that Oprah essay contest and got to go on her show. That's what anyone would remember me for, and it was certainly a dream to be thought of in that way, but a nightmare trying to keep being thought of in that way. I suddenly filled my generation from my community with a strong sense of hope for their own futures as they began paying close attention to mine. Yet, here "Oprah Girl" was, ditching seven-hundred dollar classes that only federal student loans could pay for, and I would eventually find myself cemented in more than just financial debt. If everyone knew what I was up to, I would fall right out of the .1%

category and drown in the statistics that pervaded my daily existence. I would die without anyone ever knowing my plan to find a solution. I would die being just another part of the problem.

I wiped one last rebellious tear from my face when I felt it race down to my chin. I could still be happy and excited about my future like the girl with the perfect smile in the DeVry poster. Everyone would know the truth when the time was right. There was no use crying about it now.

CHAPTER FOUR

Mom and I were greeted by a friendly group of smiling women handing out name tags. I beamed at the sight of my name and placed the sticker on the top pocket of my unkempt blazer. Oprah's warm, inviting team directed us over to a table covered in platters of fresh berries, raw veggies, imported cheeses of all different colors and textures, and mini deli-style Italian sandwiches that instantly made me forget the "meat lovers" Chicago deep-dish pizza I fantasized about for most of the flight. On a separate table laid a neat arrangement of sweets, including chocolate brownies, coffee cakes, and chocolate chip cookies I was almost sure were the soft, gooey kind.

"How was the trip?" one of the nice team members asked and smiled our way.

To no surprise, my mother took the opportunity to engage in an elaborate conversation with the smiling woman, just a few feet before we reached the table. I looked to my right, half-listening to Mom talk the poor lady to death; then to my left, at the glorious display of sandwiches and cookies calling my name; then back to Mom, my eyes begging her to have mercy on both me and the sweet staff member who meant no harm. I tried to play it cool, but my stomach scolded me for hesitating to grab a plate for fear of being the only one at the food spread. Then finally, my super peripheral vision spotted another girl about my age swoop in to collect what looked like a small turkey sandwich *and* a brownie square. An older lady, with the girl's same olive complexion, followed the teen's lead and handpicked a small branch of red grapes for herself. I gave it a few more beats before escaping my ruthless mother and the kind woman who was suffering from a loss of hearing in at least one ear at this point.

I walked over casually, despite the alarms going off in my brain telling me to run like Forest, and grabbed a small paper plate. I approached the table with ease and scanned the amazing, colorful display of fresh fruit and veggies. But the smell of toasted cinnamon invaded my nostrils and lured me over to the next table where I had no choice but to take a piece of coffee cake, browned to perfection. Some of its sweet, powdery crumbs tumbled from the top of the square onto the plate as I placed it down in its new home. I picked up a fallen crumb between my thumb and index finger and brought it to my excited mouth. The smell of cinnamon and brown sugar was so soothing I planned to hunt down a coffee-cake-fragranced candle for my room once I got back to New York.

"Kaylah, right?"

I closed my mouth quickly and looked up from the crumb in-between my fingers to find the beautiful girl with the smooth olive skin eyeing my name tag. I glanced down at my pocket, as though double checking to see if she had the right girl. I gave a weak smile as I let the crumb go, wiped my powdered fingers on my (cream-colored) slacks, and extended a hand.

"Hey. Yes, I'm Kaylah."

"I'm Leilani," she accepted my handshake with a surprisingly assertive one of her own and showed off an impressive straight row of pearly white teeth.

My eyes automatically searched for the name tag she placed neatly on the left side of her wrinkle-free button down to check out the spelling of whatever she just said. Had to be from Hawaii, I thought. She had a name that rang with the spirit of some sort of tribal queen, which matched her confident tone of voice, glowing complexion, and extraordinary posture.

"Where are you from?" Leilani's authoritative voice commanded an answer, and I quickly lost all hope of ever biting into the coffee cake square I painfully held in my hand.

"New York. Yonkers, New York."

Like most people I get into these kinds of small talks with, she had no clue a place called "Yonkers" even existed. Therefore, I had no choice but to offer the same enlightening spiel that I reserve for all the virgin ears who had never heard of my great place of origin. For starters, we were the fourth largest city in New York State and the most populous city in Westchester County. Why the founding fathers of New York City categorized Staten Island as a borough instead of Yonkers was a subject matter I could never resist putting up for debate.

Okay, Staten Island had two times as many people than we did, but it was an actual *island* more than five miles off the mainland, with its most convenient form of public transportation being a *ferry*. No, I couldn't ignore fun-facts like how the Corleone Family house was set on Staten Island in the first *Godfather*; however, Don Vito does have a fatal heart attack in the backyard towards the end of the movie, so cool points are automatically subtracted. Furthermore, in the John Travolta classic, *Saturday Night Fever*, Tony shares a really romantic moment with Stephanie in front of Staten Island's Verrazano-Narrows Bridge; but keep in mind, Bobby C. falls to his death on that same bridge just a few scenes later. Further-furthermore, there was no discussing "the lost borough" without mentioning the real-life boogeyman, Cropsey; a serial killer who kidnaps and murders children for satanic rituals in the underground tunnels of a hospital. Staten Island officials claim the man responsible for the crimes is currently behind bars, but rumor has it they've got the wrong guy. The island is a death trap. I digress.

Yonkers, however, was the sweetest part of New York State, providing the last operating sugar refining factory in the whole Northeast. Ever heard of Domino Sugar? (You're welcome). We rested just a *little* north of New York City, which we referred to simply as "the city," so there was no need to sail the New York Harbor to reach us from the south. We were the part of the mainland without the clutter of yellow taxis, road rage, and fancy glass buildings. Out-of-towners commonly referred to Yonkers as "upstate," but I was never a fan of the technical term because of how closely we rubbed up against the five boroughs. For example, leaving YO to visit our neighbor—the BX—was as simple as a fifteen-minute ride on the 2 bus. It was only ten more minutes on the 1 train to catch the rainbow in Washington Heights where walking down the street was like walking through a live Broadway musical in Spanish. You didn't need to speak the language because the bright faces and rhythmic mix of African and Taino beats made the story easy to follow. If the heavenly smells of a Dominican food truck didn't enchant you long enough to stop and devour a *chimichurri* with a side of *frituras*, then it was just another comfortable thirty minutes aboard the 1 train to 42nd

St. Times Square. Coining Yonkers as "upstate" was just another one of those New Yorker hyperboles.

What I appreciated most about my side of the Big Apple was that it was well-known for developing some of the most iconic entertainment artists in the world. Let's just say, School Street in the 1920s taught Ella Fitzgerald enough sass to later let the world know that *it don't mean a thing if it ain't got that swing*. Though raised in one of the worst housing projects in the city, R&B singer Mary J. Blige came up on top in 1992; successful rappers DMX and Jadakiss followed no more than a few years later; and believe it or not, we were only a fifteen-minute ride on the 7 bus from Heavy D and Denzel Washington's hometown of Mt. Vernon. It was hard for me to imagine a world without these people, but always easier to imagine my name added to the list of rags-to-riches stories created in our area.

If Leilani was *Lost in Yonkers* before, she was surely found now. I never passed up the opportunity to let someone know about where I was from, especially if they showed genuine interest. My block, specifically, was perceived as 'dangerous' to the average outsider, but like a woman accepts a destined soulmate with flaws and all, I accepted my *home*. Yes, you could hear the weekly roar of gunfire pierce through the nighttime sky, but you could also expect to taste the best slice of pizza in your life at *Alfonso's*, every day, except Sundays. No, your car was probably not safe parked out on the street, but the Yonkers Waterfront provided an incredible view of the Hudson River and the ideal first-date-hang-out just walking distance from my building. Of course, there was the occasional visit from the Yonkers SWAT unit for drug busts, but if you took the elevator up to the fifteenth floor-blue side, you could clearly see what colors the Empire State Building was wearing for the night. Like nearly everything in life, my neighborhood was diagnosed with the strange case of Dr. Jekyll and Mr. Hyde.

I didn't come from the best part of town, but I never saw any use in being ashamed of it. Riverdale Avenue was essentially the reason behind all of my success. I saw something that I was a part of, and yet completely detached from at the same time. I consumed my environment in order to help me visualize and birth a better environment the way a music producer takes a compilation of abstract beats to produce one magical sound. I had plans to leave my neighborhood behind, but not before uncovering all the beauty it had to offer and creating more of it.

Turns out, Leilani was from Utah. My guess wasn't too far off as I later learned she identified as a Samoan who lived in Utah. She was my first Samoan friend, a senior at West High School who loved creative writing just as much as I did.

The room was filling up fast with young, anxious faces of different shades and stories, many products of Holocaust survivors and other traumatic life-changing events. Our parents disappeared into another room when it was clear that every student had made it safely to Chicago and added a name tag to their well-put-together outfits. After waiting in pure shock through the most surreal two months of our lives, we found ourselves in a luxurious hotel conference room finally getting to meet each other and reality. All fifty winners and twenty-two states were represented in one room for the next sixty minutes. I took great pleasure in finding out that the state of New York had produced four finalists, but out of those four, I was the only girl, the only non-White, and the only one from the hood. I felt like Michelle Rodriguez in *Girl Fight*, knocking out anyone who dared to say I didn't have what it took to be great. I was a bad ass.

The social icebreakers commenced, putting the daydream of me wearing boxing gloves and cornrows on pause and the coffee cake away indefinitely. Fortunately, my empty stomach was distracted by the fullness of the room. It was amazing to hear the voices of the .1%, to be in the presence of visions as big as mine, of innate creativity, of hope and love for the colorful lives we came from. We each carried an innocent ignorance of the distant experiences near us, and yet appreciated every story and the courageous individual behind it as though we had known each other for much longer than fifteen minutes. We were joined together with the expectation of a simple "meet-and-greet," and gratefully found ourselves recognizing a complicated amount of power in one contained space, an intelligent force of nature that only someone possessing both goddess and human qualities could manifest. A ten-word essay question invited honor students, captains of sports teams, future journalists, human rights activists and visionaries to embrace the existence of their imperfect worlds and bring to light the truth behind those imperfections.

But as diverse as we all appeared to be, it was now blatantly clear that we had more in common than good grades and a free trip to Chicago—we were all products of our environments.

We were on the outside looking in on *one* world from different angles. We used words to distinguish our realities on paper, but the truth was that there was just *one* reality. We were various samples of what products look like when they are *aware* they are products. I felt like a social science experiment for a moment, until I remembered that I believed in God more than I believed in science, and decided I was a part of something bigger than myself. The horror that Professor Elie Wiesel depicted with ironic eloquence, and all of our fifty experiences combined, were just examples of the many ways in which humans severely lacked love and understanding for humans, ultimately destroying the only world we had. Our testimonies were evidence of an unwavering cycle, rotating one nightmare after another like a never-ending ride on a Ferris wheel. Suddenly, no form of ignorance existed in the room, and our definitions of tragedy were the same. Our experiences were the same. Our goals were the same. I identified as a Rwandan genocide survivor whose parents were slaughtered at the hands of the Hutu government; I lived in a small motel room and was forced to take a two-hour bus ride to school after my mother and I were evicted from our apartment in Irving, Texas; I was exposed to an "ethnic cleansing" in Darfur and witnessed the massacre of men, women, and children in my village. They were all from Downtown Yonkers and watched a crack addict offer her *Benefit* card in exchange for a vial while her toddler waited patiently on the side.

Each story was about family, loss, faith, love, fear and survival told from different perspectives, possessing the same level of courage, honesty, and awareness. For the first time ever, amidst fifty strangers, I saw passion meet purpose in my own life.

I embraced the epiphany with immense gratitude as I remembered feeling uninspired just over a year before. It was like my full potential was lost and stagnate in the wilderness somewhere and wouldn't find me until the following lifetime, all because I was sad about falling in love with a boy who dumped me for one of the popular skinny girls at his school. He was my second boyfriend, whom I dated a year after breaking up with my first boyfriend due to my relentless insecurities. I journaled a way through self-reflection and even wrote about my first boyfriend and first broken heart in letters to my father who gladly helped me conclude that I wasn't ready for a serious relationship at the age of fourteen anyway. I proceeded to allow myself as much time as necessary to strictly focus on strengthening my young brain academically and emotionally.

Then, as if the universe was rewarding me for all my mental growth and new-found maturity, there was Alexander Justin Mitchell. The gift included sweet cinnamon brown eyes unusually bigger than the average pair, but were the perfect fit for a face as strong and dark as the trunk of a baobab tree that only God Himself could have sculpted from. His laid-back, street-smart demeanor was enticing, yet the swag made him appear awkward once I recognized the humility in his candied-pecan eyes. I took one look at him, and brown was instantly my new favorite color. Puberty left his buttery skin untouched and instead focused on stretching him above average height for a fifteen-year-old boy with the hands and feet of a promising NBA star to match. Alex turned out to be a superstar running back for the Blue Devils at Saunders High School, the second leading Yonkers public school in academics. (Yonkers High was the first. Just saying).

But it was his smile that would inevitably fog any recollection I had of who I was, what country I was living in, and what language(s) I spoke, for at least six seconds. Before I witnessed his with my own eyes, my smile was the greatest smile I had ever known. It was my only feature that I couldn't criticize. It was a blessedly organic grill, never needing the help of metal and pink rubber bands to keep it together. My abnormally large grin wasn't from just Mom or Dad, but a pure mix of both their naturally long, elastic lips and evenly arranged teeth. The combination of their genes created something like the sly Cheshire Cat smile that I would proudly flaunt to shine a light on anyone's bad day. But Alex's toothy grin possessed the power to brighten days for so long the world would eventually forget that once upon a time, a moon and stars and a night sky ever existed. It went against nature and couldn't possibly be understood by the naked eye. When his lips parted for the first time to present an un-photoshopped advertisement worthy of billboards in Times Square, I was left like an open-mouthed, drooling toddler watching my first magic show in awe. It was like a live Colgate commercial taking place right before my eyes, and I half-expected to run to the nearest CVS to buy out their toothpaste supply. Just when I thought the vision before me couldn't get any more flawless, I spotted one lonely dimple on his right cheek that perfectly complimented his face without the company of another. It took every ounce of willpower in my body not to attack it with a quick kiss to show my appreciation for such beauty.

He was like every lead actor I had ever fallen in love with at the movie theater combined into one human. He was the guy that made me squirm in my seat and eat popcorn mindlessly as I fantasized about being the lead actress, the one that would drive him so crazy he couldn't imagine ever loving anyone as much as he loved me. He didn't necessarily look like any one person I had seen in a movie or on TV. But if I had to pick a combination of celebrities to paint his face, he'd be the gorgeous love child of Jay Hernandez, Kal Penn, and Usher? I was lost. His face was a beautiful, confusing mess that left me completely dumbfounded with a child-like curiosity. In Yonkers, knowing if someone was Latino, Black, or Indian, was as easy as looking at them, but Alex could have passed for all three at once. I never imagined dating someone who was

Indian, partly because I didn't live around many, and partly because I was still ignorant of cultures outside my own. Even so, I effortlessly began envisioning myself dressed in a red and white panetar saree with gold trimming. I was a dancing Indian bride exuding a regal aura alongside my glistening groom. Our chemistry on the dance floor was undeniable as we laughed and moved to the melodies of a sitar, our feet and smiles putting on a spectacular show for his family and mine.

I could feel myself staring at Alex for an uncomfortable amount of time, trying to find our future in his face. I was lost for words and the butterflies in my stomach felt so real, I thought I might burp one out when I heard him speak for the first time, "I'm hungry. You ate?"

Even at fifteen, I was a big critic of the "love at first sight" theme in movies, believing the concept was obviously solely based on superficial qualities. I wanted a man to put forth a real effort into soul-searching and fall head over heels with the end result, leaving my looks behind as a distant afterthought. I was an advocate for the righteous idea of "getting to know a person," because it just made the most sense. But, nothing about Alex made sense. His eyes told me that falling in love with a stranger was normal, totally acceptable, and everyone else was a fool to think otherwise. I was held in a trance, an outer body experience that teleported me back in time to 1877 in Paris, France. My secret lover curled up on the balcony outside my bedroom window every night because it was the closest he could be to my sleeping body without my conservative mother catching him. My beau from a past life was the same beautiful boy standing in front of me. We had searched each other's souls and fell wildly in love before, and I had grown to know him better than I knew myself. I just couldn't say that in the present day without him running away in the opposite direction.

Unfortunately, we would only be boyfriend and girlfriend in this lifetime for three short months before he moved onto a girl named Tanya who was well-known for an over-developed butt disproportionate to her My-Size-Barbie frame and a forehead slightly too large for her tiny face. But, she was also a member of the Match-Your-Belt-With-Your-Jordans Club, which was a key characteristic only the "freshest" boys from New York looked for in a girl at that time.

I knew Big Butt Tanya was just a cover-up, though. What began to attract Alex more than anything was the jungle. Alexander J. Mitchell was one of the good ones, but his stunning face, "fresh" attire, and talent on the football field garnered a social life that would inevitably hinder his academic career. The constant excitement surrounding the football star at school would leave him looking for more in a place where he didn't belong. We continued a distant friendship from opposite sides of the spectrum as I stayed in the library, and he stayed in the streets. I eventually found some relief in Alex's absence after convincing myself that watching him officially transform from a good one into a lost one would be the real heartbreak, so we were better off apart. I still loved him, though. The rest of the year, my sixteenth birthday included, was a blur with clear images of his brown face from time to time. My journal entries, poems, and short story pieces were like sad babies birthed by a mother suffering from postpartum depression. For months, my creativity could remember only one emotion.

My best friend, Yanel Pineda, often deserved credit for pulling me out of my melodramatic funks. We had literally known each other since kindergarten, so when she asked me what was wrong, there was no hiding it.

"What if hard work never pays off?"

"What, Kaylah?" She knew I was getting ready for one of my usual life reflections over the phone, but humored me anyway.

"I feel like I work so hard for nothing sometimes. I feel like I'm in an elevator that goes up to the three-hundredth floor, and no matter how many times I press the other buttons, I stay stuck at like the sixth floor...blue side."

"Well, sounds like another poem to me," Yanel teased using very little sarcasm, and I could see her eyeballs rolling through the phone. "Girl, listen...you're sixteen years old. Please stop talkin' like we're in our forties. You have plenty of time to do what you want to do. Don't let a dude make you doubt your skills."

She got me. But my break-up with Alex had just been the cherry on top of a long history with fear. I was always afraid of not being good enough for a guy, for my mother, but mainly not good enough for the success I wanted so badly for myself.

"I want to be successful."

"Then you will be. You just gotta have patience and know that God has your back."

On top of attending almost every grade school together, Yanel and I also went to Sunday school at St. Peter's Catholic Church before she and her family left the neighborhood for a Section 8 apartment on the semi-nice side of Yonkers. She was first-generation Dominican who adopted her faith in the Holy Spirit from her God-fearing mother, while I was second-generation and learned to respect the power of the Holy Spirit as I watched my God-fearing Nana kneel at her bedside every night.

Yanel was right. I couldn't pray and worry at the same time. What I also had to admit to myself was how successful a project of mine turned out whenever I genuinely worked with my heart. It was something I didn't know how to explain, just a feeling that came over me when I handed in a creative essay or recited a Shakespearean soliloquy. If the inspiration and opportunity were there to create something great, then I wouldn't let it go until I thought it was great. My heart was always the common denominator for these projects that had positively affected my teacher or my whole class. Whether I was chatting it up with Oprah or a local news anchor on *Channel 12*, I always closed my eyes to find myself standing somewhere bigger than Riverdale, which helped me fall fast asleep with a smile on my face. With all the pictures constantly dancing around in my imagination, there had to be a reason the ones of my future influence were the most vivid.

Just the way my first callow relationship dared me to reinvent myself, I used Alex to do the same. School was always my go-to catalyst for rejuvenating my spirit. I made sure to excel in all subjects until I finally reached junior year and found myself comfortably smothered by inspiration in every class, but mainly English and creative writing.

Now I stood in the middle of a fancy hotel conference room among forty-nine new friends who could all relate to my level of passion. Winning the contest was my wake-up call; it was an alarm clock labeled "Purpose," and there was no pressing the snooze button. I had to get up and recognize the calling. I only knew what desperately wanting a better life for myself and my family felt like, but didn't know how to take us to the other side. Though I still didn't fully understand, I recognized God in the contest, and it was more obvious than ever that He had no plans to keep me on Riverdale Avenue doing nothing for the rest of my existence. I was in the presence of greatness, I was being used with the .1% to make a difference, and it was our love for mankind that ultimately inspired me to stay on this path because it could only lead to more miracles. The next day, I was certain that all forty-nine contest winners had also found me in a past life as we sat patiently waiting at Harpo Studios for the miracle worker to make an entrance.

CHAPTER FIVE

The wind was like a sweet, hyper dog hovering me with excitement but not realizing how roughly I was being swayed from side to side. If it were not for its overzealous gusts, the temperature at two o'clock in the morning probably wouldn't have felt so unbearable. I was grateful for my big, ugly North Face coat that I almost left behind for a more attractive and less practical peacoat I got on sale at H&M. Prayers were finally answered when *Danny's* fifty-seat coach bus came out from hiding behind a giant Frito-Lay truck down the street and slowly pulled up to the crowd of freezing women and children waiting to be rescued at E. 149th St. and Grand Concourse in the Bronx.

I never thought I'd be so happy to see the badly beaten bus park and nearly break down in front of us. Danny, a retired locksmith from Jamaica, arrived fifteen minutes late and apologized with as much projection as his emphysema-stricken vocal cords could carry. I was looking forward to warming up, but most of my excitement was reserved for being one step closer to the final destination. The journey felt weeks-long before the moment finally came to find my place in line among the nearly frostbitten loved ones, ready to hand fifty dollars in cash over to Danny in return for his heroic services. It was February 14, 2008, and I had just made it safely off the

Greyhound, off the Uptown 2 train, and said a silent prayer to eventually make it off *Danny's* coach bus in another four hours.

My pestering guilty conscience was being fed by the cold beating against my bare face as I started to do more than just half-wish I had never left my dorm room. I was the only one responsible for bringing the unyielding paranoia and sickening anxiety on myself, knowing all too well that the illness was an inescapable consequence of my disloyalty. My present worries smothered me with an intense feeling of déjà vu when I boarded the bus and found an empty, torn seat by an icy window toward the front. I remembered how my very first series of secrets started with regular detours to Steven's house after the last bell dismissed Riverside Middle School for the day. Steven was my first boyfriend—a skinny, sluggish, porn-addicted fifteen-year-old Puerto Rican disguised as an exemplary student and God-fearing young man in a Catholic school uniform. I liked to imagine he was standing as tall as me at 5'6", but reality kept him a half inch away from my delusion. He called me his "girlfriend," and that's all that really mattered to me anyway.

My mother made her mind up about my new friend the moment he flashed an obnoxious grin and opened his mouth to speak his first words to her.

"Hi, Mom."

I could see her bulging eyes burning the flesh off of his face and quickly tried to distract her by offering some of our leftover popcorn. She had come to pick me up at the Cross County Mall at exactly 8:45 p.m. (fifteen minutes before the time we actually agreed to) where Steven and I had just enjoyed watching *8 Mile* together. I thought my mother would be impressed by the sweet way he opened the passenger door to her red Dodge Caravan and made sure I was safely tucked in before closing it. But as soon as we said our good nights and drove off, she used her Psychic Mom abilities to predict trouble.

"He looks like a dirtbag. The last thing we need is another nasty priest in these streets."

Dirtbag, maybe. But Steven had no intention of ever entering the priesthood, especially with the kind of extra-curricular activities he was in to. He loved being in a relationship with a sex novice like myself, even though I confessed to reading Zane's *Addicted* from start to finish in less than forty-eight hours. Nia, the most promiscuous girl in my eighth-grade class, claimed it was a "must read" when inconspicuously tucking it into my JanSport backpack. But Steven insisted nothing compared to the "real deal" and enthusiastically volunteered to teach me how to "French kiss real good" and give the "flavaz hand job" all in the same hour. Naturally, this kind of private schooling made me nervous, and I was usually hesitant to participate in the entire lesson, always leaving Steven with a painful pair of blue balls after make-out practice. I also felt queasy about sneaking around behind my mother's back, knowing very well how much she despised my boyfriend. Mom wouldn't even acknowledge the relationship, hoping that if she pretended Steven never existed, I would eventually follow her lead. Nana was much more excited when I shared the news with her, hopeful that she'd be alive to attend my wedding and meet her great-grandchildren in the next few years. However, as much as my grandmother wanted to see me living the happy Dominican-style family life, I knew she wouldn't approve of all the sinful experience I had obtained so soon. I wanted to give into my mother's wishes, partly because her happiness was important to me and partly because she was right about Steven. No good could come from this relationship at my age, so I had to move on...or just pretend to.

The less of Steven I saw, the wilder my curiosity grew, and it would eventually influence most of my bad decisions during the last year of junior high. I found the more often I ditched my after-school algebra tutor to visit my after-school sex-ed tutor, the more comfortable the lessons made me feel. Years of being the subject of fat girl jokes convinced me that I would go a lifetime without being loved by a guy, let alone intimate with him. Then Steven came along and offered hope in the form of soft kisses on the side of my neck. I was a foreplay pro by the age of fourteen, discovering the magic of fingers and the electric power of the tongue, ultimately learning how to please and be pleased without ever spreading my legs. Until, of course, I decided to spread my legs.

We planned to do it the night of our nine-month anniversary on March 1, 2003, while his parents were out having dinner in the Bronx and my mother lay in bed thinking I was hanging out at Yanel's house. Steven had a small room on the third floor of his parents' Victorian style home in the nicer part of Yonkers. The pastel blue sheets on his twin-size bed had been tucked, pillows fluffed, and all dirty clothes had found a way to the hamper, revealing to me a forest green carpet for the first time. I cracked open the one foggy window in the room to invite some much-needed fresh air. Steven had also taken it upon himself to light several powerful potpourri candles that made the room smell like the nursing home my 94-year-old aunt Juana lived in. I had a feeling his mother would soon wonder where all of her decorative bathroom candles disappeared to.

I explored the tiny bedroom that appeared two times bigger since the first time I stepped into it. Steven clearly made an effort to make this night special for me, and I couldn't help but love him for that.

I thought rose petals were the only thing missing to complete the romantic cliché until I heard the music start from the other side of the door. Steven searched through an iTunes playlist on the family Mac computer and pressed play when he found "I'll Make Love to You," by Boyz II Men. He succeeded in creating the ultimate sexy cliché moment without harming any roses in the process, suddenly making me feel more comfortable and excited. Just when nerves started to subside and I began to think there was no better time to lose my virginity, Steven barged into his room wearing nothing but floppy white socks and plaid boxers that drooped around his small waist.

"We got a problem."

Those were exactly the words I didn't want to hear. I knew I shouldn't have come. I knew I shouldn't have lied to my mother. She would eventually find out anyway. What was I thinking? How upset was she? Oh, my God, was she here? Was she outside waiting to kick my ass? Hopefully, I would get the chance to apologize before she turned on the dragon breath to torch my face off. Lord, if you get me out of this one, I promise to never lie to Mom again. Please, please, please.

My thoughts moved as sporadically as a million little snow flurries in the windy sky. I forgot Steven still hadn't announced what our problem actually was until he finally spoke again.

"My mom and dad are heading back now."

My rubbery body collapsed onto his bed, relief embracing my heart and taming the beats.

"That's awesome," exhaustion clouded my voice as I shared a single thought aloud with the ceiling.

"Awesome? No way. I wanted to spend so much more time with you."

Steven found a small space on the bed and sat next to me. The candle flames fluttered enough light in the room to illuminate the disappointment on his face.

"It's okay. We'll plan it again for another night," I spoke softly, too high on gratitude to console him further.

But instead of agreeing with me and putting his baggy jeans back on, my boyfriend leaned over to give me a kiss on the lips just as we practiced countless times before.

The Boys II Men track was on replay and started again for the second time. In-between each gentle kiss on my collarbone, he sang along to the words as he usually liked to do with all his favorite songs, because once upon a time, someone told him he was a really good singer. I imagined the liar was one of his past girlfriends trying to impress him. Yet here I was doing the same, listening to his off-key serenade of "I'll Make Love to You"— a really nice song that I would regrettably associate with this moment for the rest of my life.

I watched him apply the condom onto a penis that suddenly appeared much larger than I remembered, disproportionate to the size of his frail figure and nothing like the pictures in my health textbook. My merciless jeans stuck to my sweaty thighs as my body temperature skyrocketed, making their removal more awkward than I imagined. I didn't take my sweater off so that I would only have to worry about throwing my pants and sneakers back on before jumping out the window in case his parents arrived sooner than later. I was also too conscious of my body to expose it all for him. He kept his boxers and socks on.

"Ready?"

"Yes," I answered quickly, wanting to just get it over with, wanting to know what the big deal was, to know if it was as good as Rose and Jack made it seem in *Titanic*, to report back to my girlfriends who had already lost their V-cards the summer before, to take a cab home and find my mother sleeping peacefully in her bed.

I could feel him down there searching for the hidden entryway. I closed my eyes tight, embracing myself for impact. A few tormenting seconds later, he was in.

I wanted to jump from the bed to blow out all the candles and bust the window open because the room instantly became too hot to bear. In my mind, the Devil had set the bed on fire, and I begged for my life as his flames threatened to swallow me up whole. Something was moving inside of me, something that didn't feel good at all, something wrong and I wanted it out.

"Stevie?"

We heard a female's voice call from three floors down.

"Fuck," Steven panicked from inside of me.

I wanted to vomit and warned him to get off before I did.

"But I'm not even all the way in yet," he resisted against my shoving hands on his chest.

"Are you fuckin' crazy? Get off *now*," I spoke in a loud, aggressive whisper, completely taken aback by his willingness to continue.

He gave me a frustrated grunt, and I could feel the slimy, rubbery monster abruptly leave my body like something out of *Alien*.

I was too frantic to pay attention to the soreness in-between my thighs and rushed to put my cotton panties and jeans on, moving fast as if my mother had just stepped into the bedroom. Steven quietly redressed himself, blew out the candles, walked out into the hall and down the stairs to greet his parents. I felt abandoned and alone in a room I thought would do the complete opposite as the nauseating smell of potpourri filled my nostrils. I imagined finding the power of confidence and self-love like Ana did after she lost her virginity in *Real Women Have Curves*. But the hope of that new identity was vanishing around me like the smoky remnants of burnt candle wicks.

Apparently, Steven's mother wasn't buying his "just listening to music" alibi and barked at the both of us as she dialed the number of a cab company and my home number immediately after. His father was stone-faced as usual when he walked past me and up the stairs, without a word or a glance in my direction. If I didn't mind the risk of breaking both kneecaps, I would've jumped out the window like I planned to in the first place.

The only person who could make the empty feeling go away was the person on the other side of the phone listening to Steven's mother dramatize her assumptions of the evening's events. But any expectation of Mom's comfort that night was non-existent when the ruthless ranting woman decided to rip out her heart and soul through the cordless phone.

Just as my instincts had warned, Mom was already aware of my plans at Steven's house that night because the mother of one of my girlfriends at school called to break the news to her after her daughter spilled the beans during dinner a couple hours earlier. The phone call from Steven's mother later in the evening was just confirmation. I ran to the cab when it arrived, silently asking God for all the forgiveness in the world and a new set of friends.

My clammy fingers could barely grip the keys in my hand long enough to open the green apartment door. There were three sides to my building complex—the blue side, red side, and green side. You knew which side you had stumbled upon by looking at the peeling paint color of the bulletproof doors. We had recently moved from a two-bedroom on the sixth floor-blue side to a three-bedroom on the fifteenth floor-green side to make room for my little brother. We had upgraded to a better view of the Hudson River and the luxury condominium complex down by the waterfront. I wished I had enough money to live in one of those condos by myself. I wished I lived anywhere but inside the apartment I was most likely getting thrown out of that night.

What was waiting for me on the other side of the green door? The unknown choked my lungs, preventing the deep breath I desperately needed to inhale before walking in. I turned the lock before I could pass out from the lack of oxygen and stepped into the black abyss. I moved around blindly in a pitch-black space searching for the light switch, afraid of hands wrapping around my neck and strangling me to death at any second. The darkness alone was enough to suffocate me in the meantime, unable to get the idea of walking through a Wes Craven film out of my head. My fingertips finally felt the switch, and fear snatched my breath away when I turned the light on. There was Mom.

I found her sitting on the couch fully dressed to go out into the first cold night of March. She was ready to come pick me up and bring me home, but the water in her eyes must have blurred her vision too much to drive. Her swollen face was shiny with tears just as I remembered when I was a little girl. I was ready to deny everything, but the pain in her eyes told me another lie would do no good. Telling her the truth about the whole thing literally lasting less than ten seconds crossed my mind too, but I thought we were both better off if I spared the details.

"I'm sorry." It was my turn to cry.

It was the only logical thing to say, yet completely inappropriate at the same time. How dare I expect an apology and a few tears to fix anything? I tried to reconcile by promising to never see Steven again, but the damage was already done. She didn't have the strength to hear anymore, only enough to hang her coat up in the closet and make her way back to bed. Once again, I was left alone in a room knowing that I had broken my mother's heart and the promise to never do so.

I had to dig for the courage to write about the kind of misbehaving I was up to in a long letter to my father. He was the hardest person to tell, especially because instead of giving a depthless confession over a thirty-minute collect call I decided to mark my thoughts down on paper where they would live forever. I needed to know that someone could read my story and still find me worthy of forgiveness no matter how much pain it cost them.

I left Steven and the thoughts of that night alone, wanting nothing more than to move on and pretend like the last nine months never happened. The real punishment was that I hurt Mom and destroyed all the trust she had in me. Who knew three years later Oprah would be the one to help my mother fully forgive me?

Now, here I was doing something I considered one-hundred times worse. But when I compared my feelings and state of mind in the present situation to my past, I couldn't ignore the maturity of my emotions over the duration of five years. I knew that being on *Danny's* bus was wrong just like I knew that being in Steven's bed was wrong. But it was different this time because my heart was in the right place. Unfortunately, no matter how genuine my intentions were years later, there were no words I could say or write to convince my mother that everything would be okay. I was really in love, and though it was painful for me to keep these bottomless secrets from her, a part of me believed my relationship was worth lying and living the foggy double life for.

I had known this kind of love before, a complete soul-searching-love-at-first-sight-better-than-the-movies kind of love. However, I was now nineteen years old and more aware of the mechanics of my heart. I was one of the most emotionally fragile creatures I had ever known, effortlessly—and often simultaneously—crying out of both happiness and sadness (especially every time I watched *Moulin Rouge*). Nonetheless, I was stronger and fully prepared to do whatever necessary to spend Valentine's Day with my leading man, even if it meant spending the day in New York at Great Meadow Correctional Facility.

CHAPTER SIX

I jolted out of dreams at the sound of a bomb followed by the frantic sirens of police cars and fire trucks. There was a strong force over my body preventing me from leaving the unfamiliar bed to check on my mother. My weak limbs played dead hoping to trick my captor into walking away so that I could free myself behind his back. But he wasn't fooled by the defense mechanism I picked up from a horror movie I couldn't remember the name of. Instead, he held me down with the chilling steel head of a gun against my chest, maliciously ordering me to "Get up!" at the same time.

Mom set the hotel alarm clock the night before as we lay down to sleep in our own individual queen-sized beds and disarmed it early in the morning. It wasn't until she came to strip me from the warmth of the royal white comforter before sunrise that I remembered Chicago's aggressive spring breeze. I was relieved that there was no real bomb or armed kidnapper in the room, but distraught when I realized that my one night on the unbelievably comfortable mattress at the Chicago Omni Hotel had come to an end. It was the softest bed I had ever slept in, so much more generous than the dented prune of a futon waiting for me at home. I found it easy to plop my head back into the pillow of cotton candy and whipped cream even after Mom made it clear that it was time to stop drooling and get up. Then she turned the bedroom lamp on, and through one squinted eye I saw her arched eyebrow illuminated in the shadows. I immediately hopped off the mattress and its cool linens like she had just set it all on fire. I found solace on my way to the shower as I made a mental note to have a fancy bed just like that when I grew up and had a place of my own.

Mom and I were both quiet that morning. But it was too hard to suppress my laughter when she broke a nail and temporarily glued her top lip to her pinky finger after attempting to fix the nail with crazy-glue. It was exactly the kind of scene I needed to save me from the overwhelming anxiety of the morning. Hot water and petroleum jelly finally freed Mom's lip from her pinky after about ten minutes. She couldn't help but smile through her frustration as she reminded me to re-iron my outfit for the taping and organize all my stuff back into our one suitcase. We had to pack our things because we'd be driven straight to the airport from Harpo Studios after the show. We lived like royalty for twenty-four hours, and I knew both of us secretly wished it could have lasted a little longer. It was the most exciting day of our lives because I was going to be on *Oprah*, and yet the idea of having to return to reality so soon found us and pinched us both like an unwelcomed bee sting. I massaged my pain with fantasies of being like Jenny from the Block who reached superstardom and earned the world's love through hard work and dedication to her talents. I was still on cloud nine after meeting my epiphany in the hotel conference room the day before. I was surrounded by greatness the whole time, so why couldn't I think that I too was destined for it even if I was headed back to Yonkers at the end of the day? I prayed that my mother found a similar way to cope with her sting.

Mom and I were separated when we arrived at Harpo Studios a couple hours later. I gave her a kiss on the cheek before leaving to join my forty-nine new friends backstage. I wouldn't see her again until after the taping.

All fifty antsy finalists were greeted by staff members wearing microphone earpieces and walkie-talkies attached to the side of their hips. This crew, mostly women again, were a lot hastier than the ones that moderated our meet-and-greet on the first day. Nonetheless, the ladies were all still smiling as they instructed us to cautiously form one straight line among loads of camera equipment and long cable cords that led to nowhere. We organized ourselves and chatted softly with each other to ease our nerves when one of the happily busy women abruptly left her walkie-talkie conversation and looked at us. She gestured for the line-leader to step forward and the student disappeared behind a massive, solid black wall and wasn't seen again. The winner behind the line-leader was directed to do the same and so was the winner behind her until our line gradually shrunk well below fifty. Was this it? Were we headed on stage one-at-a-time in front of a crowd of God-knows-how-many-people and cameras and the entire world just like that? What happened to "lights, camera, action"? Wasn't that the cue for movies and TV shows? Wasn't there a director around directing people through a megaphone before we started filming? What about breathing instructions? How was I supposed to breathe right now? Oh, my God—what if I fell on national television? I would forever be remembered as "the girl who fell and broke an ankle on *Oprah*." Even though I was wearing just one-inch wedge heels, it was obvious that Steve Urkel could have done a better job walking in them. And my hair? I could easily set the studio on fire with the static energy coming from my head. My face? The only makeup I had on was the roll-on lip gloss I bought for a dollar at the corner beauty supply store. Surely, that wasn't good enough for Oprah.

There were no mirrors backstage for me to take a quick look at all my uncertainties. I half-wished Mom was around to conduct her usual check-up and do that thing I hated when she licked her thumb and jammed it in my eye to wipe it clean from sleepy crust with her saliva. I took a few seconds to chat with God, asking for as much Holy Spirit Assistance He could offer for the day. I just needed someone to tell me I was ready for my first television debut. I needed someone to tell me I was ready.

Then, before I could ask where the nearest restroom was located to vomit up my continental hotel breakfast, the happy lady with the walkie-talkie smiled at me and used a graceful hand to call her next victim. I decided the only thing I could do then was stop thinking so much and just smile back. I was really good at smiling and pretending to know what was going on in biology. This situation didn't have to be any different.

"I'm smiling. I'm not falling. I'm smiling. I'm not..." I muttered through chiclet-sized teeth on my way around the giant, black wall and onto the stage.

I expected to get slapped in the face by blinding fluorescent lights and my hair blown away stiff by the roar of applauding strangers covering the arena from one corner to another. Instead, I walked out into a peaceful space lined with empty seats and a man wearing a fancy camera around his neck. A few feet in front of the photographer was another jovial woman who flaunted a rich nest of lively, salon-done hair and an impeccably ironed and superbly color-coordinated outfit. She stood next to an old man who appeared to sink in a suit and tie, but his high-leveled chin signaled he was afloat and well. I saw a sweet sparkle overshadow exhaustion in the man's eyes as I timidly approached the odd couple. I was going to take a picture with Oprah Winfrey and Elie Wiesel.

I didn't have to try hard to focus on smiling and freezing all activity inside my head; it was my brain's natural reaction when it realized exactly what was happening. Oprah reached out her soft hand to shake mine and casually greeted me with a breathtaking "good morning." I held her fingers for a much shorter amount of time than I did in my dreams for fear of grossing her out with my sweaty palm. I turned to the Professor and allocated the same half-second to his fragile, cold hand and let it go wishing I could have held on longer just to warm it up some. He exchanged my abnormally large grin with a slight twitch at the corner of his mouth. The Professor's forced smirk automatically triggered my lips to stretch to their full capacity as I nestled my way between the two super humans for our epic photo.

I reached my arms around Oprah and Elie like the three of us had last seen each other in Oprah's dining room for Thanksgiving a few months prior and maybe even enjoyed lighting the menorah at Elie's place on the first night of Hanukkah. The photographer himself must've thought the scholarly pair and I were headed to brunch to discuss books and such over virgin mimosas as soon as we finished taping. I was nervous enough to chew all my manicured fingernails off and completely comfortable in their extraordinary company at the same time.

"This is insane!" I spoke suddenly, my lips never touching. *Insane?* I had never used that word for a "cool" substitute before in my life! Where had I heard the phrase? It definitely wasn't a trendy line commonly thrown around my predominately Black neighborhood. I had to have picked it up from one of my favorite TV shows—*Full House*; *Saved by the Bell*, and maybe even quirky Carlton naturally recited the line while dancing on an episode of *The Fresh Prince of Belair*. Nonetheless, the unfamiliar words had come from a mouth that I dreaded ever having to open again.

I tried to read the Professor's face without moving my head, but my eyeballs could only stretch so far to the left. I could almost hear him trash-talking my silly American lingo under all his white hair. It wasn't hard to believe that my brain could fail me at the most defining moment of my life—the first time Oprah Winfrey and Elie Wiesel heard my voice. I was morphing into an armadillo, cringing into a fetal position and preparing to roll myself back to Yonkers at any second.

My self-loathing was so loud I almost missed the laugh. It wasn't a "LOL" kind of laugh. It was a soft, pleasant sound that put my organs back in place and reminded me to exhale. I, Kaylah Pantaleón, made *the* Oprah Winfrey giggle. Yes, *I* spoke, and *she* giggled. It was very possible that she had feigned amusement just to save the atmosphere from the awkwardness I effortlessly created. If that was the case, then she was as amazing as two Oprahs in one. Either way, the giggle's authenticity was irrelevant. I had made an angel on Earth "LAL" (laugh a little), and the only ones who heard it were the three of us and God. I was definitely going to heaven.

During my last few seconds in her presence, I wished more than anything that I could step inside of Oprah's body. I imagined the process looking something like Patrick Swayze's spirit entering Whoopi Goldberg's body when connecting with Demi Moore in *Ghost*. My intention was not to speak through her and scare the hell out of people but to understand how someone like Oprah Winfrey worked. She was comparable to a rare grandfather clock with golden pieces so intricate that it would take another lifetime to pick apart and find its beginning.

If I could get inside Oprah's mind and soul, I was bound to find all of life's secrets to everlasting success. How did she define hard work? How did she avoid her greatest distractions? How much patience did a global influencer have to learn? How much faith did it take to stand in her shiny, pointed-toe pumps and speak to millions? There was so much I wanted to know from the tree of knowledge that stood in full bloom right next to me. But, the apple was still too far for me to reach.

The fancy camera in front of us flashed once, then twice. As I dropped my arms and broke away from our embrace, I decided the "exclusive" look inside Oprah's being would only be found in a Google article or her lifestyle magazine. Admittedly, it was a lot more feasible than taking her soul hostage.

I spoke once more to say "thank you," and made eye contact with the divine couple for the last time before exiting stage left. I made it down the three steps without breaking either of my ankles and followed one of the happy walkie-talkie ladies to an empty seat in the second row from the stage. I joined about thirty of the winners who sat in silence after their photo shoot. Everyone was still probably struggling to accept that they had actually woken up this morning. I couldn't blame them. I was in total disbelief over my sixty-second moment, and the only thing that told me it was all very real was the throbbing pain in both my pinky toes. I wanted so badly to kick off the wedge heels and give my feet a breather, but I had to spare my fellow finalists the inevitable stench of nervous, sticky toes.

On the TV, *Oprah* appeared to take place inside a coliseum about the size of Madison Square Garden. But in real life, Yonkers High School's gymnasium was probably twice as big as the studio. There definitely wasn't enough space for a Yonkers Bull Dogs' pep-rally, holding probably no more than three-hundred seats in the room. I remember being amazed by the magic of television even before the cameras started rolling.

I was as quiet as the rest of my friends who completely filled up the first three rows when the last winner walked over to us in a star-struck daze and sat down. We were the first of the audience members to arrive and got dibs on the best seats in the house. There was no reason to be so self-conscious because we were not expected to stay on stage during the taping. I dried my moist palms on the pretty, white skirt Mom picked out for me and started breathing normally again. Lights shined from the high ceiling, brightening the stage in an effervescent white and blue glow with purple hints. The floors looked clean enough to sleep and eat on, which I wouldn't have minded doing just to say that I did it.

The only things on display for us to gawk at were Oprah's world-renowned couch chairs. How many awesome people had sat in those giant pillow cushions over the years? I vividly recalled the episode when Tom Cruise expressed his love for Katie Holmes by jumping on top of them. I thought it was a beautiful thing to see a man act like a psycho over his girlfriend. However, Nana barely touched her lips to a freshly blended glass of chocolate-flavored SlimFast before shouting *¡qué idiota!* because she was genuinely upset about the footprints the actor must have left on the expensive furniture. Only my grandmother noticed that Oprah's chairs had been replaced a few episodes later with a slightly different looking set of chairs and was convinced that *el loco enamorado* ruined the others with his dirty shoes and reckless behavior.

Then a flashback of Alex's face snuck into my memory unexpectedly as I dazed out on Oprah's couch chairs, wishing a guy would go *loco* on national television to declare his love for me. I took a few seconds to daydream about my first true love jumping onto the futon in my bedroom and shouting to the top of his lungs so that my mother and all of Riverdale Avenue could hear about how much he adored me. Alex was more the type to whisper his feelings in my ear rather than risk losing any cool points in public, however. My mouth watered at the short-lived mirage anyway, and a sharp pinch of regret tightened my chest when I thought about the last conversation we just had the week before.

"Hey, Kaylah."

"Who's this?"

I hadn't heard Alex's voice in over a year since he started living in the streets part-time and messing with Tanya. Even so, I could never forget the sound of him smiling through the phone and only pretended not to know who was on the other end because the caller ID on my Nextel read "Unknown." He responded with his airy, boyish laugh that always made me feverish around my ears and cheeks. I wanted so badly to hear it in person.

"Stop. You know who this is."

Then I remembered there were two Alexanders: One Alexander who leaned over to whisper close against my ear, "You make me happy;" and the other who was too lost to remember my birthday. He hurt me when he chose life in the jungle, and as much as I wanted to reminisce the good times until the break of dawn, I had to let him go.

"Sorry, Alex. I can't talk right now."

"Oh c'mon, Kaylah. Don't be like that."

I waited to hear him complete the sentence before folding my phone closed. I knew it was the right thing to do at the time. The Oprah contest winner from Yonkers was the number one topic of discussion around town for the last month. I was sure it was Alex's mother who saw the story on *Channel 12 News* and excitedly shouted from the sofa for him to come take a look at the TV. He was probably just calling to talk about it. I suddenly realized how much I missed my ex-boyfriend, even as I sat in a VIP seat at Harpo Studios.

It wasn't long before everyone's eyes deserted the furniture and found something way more magical to absorb when Oprah and a couple of her happy helpers returned to the stage. Some hearts still hadn't healed from the first electrical shock at the photo shoot, yet here the Queen was again preparing to set off another wave through our veins that could possibly send us bouncing through the roof like a bunch of Looney Tunes. She sparkled under the lights as she took her usual seat in the couch chair on the right. Oprah made the white cloud look cozier than it did when it was vacant, and I couldn't help but imagine myself sitting in its twin directly across from her. I daydreamed about sinking into the marshmallow chair on the left, feeling snuggled all over by its sweet cushions and being added to the long list of superstar butts it had kept warm throughout its lifetime.

I dazed out on a vision of Oprah turning a smiling face toward me, the kindness in her eyes calming my nerves. She was going to interview me in front of millions of people, but for what? What was I worthy of talking about on *Oprah*? Was I an Academy Award-winning actress? A bestselling author? These were the futures that always came to mind first when I initiated my nightly conversations with God. My passions were my means to an end, my secret weapons, my solutions. Maybe I was both an actress and a writer? Of course. I had just won an Oscar the day before while my book of poems had conquered *The New York Times* Best Seller list for the eighth week in a row. No wonder I got invited to sit on the couch.

Oprah's helpers were busy fluffing her already-fluffed hair and powdering her already-perfect face when my daydream was suddenly cut short by the distinct sound of her voice.

"Boy, I can't wait to take these shoes off!"

I was in too much shock to join in on the eruption of timid giggles coming from the first three rows. Was it possible that Oprah's feet were just like mine? Her pumps were certainly a dangerous-looking pair I couldn't ever imagine taking more than two steps in, and the mere thought of her standing in them while posing for fifty individual pictures with each winner was enough to make my pinky toes bleed. Oprah's feet were clearly more experienced than mine, but it was amazing to see that she was just as anxious to run free as I was. She did have some really nice shoes on, though.

The Queen's tone of voice was different from what I was used to hearing on TV; more goofy and relaxed, like she was sharing some random, every day scoop with fifty of her closest friends. I couldn't believe that on top of everything else, Oprah was also just plain...*cool*.

After the happy stylists finished making the global icon look no different, they disappeared into a dark corner behind the stage and left her alone with us. Oprah just smiled, which I assumed was a natural reflex to the sight of speechless students with ear-to-ear grins plastered across their faces, unable to fathom the vision before them. But she was as real as the sunshine that morning. It all felt as though she had escaped from my TV to take a sixty-minute break in my world. Or maybe I had been sucked into the TV without realizing. Either way, Oprah looked exactly the way she did on the screen every day at 4:00 p.m., eastern time. I stared at her, really trying my hardest not to be rude, but I felt like I was losing control of my eyes and as usual, my mouth.

"I love you."

Yes. I seriously said that. Out loud.

Oh, dear Lord, send Mom over to crazy glue my mouth shut, please. A harmonic burst of laughter among my forty-nine friends *and* Oprah Winfrey came to my rescue instead. This time around, the angel blessed me with a "LOL" kind of laugh and its realness was undeniable.

However, the moment we shared hadn't made the history books until the Queen of Television beamed my way and said, "I love you, too!"

Yes, she seriously said that. Out loud. To me. My reckless mouth fell open in total awe, waiting for my ears to finish registering the lullaby Oprah Winfrey had just serenaded me with. I was more certain than ever that she was Love in the flesh. The couch chair was a Loveseat! The presence of pure Love was the only explanation for my racing heart, hot face, and permanent Cheshire Cat grin. All I needed now was to have Mr. Vicari come out onto Oprah's stage to announce his decision to teach twelfth-grade English the following year, and I would undoubtedly see Heaven on Earth. For the time being, the Queen alone was responsible for my minor heart attack, and I embraced the chest pains like a Chicago souvenir. I had plans to take all this overwhelming Love back with me and place it on a pedestal for the rest of my life.

The presence of Love would only grow stronger when Professor Elie Wiesel took his seat across from Oprah Winfrey, and the two spirits joined forces right before our eyes. The studio was filled to capacity at the start of the show, audience applause vibrating the walls on all sides. So many emotions had tackled me in the room over and over for the next sixty minutes. I laughed and cried and laughed again along with my fellow finalists, the surrounding strangers, and my mother who sat with the other parents a few rows behind us. I didn't have to look back often to know she was enjoying herself.

Seeing an Oprah Winfrey show live was more spectacular than *The Lion King* on Broadway. The people and the stories were real, the smiles and the tears were real, and so were the surprises. Every student had received Oprah's life-changing news while at school, and the surprise announcement along with the hilarious reaction that followed was all caught on tape. Oprah shared some of her favorite clips for us and the world to see. It was like watching a segment of *America's Funniest Home Videos* as each genuinely stunned face made us throw our heads back and "LOL." Eyes bulged, chins dropped, words and breaths were lost in every real-life scene of a student who thought it was just another day at school. I was a quadriplegic for about five seconds when I realized my surprise video shot at Yonkers High by Principal Moretti had made the cut. My hysterical reaction caught on camera was followed by a gleeful audience applause. My limbs came back to life as the clip reminded me of the pure joy one phone call had brought me that day.

Ms. Rodriguez had been in the middle of breaking down the conjugation of the verb *haber* in 8th period Spanish when there was a gentle knock at the door. Principal Moretti, a tall Mafioso-like man, attempted to walk in quietly with a camera crew and a cellphone in hand.

"Sorry to interrupt the lesson, Ms. Rodriguez, but someone in your class has a very important phone call."

Mr. Mo spoke so intensely with an expression so grim I was sure someone had failed the Spanish Regents exam and these bastards were about to punish the poor kid on tape and send it to their boss, "Johnni with an *i*," who sat waiting impatiently, smoking a Cuban cigar on his Staten Island property. Then the principal turned a determined step in my direction, holding out the small Nokia phone to me. No way. Not me. I admit my Spanish really needed some work, but I never failed anything. *Ever.* Please let me live, my eyes pleaded. A fire started in my chest and around my ears. My classmates gawked at me like I had suddenly grown two extra heads. They were just as scared for my life, but still way more concerned with who was on the phone. My desk was seconds away from getting splattered with the cheese bagel and Hot Fries I had for lunch two periods before. Then I caught a glimpse of what was an unmistakably sly smirk on Mr. Mo's face when I took the phone with a trembling hand and put it to my hot ear. This was the end.

"Hello?"

The only word that registered next was, "Oprah." I jumped up from my seat, nearly taking the desk with me across the room. Tears started in my eyes instantly as I tried really hard to catch my breath.

"No..." I said to myself, not yet capable of believing the sweet lady who called to talk to *me*. "My mom..." were the next words to dribble out of my mouth. The messenger realized that I was momentarily speech impaired and she happily spoke for me.

"Yes, make sure you call your mom and tell her the good news. You can bring her to Chicago with you in April."

I don't remember how the conversation ended. All I can recall is loving the stranger on the phone with all my heart. I loved Mr. Mo and his goons; I loved Ms. Rodriguez; my cheerful classmates; my father and my mother. I clung to the Nokia for a few minutes more to call Mom while tears and the camera kept rolling.

"What?! Seriously?! I have to lose weight!!" My mother screamed through her office phone at work. I tried to laugh at her ridiculous response, but ended up crying some more when she ended her outburst with a sincere, "I love you."

Mr. Vicari only ever got sick one day that school year—the day we heard back from Oprah. I was given exclusive permission to get the Teacher's phone number from the principal's office and called him as soon as I got home. My heart pounded in my chest, waiting anxiously for the sound of his voice after every dragging ring. But I ended up leaving a tearful voicemail instead, expressing as much gratitude as I possibly could before the machine cut me off. Overall, it was the best day of my life until I found myself sitting just a few feet away from Oprah Winfrey and Elie Wiesel two months later.

The tone of the show quickly turned solemn while we watched parts of a pre-recorded segment of a historical tour through the Auschwitz Concentration Camp guided by Elie Wiesel with Oprah Winfrey at his side. I couldn't even fathom the amount of strength the Professor needed to find before writing down the horrors of *Night*. Over fifty years later, he would give the memories life again while physically standing where hate had murdered his family and millions of others, blowing my mind once more. He was the strongest man to ever live, and I was so thankful for his existence. His story was the reason I was okay with writing my own. I knew no struggle of mine could ever be too difficult to share, especially if talking about it could potentially benefit someone else's life.

I was invited to spend this day in Chicago with Elie Wiesel because my essay provided evidence of evil truths that still clouded the world sixty-two years later. I had made the decision to fight against hate with love and hope just like Elie, just like Oprah, just like Clemantine.

Clemantine was one of the featured winners who Oprah spoke directly to during the taping. She was a Rwandan refugee separated from her parents during the genocide in 1994 when she was just six years old. It had been twelve years since Clemantine last saw her mother and father, always praying for their survival but never truly knowing if they were still alive. After the teenager shared her unbelievable story of courage with us, the miracle worker announced that her parents were, in fact, safe. The words caused an anxious stir in the audience. She invited Clemantine and her older sister, Claire, up to the stage to read a letter sent from their parents. But before Clemantine could open the envelope, her smiling family appeared from behind a sliding stage door on the right, the girl nearly collapsing from an overflow of joy in her heart.

The presence of Love and human compassion in the room was so powerful that World Peace had existed for the first time only for the duration of that beautiful moment. There were no such things as war, genocide, racism, drugs, hate, greed, or prisons. The emotions captured were raw, no use of camera tricks or rehearsals, and I couldn't believe I got to sit amidst so much glory as tears streamed down my own face. I felt for Clemantine like she was my sister and those were our parents on the stage. Her happiness was my happiness, and I thanked God for the opportunity to be a part of it all.

It was like church, the way every second that passed just called for another reason to look up and thank God. We barely got the chance to catch our breaths and bring ourselves back down to the ground before we moved onto another surprise in the amount of $10,000. Oprah shocked the audience, especially the front three rows, by announcing that AT&T had offered to gift each winner with a $5,000 scholarship to the school of their choice. After she gave the announcement a few beats to sink in as the room filled with breathless gasps and more tears of joy, Oprah inflated us yet again with her natural euphoria tank when we heard her say, "And I'm going to match AT&T's $5,000, so you'll each get a $10,000 scholarship to the college of your choice." She wouldn't stop. She was the gift that kept on giving. She was Love. We were invincible, happy balloons, and it was impossible to pop our high and bring us back down to the ground. I had never cried so much and experienced so much bliss at the same time.

I was thanking God for it all, for the opportunity, for the passion, for the visions, for my mother, for my father, for Riverdale, for Yonkers, for Yonkers High, for Mr. Vicari, for Elie Wiesel, for Oprah. Oprah was an extraordinary human doing His work on Earth, proving to the world that Love always prevails. She was the one who had all the solutions, and I prayed for guidance down the right path to find my own.

CHAPTER SEVEN

The snores of the hefty Black woman sleeping next to me grew more aggressive with every inhale. I half-expected to get swallowed whole if I fell asleep, so I stayed awake for the entire four-hour ride, which was fairly easy to do. I pressed my body up against the foggy, frosted window in an attempt to give the woman more room, but her mass somehow followed me, and I was trapped inside my North Face for the remainder of the trip.

"Alright! Wal-Mart time! Sixty minutes or your butt gets left behind!" A raspy Danny announced at five o'clock in the dark morning as he finished straightening out the giant steering wheel and parked a few yards from the superstore.

The woman grunted to consciousness, first fixing her cheetah-printed headscarf that had loosened during her deep sleep before scooting over to give me a little more breathing room. Danny had snatched most of the ladies out from their third dream and left them mindlessly rummaging for their belongings. They rushed groggily toward the open door to greet the upstate New York morning winds that instantly assured everyone they were awake for the day. I was ready to exit the bus too, but the woman blocking my way was busy readjusting her ginormous breasts inside a zebra-striped bra two sizes too small that she wore under a skin-tight spaghetti strap tank top. I rose to my feet and gave a timid smile to signal my desire to escape, and she practically snarled at me before latching onto the seat in front of her to lift her robust body up and clearing the way.

I was happier than the average person who was up before sunrise in the middle of New York's February because we had finally reached the Wal-Mart, which meant we were just about another hour out. My body ached all over as I discovered muscles I never even knew existed. I was used to riding the bus from Boston to New York City, but this was my first time extending the trip with an additional ride past the state's capital, and I was definitely feeling the consequences.

My bladder was fully awake and suddenly impatient, so I hurried through the brutal winds, toward the giant blue sign. I rushed past the automatic sliding doors into the brightly lit department store and asked the first person with a blue vest where the restrooms were located. She was a middle-aged White woman with straggly shoulder-length hair and a grossly unwelcoming tone of voice when she spoke.

"Hm."

I waited for the woman to finish...clearing her throat? I wasn't sure and almost expected no actual answer to follow. By the look on her face, one would think Wal-Mart had snubbed her on Employee-of-the-Month and given it to me.

"There." Her scrawny finger was in the air for less than a second, and I was left guessing the bathrooms were somewhere by the pharmacy. I probably would've thanked the rude sales clerk for her time if I wasn't so close to peeing all over myself, but all I could do was run off toward the huge "Pharmacy" sign.

I barged into the ladies' room to find that I had entered one of my worst nightmares. Each one of the four stalls was occupied and being waited on by at least two dozen more women. They were all Danny's ladies; the majority were half asleep in line against the bathroom wall; others brushed their teeth at the sinks; some unwrapped headscarves in the mirrors and combed out their freshly relaxed hair; and a couple others applied lipstick and heavy eyeshadow. A crying baby was getting his diaper changed on the changing table, his mother too tired to offer more than a "Shh-shh." Most of the women waiting against the wall carried traveling duffel bags, and the painfully delayed movement of the line suggested that they were preparing to change out of sweatpants and leggings and into their preferred outfit-of-the-day. Two pairs of feet could be seen underneath one of the stalls; one pair wearing open-toe pumps, and the other tiny pair wearing loosely-tied light-up sneakers. A young girl in a heavy pink coat fell asleep while standing against another stall, and the child nearly tumbled to the damp floor when her mother opened the door after completing her transformation. It was a scene too active for the time of day, and my bladder was completely devastated by all the commotion.

I ran out of the ladies' restroom and across the hall to what I figured was my last hope, but the men's room was blocked by an orange cone and a sloppily written sign that read "Closed for Plumbing Repair." I started to panic, feeling my lower abdomen get heavier by the second like a growing water balloon. God, please don't let me come all this way to piss my pants. Not today. I pleaded with Him while squeezing my thighs together tighter, afraid of what would happen if I let them detach. I looked around frantically for another restroom, but there were too many endless, white tiled halls to choose from. What if I picked the wrong way to the other side? No matter which brightly lit direction I chose, I knew I wouldn't make it down to the other end without soaking my jeans, so there was only one thing left to do. I waddled anxiously with glued thighs through the revolving doors and back outside to the parking lot in search of the most secluded, peaceful area.

I had no time to think about the ethics of what I was fully prepared to do as I made my way to the shrubs behind the giant building. I freed myself of all thoughts, pulled my jeans down and squatted low, feeling the February arctic blast like I never imagined I would. It was still too dark outside to see anything, but I knew the relief pouring out of my body had instantly crystalized once it hit the ground. I stayed alert and kept my head up high in case someone turned the corner to investigate the loud rush of water crashing to the floor that I had no control over. Though my ass had gone numb and possibly frostbitten, emptying my bladder was pure bliss and as relaxing as sitting poolside with a refreshing glass of iced-tea on a hot summer day. I was too happy to even care about not having a roll of toilet paper conveniently waiting for me in the bushes and shook myself dry before pulling my pants back up.

My lewd behavior finally registered when the blood rushed back into both sets of cheeks and the upstate New York winds punished me on my way to the Wal-Mart restroom to wash my hands. I wasn't pleased with myself for peeing like a stray dog in the back of a Wal-Mart, but I had to admit that the extraordinary situation could have been a lot worse had I decided to wait on the bathroom line with Danny's other ladies. It was a learning experience I was definitely willing to accept if it meant being one step closer to becoming another pro on the prison bus. Riding the bus wasn't something to be particularly proud of, but it was still something I wanted to perfect for the sake of spending just a few hours with my boyfriend. It didn't matter how exhausted the loved ones were before the sun came up. Every woman, with and without child in tow, still found enough energy to race off the bus and straight to the stalls because they knew what kind of gridlock awaited. It was survival of the fittest, and I almost got eaten alive, but I now knew better for next time. I even knew there would be a next time.

I didn't feel so bad about the misdemeanor as I smiled past the angry Wal-Mart employee. At least she had a reason to dislike me now. The ladies' room wasn't as crowded when I cautiously entered the second time, and I took the sink where a little boy had just rinsed his mouth after brushing his teeth with a Spiderman toothbrush. I washed my hands and looked at myself in the mirror for the first time that morning. I wondered how much longer I would be this tired.

Danny's bus was exactly where we left it, and I boarded accompanied by the most butterflies since leaving Boston. There was a woman in my seat who I didn't recognize until our eyes met and she pulled herself up to let me squeeze back in by the window. She was the same loud-snoring, snarling woman from forty-five minutes ago, completely beautified for the day. Even the forced smile she greeted me with was unexpected. The headscarf was off, revealing straight, shiny black hair sprayed stiff to curve inward under her chin; a hairstyle complete with crisp side bangs. Large gold hoops dangled from her ears, noisy gold bangles chimed on both wrists, and one glistening gold cross drooped low around her neck. I wanted to appreciate the delicate, uniquely cut cross for longer, but was afraid of getting caught staring at her ginormous breasts, which actually appeared slightly less threatening under a conservative black sweater. Light makeup accentuated a set of high cheekbones, lengthy lashes, and beautiful hazel eyes that sparkled brighter against her smooth ebony skin. The faint smell of sugar cookies caught me pleasantly by surprise that I figured was a sweet holiday fragrance from Bath and Body Works she lightly spritzed on before finishing up inside the Wal-Mart bathroom. Danny's entire bus looked like a Valentine's Day special of *Extreme Makeover* (*Prison Wives Edition*). My buddy's transformation, however, was the best one I had seen so far, and it made me conscious of my own appearance. I was still wearing the same clothes from the day before; I couldn't get a comb through my mess of curls; I could've definitely used a new pair of underwear; I was overdue for a new dollar lip gloss; and I hadn't even thought to bring a toothbrush along. "Rookie" was an understatement, and the hint of excitement I felt when hopping back onto the coach bus was quickly withering away with all the naked, cold trees. This was not how I wanted to surprise my baby. But I knew there was no turning back now, and I most definitely had no intention of coming all this way to stay on a bus.

More than an hour after the Wal-Mart escapade, Danny dropped off the first group of loved ones at Washington Correctional Facility, which included a brown, wrinkled old lady I hadn't noticed before, three beautified women, and a crying toddler, kicking and screaming his way off the bus. The rest of us were taken to Great Meadow just a couple more miles down the road. It was a spa resort that offered an all-day vegan buffet, outdoor yoga, and full body massages for as long as ninety minutes. No, I'm kidding. But that was the image I got when I heard the name "Great Meadow" the first few times. It wasn't much longer until all that came to mind when hearing "Great Meadow" was the "Great Wall." The maximum-security prison was enclosed in a massive concrete wall to ensure everything and everyone stayed within its perimeters. The three-thousand-foot blockade made Great Meadow Correctional Facility its own district, the people inside governed by its own laws. The surrounding barbed wire was like prison decor because the probability of anyone ever conquering the stone wall's height and width was non-existent. I found the building itself strangely beautiful, with qualities of a European private school for boys. My father had actually spent two years of his bid in this very facility, which he and others confined within its walls referred to as "gladiator school." Needless to say, the boys that walked these halls were growing up a lot faster than all the rest.

When I was back in Yonkers for Emerson's winter break, I had ample time to visit my boyfriend with his family who was very fond of me. They conveniently used their car to make the two-and-a-half-hour trip from Yonkers to Comstock, New York and were always willing to save room for me in the backseat. This was my first attempt at traveling to see him alone, and I wished I was in their company now to lessen the soreness from the long bus rides. However, I looked forward to the inevitable moment when his face would make the entire journey worthwhile.

"Good morning." I approached a large desk and handed the completed "visitor information" form to a red-faced correctional officer who only glanced up to compare my face with my NYS permit.

"Just you?"

"Yes, sir."

"Package?"

"No, sir."

"Money?"

"No, sir."

"Okay. Have a seat."

I looked for an empty plastic chair in the crowded waiting room, spotting some familiar faces from *Danny's*, but mostly new bodies that had made it to the facility probably by a more secure form of transportation. I sat in the back corner next to an out-of-service vending machine, feeling terrible for not being able to leave any extra cash or even a package of his favorite snacks. I remember observing his mother closely as she tucked a fifty-dollar bill into a commissary envelope every time I tagged along on the family visits, always bringing back memories of my grandmother sealing a similar envelope that she signed and dropped into a box for my father's account during his twelve years inside. Fortunately, those days were over for my grandmother and for Dad. He had finally made it home just in time for Christmas in 2005 and was free to thoroughly enjoy relaxing on the couch with the family to watch my appearance on *Oprah* a few months later. He said he couldn't have dreamt of a better homecoming present.

The unfortunate part was that I would sit inside of a state penitentiary two years after Dad was paroled, waiting to see another man whom I loved very much. Though the trip in its entirety was an unforgettable struggle, I found myself at ease and familiar with the inside of the facility, with the colorful faces, and with the wait. I was by no means thrilled with my choice of venue for Valentine's Day, but comfort in my surroundings came naturally when I focused on my Valentine and not his circumstance.

The clock had finally ticked its way up to 9:00 a.m., and a second cranky officer behind the desk called the first visitor by their loved one's last name.

"Gonzalez!"

It was frustrating to watch inexperienced people underestimate the power of the metal detector. I wanted to

propose that Great Meadow use some of the money it was
hoarding to make a decent sized sign that read:

Ladies: If you are wearing an underwire bra, we will ask you to
remove the bra in the restroom, place it in the paper bag
provided for you, cover yourself with the shirt-smock also
provided for you, exit the restroom, and walk through the
metal detector to complete processing. Once you have cleared,
you may return to the restroom to put your bra back on, but
we will NOT call the next visitor until you are fully dressed
and processed. If you want to save us all from wasting precious
time, please leave your underwire bra at home.

Or something like that. I had an impressive collection of
Old Navy sports bras and never hesitated to wear one for non-
workout-related purposes, especially when trying to enter a
maximum-security prison. I personally preferred the comfort,
and in this case, the convenience of a sports bra, but there were
women who were a lot more concerned about preserving a
nice view for their honeys.

"Johnson!"

My bus buddy was up next, and it was easy to spot her
expertise from where I sat several feet away. She approached
the desk before either stone-faced officer could half-ass a
complete sentence and started removing a pair of knee-high,
black leather boots, her big hoops, bangles, rings, and the
beautiful gold cross I was so fond of. With pink socks on her
feet and hands at her side, she walked confidently through the
metal detector and cleared on the first try. I was almost
positive her flashy zebra bra was swapped out during the Wal-
Mart makeover in order to pass beep-free. My process was
bound to be just as successful as hers.

"Davis..."

"Brown..."

"Santiago..."

Belts, jewelry, shoes, and more bras set off the irritating censor every time another novice visitor stepped up to the machine. My eyes wouldn't look away from the clock as I sat calculating the minutes that were quickly being subtracted from my visit.

"Mitchell!"

It was 9:47 a.m. when I finally heard his name and my spirits lifted instantly. I knew all I had to remove was my North Face, dusty Converses and the gold star I wore around my neck that Tío Edgard gave me for my sixteenth birthday. I was a winner on the first walk-through, and my right hand was stamped with invisible ink to complete the record-breaking process. Even the red-faced correctional officer couldn't help but compliment my speedy and savvy prison-visitor skills in his own way.

"Thanks for having a brain."

I was having a hard time stuffing my feet back into my sneakers and put the struggle on pause to reply with one of my signature smiles in hopes it would make his life a little less miserable, at least for the day. But the shameless officer's well-being was the furthest thing from my mind when I finally double-knotted my laces and went for the giant steel door to wait for the *buzz*. This moment was by far the most impatient I had been since leaving Boston the day before. The visiting room was just seconds away, but it felt like hours passing by as I stood gripping the cold metal handle. Waiting. The buzz finally came like a Mariah Carey Christmas song to my ears. I pushed the heavy door open to find myself in front of another. It was my belief that the purpose of the double door thing was only for the amusement of correctional officers. I always imagined a couple of bored officers watching the cameras somewhere, cracking up at excited loved ones rushing just to find themselves trapped between two securely locked doors, waiting for the bullies to grant them access through the one that would eventually lead them to the visiting room. I was buzzed to the other side after a minute too long and had the urge to stick my middle finger up aimlessly to whatever hidden camera was watching, but I took a deep breath instead and carried on.

I stopped in front of a smaller desk where another two White men in uniform sat, one sifting through papers and the other chowing down on a foot-long meatball sandwich at ten o'clock in the morning.

"Good morning." No matter how much I didn't care for correctional officers, I always treated them with respect so that they were aware of exactly the kind of people my boyfriend was associated with.

The officer with the paperwork grumbled a practically inaudible "good morning" without bothering to look up, and the other stayed busy chewing. They were both equally overweight, and the sight of them instantly reminded me of the giant baby twins, Bobo and Li'l Debil, from the Chevy Chase movie, *Nothing but Trouble*. The officer with the tomato sauce smeared around his mouth was definitely Li'l Debil. I tried really hard not to burst out laughing when handing over another sheet of paper to add to their pile.

"Twenty," said the grouch who preferred to be the one eating.

"Thank you," I said, my wide-spread grin barely strong enough to hold back the laughing fit that would've taken place if I had stayed a second longer.

I walked down the aisle in search of our assigned seats and stopped when I saw the chair marked with a faded white twenty. The corner of my lips crept up into a smirk as I placed my puffy North Face on the back of the securely bolted seat and settled in. Twenty was a good number and an okay spot, far enough from the front for me to reach over and sneak in all the kisses I wanted when the babies weren't looking. Great Meadow's visiting room was designed differently from the ones I had grown accustomed to seeing. Most of the various "playrooms" I had spent five-plus hours at a time coloring in had floors completely covered with countless square tables that were convenient enough so my father could reach around and snatch me up to tickle my ribs until I couldn't breathe. The construction of Great Meadow's tables, however, made it obvious which bolted chairs were for visitors and which were for inmates, allowing very limited contact between persons. There were several rows of one long table meant for a number of loved ones to share at the same time, with chairs spaced far enough to give each family their privacy. Visitors sat on one side of the three-foot-wide divider and inmates sat on the other, never to cross paths.

It was the limitation of human contact that I found most troubling, even as an adult. I had visited my father only once in two years during his time at Great Meadow Correctional Facility because he wasn't allowed to reach over and pick me up like he had done so many times before. He was sitting right in front of me, no window or phone to separate us like in the movies; just a table, an ocean that he couldn't cross, not even to save me. All I could do was break down and beg for his attention until our visit was finally terminated. Watching me drown brought my grandmother to start a flood with her own tears, so she decided to wait until Dad relocated before trying to take me up again, for my sake and for hers. I would write him letters in the meantime.

At nineteen years old, I still wasn't comfortable with the distance between my Valentine and me, but was mature enough to refrain from throwing a tantrum at the end of the visit. My back was to stay facing Bobo and Li'l Debil, while my boyfriend sat across from, but slightly to the right of me so that the twins could see his face and hands at all times; not that they planned to look around and do their job much, anyway. I could deal with it.

My babe wasn't expecting a visit so I knew it would be some time before he was ready to make an entrance. I hoped that he would at least skip shaving because that was usually the main reason for the delay. Even so, in my opinion, the fact that he was still even a little conscious of his appearance was a good sign that prison hadn't fully broken his spirit yet.

I pulled out some of the single dollar bills I had saved specifically for the vending machines and decided to buy breakfast while I waited. I knew from the visits with his family that the sausage, egg, and cheese on an English muffin was a must in the morning, so I bought two of those for him. I was on a diet, as usual, and opted for something with less fat and FDA-approved chemicals. The pack of no-name mints flew down to my rescue when I remembered not having the luxury of a toothbrush that morning. I used a couple more dollar bills for two bottles of water and his usual can of Snapple Peach before making my way back to table twenty, arms fully loaded.

The visiting room was filling up fast with a festive wave of reds and pinks in honor of Love. I felt a sharp pinch in my chest when I thought about powering off my busted Blackberry and leaving it in my sackpack on the bus. It was common knowledge that cellphones weren't getting through the metal detector, and I didn't bother wasting a quarter to store my belongings in one of Great Meadow's outdated lockers. But even as far away as my phone was, I was certain Mom had left a voicemail wishing me a happy Valentine's Day by now. It was the first year that I wouldn't wake up to find a chocolate rose on my pillow, so I knew she was worried that I'd be sad about it. I was, and I was also sad about heading to Boston without stopping by to tell her how much I loved her. I took a big inhale in an effort to halt the tears I felt prickling the inside of my nose. I would call Mom as soon as I got back on the bus.

CHAPTER EIGHT

I was stuck in biology trying to figure out how I could get inaugurated as Senior Class President and not know a thing about my basic genetic make-up. Then I remembered that George Bush was still President of the United States and concluded that anything was possible.

The pop quiz on the human genome had me chewing the eraser of my mechanical pencil and my right leg catching its own seizure. Beads of sweat started down the small of my back as I looked around, thinking of ways to avoid answering the two pages of twenty-five multiple choice questions. What kind of a pop quiz was this, anyway? Our midterm hadn't been nearly as long. I wished I was as cool as Ferris Bueller and had never gone to school, but playing hooky was just another thing I wasn't good at. In fact, I had plans to skip Spanish the day Mr. Moretti and company walked into Ms. Rodriguez's class to surprise me with the Oprah news the year before. Granted, my monthly friend was in town and Spanish was the last class of the day, so it was extra tempting to cut and run home to bed. Luckily, I was born a nervous wreck and remember being too paranoid about getting anything less than a 90 on the upcoming conjugations exam, so I popped a couple of Tylenol and dragged myself to class. It was more than worth sticking it out till the end. I couldn't even imagine living with the regret if I had gone home. Forget about detention. What would Oprah have thought of me? Mr. Vicari? The idea was enough to make me throw up in my mouth a little. Or maybe it was the first question about transcriptions on the pop quiz that was making me so sick. I couldn't stand it any longer. It was true, I rarely came close to failing anything, but maybe I was better off just throwing in the towel on this one and guessing every question from one to twenty-five. Students did it all the time. Why couldn't I? Because I was too scared the results wouldn't end in my favor.

That's when I slowly reached down into my messenger bag for my favorite pink folder, pulled out my genetics notes as swiftly as possible, and snuck them under the quiz. I kept a close eye on Mr. McDowell who had been too busy at his desk to pay close attention to anyone. I couldn't believe what I was doing, my shaking hands giving away my inexperience. I was finally getting answers down, but feeling more nausea after every bubble I darkened. I kept reminding myself that it was almost over, that I would pass, that no one would ever know.

Mr. McDowell abruptly stood up from his desk and hastily walked to the door, just a few feet from where I sat nearly peeing my pants.

"Okay, kids. I need to use the little boy's room. I'll collect the quizzes when I get back. Try to keep your integrity while I'm..."

The ringing fire alarm cut him off. The sound of this bell, however, wasn't going to save me.

"Oh, great. Well, that's that. Okay, I'll take 'em now. You can finish when we get back inside."

Mr. McDowell came to collect my quiz first, but I hadn't had enough time to stash the notes back inside my bag. I had given up on breathing when my teacher reached down and gathered a lot more than just the stapled two-page genetics quiz from my desk.

"What's all this?" He said loud enough for the class to hear over the blaring alarm.

I could feel everyone freeze and land their eyes on me, suddenly forgetting that there was a possible fire in the building. The fire could have easily been right in the classroom, engulfing me in its flames. I was burning alive, and no one wanted to save me.

"I'm sorry," was all I had.

Mr. McDowell released an exaggerated sigh and shook his head from side-to-side as he went around to finish collecting quizzes, my notes still in his hands.

I followed everyone out the room to the emergency exits feeling an aching emptiness. What was I thinking?

"Oprah Girl! No one ever teach you how to cheat?"

Jessica Dawson and her goons followed close behind me down the stairs, cackling like the hyenas from *The Lion King*.

"No. Unfortunately," I turned around and feigned amusement with a weak smile, stepping to the side of the staircase so their ponytails could prance merrily past me.

I wanted so badly to find as much humor in the incident and genuinely laugh it up carelessly with the hyenas, but that wasn't who I was. What bothered me the most was the tone in which Jessica Dawson's words came packaged in before setting off a bomb in my ears. It was the same unusual tone I remember hearing in Ms. Rodriguez's voice no more than a week following my appearance on *Oprah*. A classmate had simply leaned over to quietly ask which chapters we were discussing because she had arrived fifteen minutes late to class. Before I could return a whisper, Ms. Rodriguez pretended to clear her throat and shot daggers my way.

"Is it too much to ask for your attention, Oprah Girl?" The class inevitably erupted in a wave of snickers and giggles, every pair of eyes waiting to see my reaction.

"No. Of course not," I responded firmly without the use of even a fake smile. Ms. Rodriguez was my Spanish teacher three years in a row, and I had never heard such attitude directed toward me before. Over the years, she developed a keen understanding of the student I was, the insecurities I felt for not being a fluent Spanish speaker, and stood witness to all the days of undivided attention I had invested in her class in hopes of perfecting the language of my roots. But it would only take two seconds for my efforts and intentions to be forgotten for the sake of setting an example in the classroom. I had grown up a lot since my bullied elementary days and acquired a quick tongue to defend myself whenever necessary, but I saw no point in trying to prove my innocence to Ms. Rodriguez at that moment. People were going to think whatever they wanted, no matter how hard I worked. I, myself, would just add more fuel to the fire even after a whole year had gone by.

The terrible decision I made in Mr. McDowell's class crowned me, once again, the most interesting person of the day, and I wanted nothing more than to rewind the last five minutes and start again differently.

I had disappointed my teacher and myself. But the worst part was realizing that there were people waiting for me to fuck up so they could toss their heads back and laugh and say they knew it all along.

I was "Oprah Girl," winner of the American Association of University Women Writers Award, winner of the Harvard Radcliffe Book Award, winner of the Sarah Lawrence Fulbright Summer Scholarship Award, winner of the Latina Caucus Scholarship Award, Senior Class President, Yonkers'

Youth Godmother of the Puerto Rican/Hispanic Day Parade, Oprah Girl, Oprah Girl, Oprah Girl. And now a cheater. I had given the people a little piece of what they wanted, and they thoroughly enjoyed eating it up. I let the thought sink in as I walked off campus during the fire drill, not having a care in the world about cutting the rest of my classes.

A slice of *Alfonso's* pizza and Nana were the only things that could make me feel better about myself, so I planned on ordering two slices to go for my grandmother and me.

"Oprah Girl! Heeeeyyy!" John, Alfonso's oldest son, greeted me with his usual nice-guy smile as soon as I walked through the door. I wanted to throw my head back and scream loud enough to shake the universe and realign the stars to work in my favor, all the while pulling out every strand of hair. I just wanted a mushroom slice with extra cheese, but I had to first crawl through the twilight zone to get it.

"Hey, John." I requested a rush on the to-go order. I didn't know how long I could fake my smile.

"What's up? No school today?" John's genuine concern caught me off guard.

I had walked to Riverdale from school in less than an hour, making it home just in time for lunch. But I clearly wasn't in the school cafeteria, and John's question delayed my thoughts as they fished for a fib.

"Yeah. Just not feeling well." It wasn't too far from the truth.

"Ah, man. Sorry to hear that. But you just gotta stick it out a little longer. Year's almost up, right?"

I had to admit, my pizzeria guys were really proud to hear that one of Oprah's winning essays had been written by a girl who grew up eating their pizza. What I loved, just as much as their food, was their loyalty to the neighborhood. There were plenty of incidences when Riverdale Avenue proved to be undeserving of a quality place like *Alfonso's*, but they had stuck it out for over twenty years. My step-dad always said *Alfonso's* was untouchable, that no one would ever think to rob them because they were too loved and protected by the block. That didn't stop me from imagining the serious artillery they kept hidden behind their greasy counter just in case something did go down. Under those sweet smiles and tomato-sauce-stained aprons were a couple of bad ass pizzeria guys who ultimately became a vital part of all the good my neighborhood had to offer. They were Riverdale.

"Yup. I can't wait. Emerson College in the fall."

"Emerson? Where's that?"

I had gotten used to hearing the question ever since making my decision the month before. If you weren't into the Arts and the color purple, then you most likely hadn't heard of the school.

"Downtown Boston."

"Wow. Leaving us, eh?"

"Just for a little," I surrendered my first real smirk. I honestly couldn't wait to get the hell out of Yonkers and away from everyone who thought they knew anything about me. Those strong feelings didn't apply to my pizzeria guys, though. The authentic Italian-bred boys were some of the few people I was actually going to miss. Alfonso and his sons had always shown sincere happiness for me and my achievements. It was disheartening to think that not everybody was as quick to cheer me on. I decided the life lesson was inevitable and shrugged the thought off as I reached for the box of oven-fresh pizza.

"Thanks, John."

"Feel better, kid."

Every floor in our complex had long hallways lined with barred windows. Nana's floor was one of the smaller, quieter halls where you rarely found a couple of lost ones disassembling the skins of a Dutch to assemble the perfect blunt. The smell of weed would oftentimes seep through the crevices of steel apartment doors on other floors and colors, and that family was forced to inhale the earth whether they liked it or not. Dutch guts left scattered in the corner of a window sill and on the dingy tiles was a sure sign that a lost one had walked the halls, but hadn't found their way out yet. Nana lived on the fifteenth floor-blue side, and her hallway's windows were known to have the best view of the Yonkers Waterfront fireworks on the Fourth of July. It was a million dollar view you could only fully appreciate if the rusted, gray bars weren't in the way.

I rang Nana's doorbell like I was being chased by a couple of hungry armed robbers who wanted my pizza and she was my last hope for making it out alive with the box. A ridiculously urgent ring was the only way my grandmother would ever take the time to leave her bed and/or a Red Sox game to answer the door. If the sound was any less imperative, she automatically assumed Jehovah Witnesses were patiently waiting for her outside, and she was certain that no true Word from the Lord would interrupt her during a Red Sox game.

"Who?!" Nana masked her thick accent to yell at the air, appalled by such an abrasive sound. I could hear the dragging of her fluffy, cheetah-printed slippers across the plastic carpet protector as she made her way to the peephole every time.

"Kaylah!" I shouted back loud enough for her to hear on the first try. Her neighbors always knew when I was visiting.

¡Ay! Mi Kaylitaaa, she sang my name out like it was her favorite song before even opening the door. I could never help cracking a smile while listening to the clinks and clacks of the sliding chain, followed by the unlocking top big lock, then the small bottom lock and finally the slow twist and pull of the doorknob. An army couldn't get through her blue shield if they wanted to.

Nana's fair-skinned face beamed at the sight of *Alfonso's* small cardboard box in my hands. Apparently, I had abused the bell just in time. She swore she was just about to get up and blend a chocolate SlimFast shake with one of the deliciously ripe bananas she had bought for sixty-nine cents a pound at Shop Rite earlier that day. But my grandmother quickly concluded that she would drink the meal replacement for dinner instead since her lunch was going to be unexpectedly heavy. Nana was a diabetic who was far more concerned with controlling her diet for the purpose of getting as close as possible to her 1970s figure she proudly displayed in picture frames across the entire wall above her bed. One corner to the next was covered with a jaw-dropping photo collection of everyone she loved most in the world, herself included. Memories of her mother, father, husband, Tío Edgard, Mom, Janessa, Nunu, and me were protected in fragile frames of all different shapes and sizes, hanging on thin nails against the hollow, white wall. I was almost positive there was a new addition every time I looked up at the beautiful clutter that made it Nana's room. The colors of countless smiling and frowning faces presented a rare rainbow of black and whites, aging sepias to bright, modern day blues and reds. If time could be captured on a canvas, then my grandmother's wall was an artist's palette, and her photos were his paints.

Once again, I recited my half-truth to explain what I was doing home from school so early, and she immediately proceeded to give me a list of all the over-the-counter remedies in her medicine cabinet while she munched away on her slice of pizza, crust first.

¡Hay Pepto Bismól, y Robétussin, y Tylenól, y Benádril! ¡Coge lo que quiere! ¡Ay, qué pissa tan rica! ¡Gracias, mi niña bella! I heard her excitement from the bedroom as I poured myself a cup of water at the kitchen faucet. Despite her appreciation for the modern day American quick fix, Nana was a natural-born caretaker who was ready to make a lifetime supply of chicken noodle soup from scratch and her Dominican super-detox herbal tea before I ever had to step into a doctor's office. She was number one on the list of people I would miss the most when I left for college. The look on her face when I confessed to choosing a school out of state was enough to make me want to pick her up and cradle her like a baby. Nana had shrunk back into a child with pouting lips and drooping eyes that rolled away from me as if to say, "We're not friends anymore." It was the same look she gave me when I asked her to tell me stories about life during the Trujillo Era; she was completely offended by the subject and never wanted to speak on it.

I wrapped my arms around her fleshy body and squeezed tight while stamping her forehead with kisses over and over until she was forced to be my friend again. I promised to visit frequently on the *Bolt* bus and reminded her that I would spend the winter and summer breaks at home. But it was the thought of me no longer living just an elevator ride away that blocked her view of a glass half full.

Eventually, Nana found solace in knowing that Emerson had accepted me based on an acting audition for their Performing Arts Program. My grandmother knew better than anyone the thrill that came over me when I was on stage. She and Mom were front and center the day I performed my first comedy skit for my summer camp's end-of-the-summer variety show in the Bronx. As God would have it, my grandmother was a baseball fanatic watching her 11-year-old granddaughter play the role of a bitter, old accountant who had always dreamt of becoming a major-league baseball player. The accountant called for a male actor, but camp counselors thought my enthusiasm for the five-minute scene was unmatched and let me take the stage after rehearsing for two weeks. It was the first project I can remember working on with all my heart.

The only live performances I had ever come close to before the variety show were painful school holiday concerts where we sang, "I Have a Little Dreidel" and "Rudolf the Red-Nosed Reindeer," and I quickly realized singing wasn't my forte. On the other hand, this memorizing lines and just talking stuff I could definitely do.

I stood in front of a decent crowd of happy people waiting to see what I planned to perform in a gray business skirt that touched well-below my shins and a matching over-sized blazer with sleeves ending past my fingertips. I jumped right into the monologue, transforming into an accountant with dreams of a bigger and brighter future as a superstar baseball player; whining about all my shoulda-coulda-wouldas while I paced back and forth in my "office" like a desperate puppy. I felt so light and free in the middle of the auditorium, as if I was back home talking to the mirror when no one was watching. I blacked out after an overflow of adrenaline seeped through my veins until the eruption of laughing mouths, stomping feet, clapping hands, roaring praises in the form of different words and sounds brought me back to the room. The audience loved me, and I loved them. I loved them so much I stopped mid-sentence, completely forgetting the rest of my lines. I had gotten so caught up in people's pleasure that I was suddenly blanking on what came next. I could feel the pressure of the moment tease my tear ducts and dry out my throat. I wanted to apologize because at least I knew "I'm sorry" were always the next words that came after a mess up. Then my eyes fell on Nana's joyful face, and I remembered that no matter how badly I messed up the scene, she had loved me a long time before the show and no one else mattered. The words came back to me, abruptly ending the temporary amnesia, and I would see my first standing ovation when it was my turn to bow.

For years, Nana could recall my lines and recite them better than me whenever she wanted to reminisce that day (which was often). Her infamous broken English always made the skit sound way funnier than I think the writer intended it to be.

"I can hit da ból! I can cash da ból! An' I can throw da ból bedder den anywon! I yam grrreeaaatt! Why can't dey see?!" She even attempted to imitate my rehearsed body movements with the words every time, flailing her weak arms from left to right. I could see how much my grandmother appreciated being in the audience that day, and I found it easy to feed off her happiness. She would nickname me La Artista from that day forward, planting the seed for a future in Hollywood.

I chose Emerson College after a long and relentless inner conflict that was keeping me up at night for weeks at a time. The mailman had blessed me with several acceptance letters in the last few months. However, when I tore open the envelopes to find out both of my top choice schools were interested in having me, my heart was thrown into a bloody tug o' war battle while my brain helplessly watched from the sideline. Emerson College honored me with an offer to join their Performing Arts BA Program in the fall of 2007. Unfortunately, no financial assistance was included in my package sent from the private institution robbing out-of-state students of over fifty-thousand dollars a year for tuition and on-campus living. Every time my school guidance counselor saw me in the hallway, he praised me for being a first-generation college student and then reminded me that Oprah's generosity would barely cover half of my first semester at Emerson. Mr. Sloansburg was either very serious about the art of guidance counseling or beginning to show signs of early onset Alzheimer's. Though his efforts were appreciated, I found myself more concerned with failing to apply to Harvard when I had the chance because Emerson was nearly as expensive as an Ivy League school I always considered too far out of my reach.

The other school of my dreams was Purchase State College, a SUNY institution that sent an offer letter stating I had full coverage for all four years and a free five-week trip to France to participate in a creative writing workshop. I was blown away by the generosity and elated that Purchase, a leading Arts school in New York, had found my love of storytelling worth so many gifts. But, I just couldn't silence the rambunctious part of me that desperately wanted to leave the state.

The real dilemma that caused the most heartache and confusion was choosing between writing and acting. It was like falling in love with two Prince Charmings, both equally handsome and loyal, but having to marry the one man I foresaw the greater future with. I was honestly hoping one of them would dump me with a rejection letter in the mail first so I wouldn't have to do all the dirty work myself.

I figured somehow, someway the two passions could eventually co-exist in my life, and one day, I'd happily thrive while doing everything I absolutely loved to do. However, for the sake of having a home away from home in the fall, I was forced to prioritize one dream at a time. Money was the last deciding factor and my father's parents, who were more comfortable financially than my mother's, offered to help me pay off some loans when the time came if I chose Emerson. They insisted I get far away from Riverdale Avenue, explore a life outside of New York, and take part in the real, on-campus college experience. I couldn't agree with my grandparents more and yet found myself staring up at the ceiling at night suppressing another stinging reason why I wanted Emerson. I had begun to think that maybe when it came to writing, *Oprah* was the best I could do. What other achievements in the written word did I have to look forward to when I had already exhausted the ultimate dream of being recognized by Oprah Winfrey? I would probably never create a better one-thousand-word essay for as long as I lived, so why waste a precious four years in trying? The idea that I had reached my peak success at seventeen years old was frightening enough for me to turn down Purchase and pursue an acting career at Emerson. At least, I hadn't yet won any notorious acting awards, and there was more room for growth at a school where I didn't feel pressured to remain Oprah Girl. I had higher hopes of going to college and doing justice to the nickname *La Artista* that Nana so proudly marked me with. More than anything, I was looking forward to leaving Yonkers and forgetting Oprah Girl ever existed.

Nana's dentures made her a slow eater, so she was still enjoying her slice of pizza when she passed me the remote control as she usually did if there was no baseball game or news on *CNN* that interested her.

Ver peícua. She mocked the five-year-old me who was very into watching scary *películas* when spending the night at her place, always having a hard time pronouncing the word "movies" correctly in Spanish. I did grow up loving a good horror flick and generally anything spooky related, which my grandmother was gleefully at fault for. Nana was born on my favorite day of the year—Halloween. No one loved celebrating my grandmother's birthday more than she did, however. Every year, no matter how old she was turning, Nana invited all of her over-the-hill friends and family to the orange and black color schemed birthday party that took place in the living room of her small one-bedroom apartment on the fifteenth floor-blue side. She always prepared her own buffet and in the center of *moro de guandules, pollo guisado, pastelitos, y plátanos maduros,* my grandmother placed a guava-filled Dominican cake decorated with orange cream frosting and edible pumpkin heads that her best friend baked all from scratch every year. Nana's birthday was a highly anticipated social event that even my little sister and I looked forward to attending after Mom took us trick-or-treating on the really nice side of Yonkers. We always walked into the lively apartment and attracted everyone's attention with our Halloween costumes for about two minutes before they all resumed drinking cans of Coors Light and laughing about something that happened years before either of us were born. Mom would serve Janessa and me each a full plate of delicious, steamy food that we cautiously walked into Nana's bedroom to escape the deafening sounds of *chisme* overlapping *meregue típico* and the merciless aroma of conflicting floral perfumes. We settled in her bed, careful not to dirty the fresh sheets, and

I would take the remote control from its usual spot on the night table to scan through the channels for *peícuas*.

Nana loved when I hung out to channel surf with her, but I wasn't in the mood for TV the day of my voluntary early dismissal from school. I rejected the remote and pretended to find interest in ESPN's news coverage of Alex Rodriguez's impressive home run streak during the month of April. Then, of course, hearing the name "Alex" dug me into a deeper funk when I remembered that I hadn't been in the mood to watch TV all year because of my ex-boyfriend. It was less than a month after the *Oprah* episode aired when I caught a disturbing story on *Channel 12 News* about the robbery and brutal beating of thirty-two-year-old Yonkers Latino, Jose Velasquez. The man had been in critical condition for three days before passing away due to a severe head injury. *Channel 12 News* provided a list of several suspects in custody, ranging from sixteen to nineteen years old, and I instantly lost all sense of time and space when I saw the name "Alexander Mitchell" glaring across my screen. The reporter's perfect pronunciation continued to ring in my ears over and over, making it nearly impossible to hear the rest of the story. Alexander Mitchell. No news anchor had taken the time to include the "J" in the middle, a single letter that completed the elegance of his actual birth name and made him sound like a student entering Ohio State University on a full football scholarship. Alexander J. Mitchell was a future first-round draft pick for the Jets. Did they know Alexander J. Mitchell loved the Jets? Did they know Alexander J. Mitchell was working on his GPA and counted scholarships in his dreams? Did they know that Alexander J. Mitchell had dreams? Did they know that Alexander J. Mitchell had never spoken about murder? That Alexander J. Mitchell wasn't a murderer? Alexander Mitchell could've been anyone. Alexander Mitchell could've been any other seventeen-year-old lost one from Yonkers that I had never crossed paths with before. But, my city was too small for such a coincidence.

The flashback almost prompted me to update Nana on Alex's current unfortunate situation after keeping it from her all year. She had been fond of my boyfriend, nicknaming him *El Indio* because of his handsome, dark Indian features that stood out to her when he carried her Shop Rite bags up to the fifteenth floor-blue side after just meeting for the first time. I remember laughing at Nana's lack of creativity and the nickname that made my first love sound like a hurricane; ironically, Alex would turn out to be just as destructive. My grandmother asked for *El Indio* often until she caught the pained look on my face one day and dropped the subject. I wanted to share the bad news that was a hundred times worse than my stupid, little high school break-up, but two broken hearts in a tiny room wasn't going to do anybody any good. I kissed Nana's forehead and promised to come back when I was feeling better.

CHAPTER NINE

I tried to pretend like I wasn't obsessed with the sound of the prison door unlocking every time a new inmate appeared and strolled into the visiting room. I focused on setting up Hang Man on a scrap of paper I found in the corner where incomplete decks of playing cards, an ancient Candy Land box, Checkers, and Dominoes with missing numbers sat waiting for attention. I drew sticks to form my hanging station with a small number two pencil in need of a sharpener and poked my head up immediately when I heard the door again, but he wasn't mine. I was like a lonely puppy jumping at every sound until her best friend made it home.

The tall, dark-skinned man who opened the door was shaped like a competitive bodybuilder in forest green pants and a burgundy short-sleeved polo. The sleeves seemed to choke around his over-trained, bulging biceps, but I had a feeling that's the look he was going for. On visits, the guys usually wore a nice, standard-colored top that their mom, girlfriend, or wife most likely bought for them. Visits, no matter the day, were always a reason to dress up. The body builder walked in confidently with an intimidating, stone-cold face that looked like it hadn't known happiness in a very long time. Surprisingly, within seconds, the face morphed into a ray of sunshine when his ear-to-ear grin displayed every sparkling tooth in his mouth, including a perfectly-spaced gap in-between the front two. He spread his big, muscular arms wide like airplane wings and landed them around my bus buddy's voluptuous waist. He was Johnson. The two embraced for several beats over the three-foot-wide table before sneaking in two quick, wet kisses and sitting down in their individual bolted chairs across from one another. They held hands, neither pair of eyes aware of anyone else in the room.

The visiting area wasn't very big and near full capacity by 10:30 a.m., mostly of patient women coming to celebrate Love with their chosen Valentines. I remembered visiting my father in rooms nearly five times the size of Great Meadow's. As grand as those floors were, the surface area and seating arrangements were the only differences between this room and the others I had frequented over twelve years. The overflow of love around me was the same, and so were the colors. I had been visiting prisons since 1993, and the colors were always the same. In every row sat a line of black and brown bodies wearing tops in the permitted earth tones like cream or burgundy and the state's standard green pants. In every two rows was a White sprinkle in the same green pants. There were definitely a lot more Blacks occupying seats than as depicted in *Shawshank Redemption*, which made everyone seem familiar to me, as though I had crossed paths with them while walking down Riverdale; like I could say, "Hi," and they wouldn't hesitate to say it right back. The only ones allowed to wear blue or gray were the other Whites in the room that sat in corners watching all the smiling blacks and browns in greens from a distance, feeling outnumbered but not out-powered. I was in a Bob Ross painting of a colorful, happy forest being threatened by the shadows of storm clouds. I wished for a brush of my own so that I could move mountains and brighten the sky.

My eyes smiled at the sight of a little girl wearing two neat buns, one on either side of her well-groomed head, playing an intense game of Connect 4 with her dad who was about to let her win for the second time. She shrieked with joy when her last red coin dropped to complete a horizontal row of four.

"I beat you again, Daddy!" Her father shook his head and feigned devastation. She had his island dark skin and her mother's strength.

My eyes darted away from the joyful family toward the door when I heard the click and clack of steel against steel. Alex finally made an appearance at 10:42 a.m. with a perplexed look on his sweet, chocolate brown face as he scanned the room for his surprise visitor. I stood up grinning in a red hoodie that he spotted immediately and responded with raised eyebrows and a mouth that formed the word, "Oh!" His heavy black Tims quickened their pace over to table twenty, and he blessed me with his signature smile just before smothering me in his signature bear hug.

"This is a nice surprise," he muffled the words against my neck.

"Really? I was just leaving," I managed to tease through a small airway passage near his elbow before he finally released me and found my eyes. He attempted to bring my face closer to his by sneaking his fingers up the back of my neck and through my curls.

"Uh, that's one way to lose a hand," I said, half-jokingly.

We laughed together as he opted to leave his big hands on my cheeks instead and leaned over the dividing table to properly greet me with a soft kiss on Valentine's Day.

We took our seats on opposite sides, and each exchanged a ridiculous grin, taking each other in until I got too self-conscious and looked away.

"Stop," I said while covering my face, then peeking through the spaces between my fingers because my eyes loved the sight of him too much to stay away for long.

"I can't. I'm so happy right now," the light in his brown eyes proved he was telling the truth. "Sorry for taking so long. I was knocked out when they called me for a visit. I stayed up all night finishing *Eclipse*." He took both of my hands in his and stared into my eyes, "I don't know about you, but I'm Team Jacob."

Alex had just finished reading the last of the Harry Potter series during the holidays. I sat feeling ashamed of myself for not having even read past *Prisoner of Azkaban* while he had already moved on to conquer *Twilight*. It was an exciting day when I realized I could say, "Alexander J. Mitchell is an avid reader." He was definitely into his guilty pleasures like *Twilight* but developed a strong relationship with literature shortly after passing the G.E.D. test during his first year upstate.

"I'm in love with you, Kaylah. Kaylah, I love you, and I want you to pick me instead of him," Alex landed a soft kiss on the backside of each of my hands as he replaced Bella's name with mine in his dramatic portrayal of Jacob in *Eclipse*.

"You're crazy," I tried to seem unfazed by his goofiness, but my smile gave me away.

"Crazy about you."

"Okay, fool. Are you hungry?" I snatched my hands back. Nerves always forced me out of a moment before it turned too mushy.

He stared at me for another awkward beat, still unable to relax his incredible smile.

"Always."

"Is that a vampire joke?" I playfully rolled my eyes and got up to warm his egg sandwiches in the mistreated microwave by the vending machines. He was good at making double entendre jokes that increased my heart rate in his presence. Ironically, when we were kids, I would always be the one to make the first move because Alex was surprisingly more bashful when alone with me than when hanging out with his friends. I had acquired a false confidence while dating Steven, causing me to use what sexual experience I gained from him to try to be more attractive for my second boyfriend. But Alex didn't understand my efforts and rejected me one night in the back of my mother's Dodge Caravan.

We were on our way to drop my boyfriend off at home after eating dinner at Bennigan's and driving around the nice part of Yonkers to look at pretty houses with Christmas lights and decorations. My mother was known to make last-minute pit stops at Shop Rite before heading home for the night, so we took a detour to the supermarket when she remembered we were out of milk. She parked and cracked the windows open, leaving Alex and me in charge of watching Janessa and Nunu who were both snoring softly in the front row.

"I'll be right back." But knowing Mom, she would return to the van in no less than thirty minutes with a lot more than just milk after discovering all the unnecessary sale items she suddenly needed.

"Your mom is mad cool," Alex complimented as we watched her go for a huge shopping cart and roll it into the building.

"Kiss me," I replied, abrupt and serious.

"What?" Alex was genuinely concerned about waking my brother and sister, but before he could say another word, I pounced on his lap like a wild gazelle, my tongue on a mission to find his. "Whoooaaa! Wait! What if"— My mouth muffled his words. My assertiveness was new to him, but it wasn't long before the muscles in his face relaxed and he wrapped his puffy, bubble coat arms around my waist to prove that he loved kissing me just as much.

We kissed and we kissed, taking in each other's mouths and forgetting that oxygen was a necessity as our tongues wrestled, neither one with any intention of surrendering. I pulled on his face, trying to bring him closer against my lips but the tickle of his peach fuzz warned it was impossible to get any closer without risking a rug burn on my chin. I lowered my excited kisses down to the side of his neck, gently sucking his warm skin to avoid marking up the smooth brown color I loved so much. My hands explored his sculpted torso, running my fingertips up the front of his shirt to find warmth on his chest like it was my fireplace. I could feel his heartbeat and breaths grow heavy as his arms tightened around my backside while my mouth alternated between both sides of his strong neck. Without much thought before acting, I crept one hand down his stomach and stopped just at the edge of his pants.

"Kaylah," Alex breathed my name with closed eyelids.

I responded by taking back his tongue, encouraging him to talk less and act more. I then snuck my one hand down into his jeans, and before I could feel anything, Alex jumped to take hold of both my wrists, almost knocking me off his lap.

"What's wrong?" I was caught off-guard by his sudden outburst, feeling the itchy beginnings of a burn on my chin, and I couldn't care less. I could've made out with my boyfriend until death do us part. He looked lost and worried as he searched for an answer. "Alex?" I was still trying to catch my breath while he continued avoiding my eyes.

"I think I'm horny," he finally admitted.

I dropped my head back in relentless laughter, finding it hard to keep quiet while my brother and sister slept. My wrists stayed secure in his more relaxed grip as I took the beautiful face in my hands and planted a comforting kiss on its soft lips. I fell in love with the innocence in his voice and suddenly had the strong desire to take care of all his needs—physical, emotional, and spiritual—for the rest of my life. I had conquered the smooth Alexander J. Mitchell with my make-out skills alone.

"It's okay. That's usually what happens," I teased him, reaching for another peck, but he turned his face away from me again before I could inch any closer.

"I'm sorry. Can we just chill? I don't wanna feel this way in your mom's car. Plus, Janessa and Nunu..."

I was shocked and slightly embarrassed as I unhinged my legs from his lap and sat back in the space beside him. It wasn't until a few seconds later when Alex pulled a puffy arm up and over my neck to embrace me that I realized how relieved I actually was. The sounds of our crisp winter coats brushing against each other were the only noises we made in the quiet van as I scooted in closer and settled underneath his arm. Alex genuinely didn't want to do anything, and though it was hard for my brain to grasp at first, I was soon overwhelmed by the peace of just being in his presence. He was perfectly happy with holding me in his arms the way he had done so many times before. I had assumed that our lack of sexual activity during one month of dating was boring him, but I was wrong. I had projected my insecurities onto him and his rejection of them was not only a show of respect for me, but also for my mother, and I fell deeper in love with him at that moment of clarity.

"Here," I put the two steamy egg sandwiches, napkins, and a couple of ketchup packets down on the table.

"Thanks, babe."

"First guess?" I grabbed the withered pencil, turning the scrap of paper toward Alex so he could get a good look at the empty spaces on my Hang Man station and guess the first letter.

"Happy Valentine's Day," he barely formed the words through a mouth full of sausage and egg, but it was clear he had figured out my whole puzzle on the first try.

"You're no fun." I slammed the pencil on the table.

"That was too easy. My turn," he was still chewing when he grabbed a few napkins to wipe the corners of his mouth and hands before clearing every crumb off the table, then standing up to dispose of the dirty napkins and crumpled sandwich wrapper. I guessed that he would proceed to enter the "Inmate Only" bathroom just to wash his hands next. His case of OCD for cleanliness had intensified ever since getting locked up.

"We're gonna have a big house," Alex broke the silence in the van when I was halfway to reliving our awesome night together in my dreams.

"Like the ones we saw tonight?" I kept my eyes closed. I could see the vision in his head.

"Yeah."

"Christmas decorations?"

"Yeah. All that." His answers were certain as if he had plans to put a down-payment on a three-story house in the really nice part of Yonkers the very next day.

"Okay," I smiled in the comfort of his warmth, not wanting to open my eyes for fear of losing the sight of our bright and colorful future.

"Okay."

My eyes followed him on his walk back to table twenty. He was wearing the rusty-red Ralph Lauren sweater I bought him for Christmas during one of Macy's "one-day" sales. It took me a few visits, but I eventually learned to disregard the ugly green pants that would never compliment his outfit-of-the-day, so my boyfriend always looked beautiful and rare, like a Black model in a *GQ* magazine. I loved looking at him, taking him in every chance I got, and he knew it. He leaned over to treat me to a kiss on the forehead before sitting back down and starting to draw.

I couldn't believe Alexander J. Mitchell sat across from me as my boyfriend again. I watched while he constructed the game and thought about how far we had come. I didn't think we would ever speak again after our petty break-up, but there was no way I could resist reaching out when the news spread around town, and he was instantly characterized as a monster. Alex was in custody at Valhalla County Jail when I wrote my first letter to him the summer of 2006. I had to let him know that no matter what, I would always be his friend, especially at a time when he needed one the most. I sent a reminder at least once a month, even citing the lyrics to my new favorite song, "Umbrella" by Rihanna, in a birthday card that he received when he turned eighteen on April 8, 2007. The song had debuted at the perfect time, embodying my exact feelings toward my ex and his unfortunate situation without being too forward. Our correspondence remained limited because he was technically still with Tanya throughout his first year behind bars. Their long-lasting relationship hit me like a punch to the gut, but the pain and pride began to subside when I realized the most important thing for me was Alex's well-being. I just wanted to make sure he was safe and as close to happy as one could possibly be without freedom.

The mailbox was my sanctuary, a small compartment carrying primary, handwritten evidence that my first love was alive and well. I checked the mail often, even when I wasn't expecting a response, just in case my mother saw the address on the envelope before I did and threw it away; or worse, hid it from me like Allie's mother did to all her letters from Noah in *The Notebook*. Her feelings about Alex had changed dramatically from hot to cold along with everyone else's, and I knew the last thing she would allow was communication with a *murderer*.

I turned eighteen during senior year and only wanted to celebrate by visiting Alex at Valhalla without parental supervision. Luckily, the county jail was just a forty-five-minute bus ride north of Yonkers, so I took a detour after 8th period one day and hopped on two Bee-Line buses to make it to the last visiting hour. The wild butterflies in my stomach were hard to control as I sat at a 3x3 foot square table, waiting for my ex-boyfriend who I hadn't seen in over a year and was still in love with. But their wings would quickly fall flat at the sight of someone I hardly knew. Alex's face was unrecognizable without his smile and the one dimple that stayed in hiding. I cringed at the sight of his orange scrubs that were a size too big. I had never even seen my father wear the oranges that I thought were only reserved as costumes for prisoners in the movies. Alex looked like he hadn't slept in days and the fresh cut on the corner of his eyebrow explained itself. His beautiful brown face, usually filled with so much light and adventure stories, was a blank page leaving me with nothing to read. It was not the face I pictured when reading his high-spirited scrawl in the letters I rushed to retrieve from the mailbox every day. The person writing the letters was who I was excited to see, but reality walked into the visiting room and sat across from me instead. I wanted so badly to cradle him like a baby and tell him everything was going to be okay, but I had no way of knowing for sure, and I didn't want to lie.

"Go," Alex flipped the paper over so I could make my first educated guess.

"A," I announced my favorite letter. He looked down at his empty spaces, trying to remember how many "A's" he had included in his hanging station and only marked down one.

I only snuck back to Valhalla one more time to say "good bye" a few days before leaving for Boston. Alex was as distant as he had been on the last visit, and just when I was getting up to leave sooner than expected, he held eye contact with me for the first time in thirty minutes.

"I'm proud of you."

The words tightened my chest and shoved me to the edge of tears. Then, I saw that his words had done the same to him. I threw my jacket on, rushed a hug and one last kiss on his cheek to save us both from crying at the table together. I didn't want to break him down before he went back inside. Strength was a requirement in the wild, and he was going to need as much of it as possible to survive the next fifteen years.

"C," was my next guess and Alex drew a circle on the noose to mark my error.

"Babe, do me a favor," he requested suddenly when looking up from his doodle.

"Yeah?" His eyes put me under hypnosis, forcing me to admit that I would do absolutely anything for him.

"Try not to be so bad at this game," he flipped the paper back over to me with a smirk big enough to invite the one dimple out to play.

I snatched the flimsy scrap from him and pretended I was appalled before cracking my dimpleless grin.

"O," I decided to play smarter and knock out all the vowels first. There was one "O."

"Okay, all jokes aside. Can you do me a favor and mail a copy of the book that got you on Oprah? *Night*, right? They don't have it in my library."

Alex got arrested before reaching *Night* on his English curriculum at school. The streets were taking a bigger bite out of his soul each day leading up to that night, keeping him too busy to even watch TV and hear about the book during my *Oprah* episode. The deep-zoning daydream that I frequently had of his mother yelling from the couch for him to come take a look at my story on *Channel 12* was only a daydream because he was rarely ever home. How could I expect Alex to have the time to learn about *Night* when he was too caught up living through his own? The love of my life was growing into a lost one and feeding into our environment, which was a lot easier for little Black boys to do when no one in a position of power looked like them unless they came face to face with the leader of the Crips. He was quickly losing sight of all his God-given gifts, failing to recognize that he was a product and not just a victim of our world. The average outsider looking in on Alex's situation could easily say this kid wouldn't realize his potential until it was too late. But "too late" to me meant that the body of this seventeen-year-old kid lay in a pool of blood, sprawled limbs on the dirty concrete, bullet wound in his chest. Alex's incarceration would not only save him from himself but force a connection with the purpose he had way before making the biggest mistake of his life.

"Yeah, I can do that. We should have it at the Barnes and Noble on campus. Is there an 'I'?" I replied casually, trying to hide the fact that I was slightly turned on by his simple request.

"Cool. I wanna add it to my spring reading list." Alex marked one "I" down on the paper. My God, he was so hot.

I would spend the whole summer of 2007 thinking about the last words my ex-boyfriend said to me before I left him behind in New York. It didn't help that my first part-time job in Boston was a hostess position at a Bennigan's around the corner from my Emerson dorm. I dazed out into space at the start of every shift, reminiscing the food we ate and the fun we had that one night Mom took us all out for dinner. Luckily, the bond I formed with my co-workers, my Puerto Rican soul-sisters, Flaca and Mishie, would eventually help keep my mind busy until the past began settling in a place behind me where it belonged.

What I was surprised to see, however, was Flaca and Mishie as my only friends in Boston, despite being enrolled at a school with nearly five-thousand students on campus. As much as I wanted to, it was hard for me to connect with White kids whose families were paying more than fifty-thousand dollars a year out of pocket for them to attend the private institution to pursue their dreams in Communications and the Arts. I had suddenly become a Brown sprinkle in someone else's world. There was no one around who could honestly say that I had a good shot at making it in Hollywood because none of them looked like me. There was no one around who could even begin to relate to my struggle unless they chose to interview me for a research paper on the psycho-analysis of inner city youth in some race relations class they only registered for because it fulfilled their history requirement and the course description sounded the least "boring." My freshman year consisted of courses like basic improv, movement, and voice, and it was so far the most challenging academic year of my life.

Thankfully, I got a phone call just when I had suppressed my memories long enough and was in desperate need of a distraction from my sickening culture shock. On November 20, 2007, my outdated Nextel buzzed, its blue light illuminating a "914" area code, and I immediately jumped on the cell when I recognized the number as if God Himself was calling me from Yonkers.

"Hi, Kaylah." It was Alex's sweet mother, Judy.

"Hey, Judy! How've you been?" My heart was instantly filled with joy by the sound of her voice alone. Judy always treated me with so much kindness during my premature relationship with her son, even buying and wrapping a sky-blue journal for him to pass on as his Christmas gift to me. The unique cover came adorned with floating white clouds and pictures of classical angels holding harps printed on the corners of the book's thick, blank pages like it had been specifically "made in heaven" to hold all my wild dreams. It was the perfect Christmas present and would inevitably become my favorite addition to my growing journal collection.

I was just as worried about Judy as I was about Alex when watching the story for the first time on *Channel 12*. I hadn't hesitated to give her a call to extend all my love and support at the time of his sentencing. She was someone I truly empathized with and respected, especially after she lost her youngest son to the system.

"I'm hanging in there. We miss you. I hear you're doing your thing in Boston now."

"Yes, ma'am. I'm trying my best." My cheeks started to heat up as I thought about the only person who could've told her I was currently living in Boston, and who exactly was included in the "we" in her sentence.

"That's all you can ever do, sweetie. Hold on. Alex, you there?" My heart leaped into my throat at the sound of his name. I was on a three-way call with my first love and his mother.

"Yup. I'm here." His booming voice chimed in and knocked me backward onto my twin-sized bed, my Cheshire Cat grin in full effect.

"Okay. I'm gonna put the phone down while you guys talk. I think there's about twenty minutes left. Keep up the good work, Kaylah. Talk to you soon," Judy's nurturing tone set my nerves at ease long enough to think of a few words.

"Thank you so much, Judy. Take care." She couldn't even begin to suspect how thankful I actually was. "This is a nice surprise," I directed a calmer voice than the one inside my head toward my favorite stranger on the phone.

"Kaylah N. Pantaleón. Always doing her best," Alex teased from the other side, and I could sense his one dimple creeping up to make an appearance.

"I'm just trying, Alexander J. Mitchell," I corrected him. I could have been doing a lot better in school, but this was not the time to vent about my freshman blues. My leading man was on the phone, and all I wanted to do was hear him talk. Of course, he wasn't aware that his random phone call came on the exact day we had met three years before. I was the psycho teenager who went through several journals in high school, recording almost every significant event in my life, which is how I knew for a fact we had met for the first time at the Cross County Multiplex Cinema on November 20, 2004. He was impressed and flattered by my recollection, but more fascinated by the sudden opportune moment to reach me on the twentieth of all days.

"I don't really believe in coincidences anymore. I'm happy you picked up the phone."

"So am I," I replied through a smile which was all the proof he needed to know I was telling the truth. I wished he could see it.

As I expected, Alex's relationship with Tanya had ended over the summer before he was due to move from county jail to a maximum-security prison in upstate New York. The realness of his situation had sent more than just his tiny ex-girlfriend running in the opposite direction, leaving Alex alone long enough to conclude he had less than a handful of people he could count on. I wasn't afraid to tell him how much I had missed him after he clearly implied I was one of those few trustworthy people left in his life. In fact, I told him everything I was feeling at that moment, how a part of me dreamt of falling asleep in his arms, and the other part of me that would never dream of taking him back after all the shit he put me through. I took up more of our precious twenty minutes than I wanted to while Alex listened patiently. When I finally shut up, he confessed to having very little expectations of rekindling a friendship, let alone a serious relationship.

"I wasted a lot of time letting people influence the way I think, so I hope I can make this as clear to you as it sounds in my head right now. I honestly called to apologize for any pain I may have caused you during that fucked up time in my life when all I really cared about was myself." I heard his voice crack at the end of his sentence. He took a few beats before continuing, slowing down the pace and distinguishing the syllables of each word. "You always saw me for who I was, and

I just wanted you to know how much I can appreciate that now. Thank you."

His thoughts were unorganized but heartfelt, and the words stayed with me long after the operator intervened to disconnect the collect call. I received the unexpected apology like an early Christmas present, a priceless gift I had waited over a year for. It was a moment worthy of writing down in the journal made by the angels who knew my dreams. I hadn't realized, that after all this time, I was still hoping Alex would apologize for choosing the streets over me, for doing what he did, and for ending up where he was because that pain was a hundred times more electrifying than leaving me for another girl. His sincere apology came second to my family for things I was most thankful for during the month of Thanksgiving.

"Gimme a 'U'," I took a swig of water while Alex wrote the letter "U" in one of the empty spaces on his hanging station and put the pencil down to unwrap his second egg and sausage sandwich of the day.

"Okay, you should be able to guess the whole thing now," he said, before taking a huge bite of his breakfast.

"What? I only got four letters down, ass face." I snatched the scrap of paper from him to look closely at the puzzle and noticed a "Y" could work to complete one of the words.

"There should be a 'Y' over here," I pointed to the empty space. Alex nodded and chewed at the same time while he filled two lines with the letter "Y."

"Two 'Y's. Cool. How 'bout an 'E?'" I used my remaining vowel. Alex marked the last space with an "E." I stared at the puzzle containing four words and fourteen possible letters altogether. I had only filled seven spaces, but I almost choked on the weak mint in my mouth when I recognized the very possible answer to the Hang Man puzzle my boyfriend had put together. I refused to guess the sentence. I bit down on the brick-hard mint instead, doing a bad job at concealing my sudden increased anxiety.

"Can I get a clue?" I said in-between crunching, looking up from the paper to find his eyes. I went for another mint. *Crunch. Crunch. Crunch.*

Alex was in the middle of his second bite when he grumbled a chuckle and took the faint pencil to give me the clue I asked for, but wasn't really sure I wanted.

WILL YOU MARRY ME? Alexander J. Mitchell filled in every empty space of the puzzle and swiveled a question mark at the end to complete the sentence.

"You really just proposed in a game of Hang Man, Alexander?" My inner superstitious crazy lady spoke for me, but I couldn't hear any sounds leave my mouth. I was completely oblivious to my surroundings and who I was trying to speak to while my eyelids suddenly lost their ability to blink. The four little words written in my boyfriend's sloppy print held me in an everlasting trance. I only lifted my head when Alex finally swallowed his food and spoke again.

"Is that a 'Yes'?"

PART TWO

CHAPTER TEN

Santa left Janessa and me the most presents we had ever seen under the tree on Christmas morning. I was worried that I wasn't going to get anything this year because I spent most of my days in school crying about Jonathan and Leo always making fun of me in class. But when I woke up to find all the red, green, and gold boxes in so many different shapes and sizes, I knew there had to be at least one present under the tree for me. I kept hoping that Santa brought the one thing I really wanted.

Mommy was more tired than Janessa and me, but she was still strong enough to pick up the presents and pass them to us. We were so excited.

"Janessa," Mommy read the name that Santa wrote on the wrapping paper and put it carefully in my little sister's hands so she wouldn't drop it. Janessa was really slow at opening the present, so I started to help her rip the paper off.

"Kaylah, this one is yours." I left Janessa alone when I heard Mommy say my name. The box she gave me was a weird shape and too small to be the thing I was looking for, but I was still really happy. I opened it right away, and I beat Janessa even though she had a head start.

Wow. I couldn't believe it. It was the same voice recorder machine that the little boy from *Home Alone* used for all his pranks, but this one was pink for girls! I started thinking about all the stuff I was going to record with it. I wasn't good at practical jokes like the *Home Alone* boy, so maybe I could just tell the machine funny stories instead.

The sun started shining into the *sala,* and all the wrapping paper looked brighter and more beautiful in the sunlight, especially one really giant box in the corner that I knew for sure couldn't be something from my wish list. I still had a feeling the present I asked Santa for was under the tree somewhere, but I waited nicely for Mommy to finish reading all the boxes. Janessa finally finished unwrapping her first toy, and it was a really pretty Barbie with a fancy, poofy dress that was silver and glittery. The Barbie was so classy and beautiful.

"Oh, gosh!" Janessa said her favorite words and Mommy put a little camera in front of our faces and told us both to say, "cheese."

My name was written on more boxes covered in sparkly wrapping paper, but they were mostly just clothes. I never liked trying on clothes because sometimes things didn't fit and Mommy had to go all the way back to the store to return them. Hopefully, I would look nice in my new shirts and jeans so she wouldn't get mad.

I only had two presents left, and there was a tickling feeling in my heart when I looked closer at one of the boxes. It was shaped almost exactly as I remembered it from the commercial. All I had to do was shake it, and the sound would tell me for sure. I brought the pretty red box to my ear and shook it very gently because I didn't want any of the pieces to break. The sounds I heard made me smile so big that my cheeks started stretching up to my ears. This had to be it. Janessa looked at me like I was crazy because I was jumping up and down even before ripping off the wrapping paper.

"What's that?" She stopped pressing the buttons on her new McDonald's register to see what kind of present I was holding in my hands. Even though she was really slow, I let her help me open my new favorite game.

"Yes! Yes! Yes! Connect 4!" The box looked the same way it did in the commercial with the smiling boy and girl. I played Connect 4 for the first time when I went to see Daddy in the hospital with Gramma Brooklyn. Daddy taught me how to play, and then I just kept winning so many times. It was really fun.

"Oh, gosh!" Janessa yelled and clapped her hands again and again, but I was pretty sure she didn't know anything about the game. I couldn't wait to teach her how to play after Mommy finished taking pictures of us both with humongous smiles. It was the best Christmas ever.

The phone rang, and I jumped up to get it because Mommy was busy cleaning up our mess in the *sala*. It was Daddy! I waited for the operator lady to tell me when to press "3" so that we could talk.

"Merry Christmas, Daddy!"

"Merry Christmas, Boobie!"

I told him about Connect 4 and he said he spoke to Santa himself and made sure that he didn't forget to put it under the tree. Daddy and Santa were really good friends.

I told him about all the cool games and the nice clothes I got. I told him that Janessa got a really humongous present that I had to help her open, too. It was a My-Size-Barbie! I didn't tell him that I was kind of sad because I didn't get one in my size. But it was okay because all I really cared about was the Connect 4 game, anyway.

Daddy asked to speak with Mommy, but Mommy said that she had to go get Nana from the fifteenth floor and help her down to our house. She slammed the door loud when she left. Janessa got scared, but I told her it was okay because Daddy was on the phone.

"Let me talk to Nessa."

I gave the phone to Janessa who didn't really want to talk because she started making fake French fries and hamburgers from McDonald's. She just said, "yes," "no," and "oh, gosh" a lot. Sometimes she shrugged her shoulders too and said nothing.

I took the phone back and finished talking to Daddy. He started asking me about school. I told him about all the really good stuff like our holiday concert and the nice notes Ms. Goldberg wrote on my report card. I didn't tell him about the mean boys making fun of me in class because he wouldn't be happy to hear that.

The operator lady's voice came back on the phone and told us that we only had sixty seconds left to talk. That was the quickest thirty minutes ever.

"Okay, Daddy. Talk to you tomorrow."

"I'm gonna call back, baby. I'm sure Mommy won't mind since it's Christmas."

I hung up, and Daddy called right back super fast. I waited for the lady's voice to tell me to press "3" so we could start talking again. Janessa left the fake foods on the floor and started combing her My-Size-Barbie's hair. Daddy asked about what I was planning to do for my birthday that was coming up soon. Mommy said she would invite my best friends over to the house for a small party if I wanted. I really wanted Yanel and Dejanee to sleep over too, but I had to ask Mommy first. I asked Daddy if the doctors were going to let him come home for my birthday. I couldn't hear his answer because all of a sudden I heard Mommy come back in the house and start screaming to the top of her lungs. Janessa and I jumped with fear.

"Who the fuck said he could call back?!" She looked at me like she was going to hit me. I guess she knew I was talking to Daddy for more than thirty minutes, but I didn't think she was going to get that mad.

I heard Nana say something in Spanish to calm her down, but Mommy wasn't listening.

"You're a slick muthafucker, Marino! Are you gonna send me money for the phone bill? NO! I didn't think so!" She kept screaming loud so that my dad could hear everything, but she wouldn't take the phone to talk to him.

"I gotta go, Daddy." I was scared, and I didn't want Mommy making him feel bad anymore.

"What's wrong with her? It's Christmas!" Daddy didn't want to get off the phone.

"I don't know. I have to go now. Bye." I whispered and hung up on him. I felt bad.

My little sister started crying, and I picked up her My-Size-Barbie and brought it to our room so she could play in there.

I heard Mommy slamming and throwing a lot of things in the kitchen. She kept screaming and saying bad words, talking about money and other stuff I didn't understand. I wanted to bring Nana to my room, but I was too scared to go back outside and get her. I couldn't hear Nana say anything. All I heard was Mommy screaming and screaming until she got so tired she just started crying. I wished my dad was here.

I wouldn't hear anger like that again until the day I told her I was getting married. The only reason I decided to tell my mother the truth was because Judy, a social worker/therapist with two masters, somehow convinced me it was the right thing to do. I was constantly sneaking back and forth from Boston to New York to visit my fiancé and had become somewhat good at it, so I knew I'd eventually be ready and fully capable of hiding something as big as a marriage. However, my future mother-in-law would hit me with the golden knowledge she had acquired throughout her impressive academic career and years of personal life experiences just to shake up the guilt I had worked so hard to suppress at the bottom of my heart. Our conversations were like three-hundred dollar therapy sessions where we not only tried to get at the core of why I was hiding my plans from my mother, but also the rationale behind my plans.

There was no doubt in my mind that Alexander J. Mitchell was who I wanted to spend the rest of my life with. I shared my thoughts with his mother for the first time, trying to describe the fully blossomed love I had for her son the second we locked eyes and could only hope she wouldn't have me admitted by the end of the session. I was good at offering details for many things, but never when it came to rationalizing my feelings for Alex or why I had to marry him. So, I stopped trying after a while, even putting my journals to rest. Words consistently failed me when I asked myself for one cohesive paragraph of how and why I cared so deeply for him. The pen had taken an idle place in my hand until I finally concluded that it was all intuition, and intuition was like a planet I called home where rationalizations and justifications and logic didn't exist. I was going to live happily ever after on Intuition because I knew Alex, I knew who we were together, and who we could be.

Judy forced my brain back to a ruthless meeting with honesty, where I also had to admit that constantly lying to my mother so that I could be with my fiancé was beginning to drain my soul. I was tired of running from her, especially at nineteen when I was old enough to make my own decisions. If she loved me, she would have to accept the choices that I was making as my own woman. If she couldn't accept my choices, then I'd have to accept the consequences, whatever those were.

Before I left Boston for Emerson's winter break, I called my mother to tell her that Alex and I were getting married on Friday, December 19, 2008. I said it like I was ripping off a Band-Aid, but this was a permanent adhesive Band-Aid that covered my entire body, and when I ripped it off I was left skinless like a specimen in the Bodies Exhibition.

Confusion hit her first. "Alex Mitchell? The one you dated for two minutes? The one in prison for murder? The *murderer?*" My insides were dissipating with every word, atoms losing dead space by the second so that I was suddenly small enough to fit inside of a dust particle. I could feel nothing. I was nothing.

Maybe it was because she barely gave me a chance to speak, but my biggest challenge was attempting to say even a few words that would help paint a picture of my connection with Alex just the way I had done when speaking to Judy. I couldn't tell her that I was living on planet Intuition where nothing had to make sense because she'd be in Boston to slap the sense back into me before I could finish my sentence. I was stuck, mute, unable to even find the courage to say, "I love him." My mother wasn't going to care either way, and I immediately regretted ever thinking for a second that telling her was a good idea.

The wrath from the other side nearly sucked my entire body through the phone and spit me out like a worthless, tasteless, over-chewed piece of gum. After morphing into a dirty truck driver and brutally beating the receiver with words that would haunt my dreams for the rest of my life, my mother finally fell into a state of denial and then hung up on me.

"Over my dead body." Click.

I assumed the dragon's next victim would be Judy, but when I called to warn her of the danger ahead, there was no answer. My mother had gotten to her before I could, and I knew that Judy was about to fully understand why I couldn't tell her.

Why couldn't I tell her? It was more obvious to me than anyone else, even a family therapist. My mother had spent most of her life being angry at her ex-husband for leaving her alone and broke in the hood with two kids. The animosity would only grow stronger as the years passed by and my little sister and I only got harder to raise. She didn't choose to marry someone in prison. Someone she married ended up in prison, and that life was too difficult for her to take on. The last thing my mother wanted for her first born was *that* life; the trapped life that many women from our neighborhood fell into. She worked hard to show me that our environment did not define who I was and that I would always be the one with a choice. I was the one with the amazing grades, talent, and charisma; the one leaving Riverdale, the one going to a private college and would graduate with a bachelor's degree before going on to save our family from generational curses. I was the One. Marrying a man in prison destroyed the possibility of saving anyone, especially myself.

What I couldn't understand was why my mother decided my future was now destined for failure. Why would marrying someone, who happened to be the love of my life, cancel out the greatness that God had already reserved for me? The only difference between me on December 18 and me on December

19, would just be a piece of paper. I was still going to have ten fingers and ten toes (if Mom didn't get too close), a brain, a heart, passion, and dreams that I fully planned to pursue. I was still going to be Kaylah. If anything, I looked forward to being a better version of Kaylah.

I took a *Bolt* back to New York for the winter break with no intention of going home once I boarded the Uptown 1 train and made my way to Yonkers. The best thing I could do was stay far away from my mother and any other negative energy threatening to sabotage my wedding day before I got to see it. I was surprised but grateful for Judy and her family who allowed me to stay with them for the three days leading up to the ceremony or until the storm between my mother and me passed, if it ever did.

Judy also took a few verbal blows via telephone that I knew were causing her unnecessary stress, which I was completely at fault for. My mother blamed Alex's mother for brainwashing me into getting married, claiming that I was being dragged along and used by her entire family. Mom sure knew how to hurt a person's feelings, but I'd be lying if I said her crazy accusations hadn't crossed my own mind. I loved Alex and everything associated with his being. I had no doubt that his family genuinely cared about my happiness and me as an individual because their love and kindness were on display since before Alex's incarceration. On the other hand, Alex wasn't as trusting as the members of his family; he also wasn't as secure, and definitely lacked the understanding that his love could be reciprocated, which was a dent in both of our personalities. I owed it to myself to at least ask if there was any part of me that felt I was being used for convenient prison company. However, I couldn't entertain the thought for more than a minute when I remembered that the night Alex got arrested was the worst night of both our lives and we had known each other long before the devil's interference. If it wasn't for the spirit in his eyes and the night we sat on my futon to watch the ball drop into 2005 before he said, "I love you," for the first time, I wouldn't try tricking myself into thinking that Alexander J. Mitchell was a good person with good intentions. Two years into his bid is when I would finally get the full, relentless love and affection I craved from him on a daily basis when he was home, running wild in the jungle. This love felt more real and accessible than ever, even as he sat behind bars. Granted, Alex had more than enough time to reflect on his teenage past and was essentially forced to grow up a lot faster than most boys his age. Behind bars is where he began to understand the kind of responsibility a man not only had in a serious relationship, but in his world.

My fiancé's epiphany came in the merciless form of incarceration, enlightening him with the vision of love he failed to show others when he was home. His circumstances were devastating, but at the same time, allowed him to confront a false identity and confess to desperately wanting to learn how to love and be loved in return. It was natural for a man in his position to want unnatural things like a woman to stay by his side for fifteen or more years. I figured that was why he proposed two ideas on Valentine's Day: 1. Marry him, and 2. Marry him but still do whatever I wanted, with whoever I wanted, just as long as I didn't mention it to him. Apparently, this was the way a man in prison proposed to a woman. It was a proposition that came with a subjective, underlying realism that a prison wife was a hundred times more unlikely to stay faithful throughout her marriage than the average, "normal" wife. Alex looked me in my eyes and shared all his insecurities at once without saying another word. I didn't hesitate to express my full willingness to hold him down and love him for as long as he loved me. I wanted to prove his theories about a prison marriage and all marriage wrong by helping him learn how to not only trust but accept the true meaning of unconditional love, because our relationship was just that. Our relationship was the poster child for unconditional love, and I promised to hold it and to cherish it until it grew up so strong and so real that no one could ever deny its existence. My fiancé and I were two rare beings that were capable of unimaginable feats, our wedding would be the first of many.

It was like my mother had toyed with the universe to work in her favor the day Alex's parents and I were headed up to Great Meadow Correctional Facility. She had already resorted to calling the cops on my future in-laws, but my legal age left the officers with very little they could do about the situation. So, Plan B must've involved a talk with Mother Nature because four inches of snow had already touched down before I settled in the back seat and we headed north into the heart of the blizzard. I was always reading too much into things, looking for signs from God around me at desperate times, but I refused to believe the heavens were attempting to object to my matrimony. The blizzard was my mother, just another hurdle to jump over before I could see my dreams become reality. The ride up was nothing short of terrifying, so I kept my eyes down and found peace glistening in the tiny diamonds on my ring. I was worried Judy would decide against standing as a witness at our wedding after my mother did more than express her opposition during their phone conversation. Thankfully, the shocking wrath overflowing from the receiver only proved to Judy how alone I was in my decision.

"...And I know what it's like to feel alone," she looked at me distantly like she had gone on a temporary flashback to her younger days. "So, are you up for ring shopping?" Her smile was soft, and her essence was filled with so much empathy that I had no choice but to nod my head and begin to cry.

I hadn't taken the time to check in on myself and realize how sad I actually was. A wedding was a time to celebrate love with those you loved the most, a day filled with happiness and memories captured in photos to look back on and cherish forever. Unfortunately, my wedding promised to be nothing like the fairytale every girl dreamed of and more like something out of Tim Burton's, *The Corpse Bride*. I was so caught up in thinking about how much I had upset my mother, I had even forgotten that Alex and I had no rings to exchange, nor the money to buy them.

Alex's parents took me downtown the day after I arrived in New York and we walked into the first shop we saw with big, clean windows displaying diamonds and gold shining from a block away. My eyes barely blinked at the sight of magical princess and pear cuts, rose gold and white gold and gold-gold, but I didn't take much time deciding. I was looking for something as simple and inexpensive as possible to avoid being any more of an inconvenience to my fiancé's family. But Judy and Alex's father, Timmy, insisted that they were more than happy to give these rings to us as a wedding present. I couldn't believe I was receiving the ultimate wedding present, and I found it harder to believe that I was getting ready to marry the man of my dreams, Alexander J. Mitchell. I was grateful for Judy and Timmy but prayed that one day my own mother would embrace my future husband and me with just as much love and understanding.

The ceremony was short and as sweet as it could possibly get at a maximum-security prison. It wasn't the Catholic way as Nana would have liked, but a kind, little, old lady judge went through all the necessary steps and got the job done. Alex and I both said "I do," exchanged our shiny white gold bands, and closed with a quick kiss before the judge signed our official license and escorted us back to the visiting room ten minutes later. The process was a lot less complicated than I had pictured in my head every night for the last ten months. I was especially relieved about choosing to wear a simple, white sweater dress for my special day because it was very easy to look overdressed in our particular venue. Alex wore a creamy vanilla button-down and the state's hideous dark green pants that I refused to give more than a second's glance. He had taken the summer to start growing out his hair, so it was the longest I had seen his healthy locks since we were fifteen. The unkempt afro was the first thing I eyeballed when he walked into the room, and just when I was about to share my thoughts on his new look, Alex's smile charmed me into silence.

"I was gonna get it braided this morning, but my barber was out sick. I'm sorry," he said before greeting me with a gentle kiss on the lips. He was good.

Needless to say, Alex's hair was the main attraction in all five of our Polaroid wedding photos taken by a nice man in green pants named Bucky. The impressive, dark head of hair created an eclipse in every photo, but it didn't stop me from obsessing over the captured memories as they slowly began revealing their pixels under the visiting room's yellowing lights. My eyes jumped from me, to him, to hair, back to him, as I studied every detail frozen in time inside the 3.5x4.5 Polaroid frame. The smiling man in the fully developed Polaroid was my husband, and I, his wife. I absorbed our faces and waited patiently for one of them to pop out of the square to say, "Sike! Wake up!" But I finally released a long overdue breath and accepted reality. I just married Alex.

Who knew my future husband would meet me for the first time on a blind date at the Cross County Multiplex Cinema in Yonkers? One of my closest and brightest girlfriends at the time, Cindy Gonzalez, had been planning to finally meet her latest prospective boyfriend in person after communicating through AOL Instant Messenger for three weeks. Her mother and father were a couple of the strictest Dominican parents I had ever known to walk the streets of Yonkers, so my friend would only ever drop the books and con her way to a house party or the movies when it was worth the risk of getting caught. She'd then go to school the next day and pass a calculus test with an A+ like nothing ever happened; a talent of hers I always admired.

Cindy deemed Dan Grossman worth an opened Dominican can of whoop-ass and cunningly strategized a plan to meet him at the movies, but that involved an accomplice to ensure a high success rate. I was always down to play Cindy's Laverne, especially because it was easier to guilt-trip her into tutoring me in math every week. This plan, however, was a tough one to shake hands on since I wasn't too keen on being the third wheel and couldn't get the image of Cindy and her boo slobbering all over each other's faces while I tried to keep my nachos down. Fortunately, the issue was resolved quickly when Dan chirped through Cindy's Nextel walkie-talkie a couple days before their official meet-and-greet, "Yo! All good. My boy's coming with me on Saturday. Later, sweet pea. Don't miss me too much." From what I could gather via Nextel conversations, Dan was a bit of a clown, but I liked him. I had high expectations that his boy would be just as cool.

On Saturday, November 20, 2004, at approximately 4:00 p.m., Cindy's dad dropped us off at the Hudson River Museum where we worked as volunteer tour guides after school and on some weekends—just not that weekend. Her dad growled something in English that sounded like, "Be outside at nine o'clock. Bye," before speeding off in his green 1977 Lincoln Continental that she and I liked to refer to as the "Plátano Mobile." We called a cab once the Plátano Mobile had absolutely vacated the premises and made it to the theater in less than thirty minutes. To our pleasant surprise, the guys had gotten there before us, which meant we could get tickets to an earlier show and have a better chance of making it back to the museum before it closed.

Cindy and I stood in line to buy our tickets to the only non-G-rated movie available at 4:45 p.m., still waiting for Dan and his friend to find us. I wasn't nervous about my blind date. All I really cared about was being there for my friend and hoped for some good company while I watched her little dating adventure unfold.

"Hey, sweet pea."

Cindy and I turned around when we recognized the unmistakable playful tone and slowly raised our chins up before dropping our heads back in unison as we searched for Dan's blue eyes in the sky. He was definitely the tallest White kid I had ever seen in real life. His young face, however, was as rosy and fleshy as a baby's bottom. It was almost as if his head was better suited to be on an eight-year-old's body, but certainly not on a fifteen-year-old who stretched up to at least 6'5".

"Hey, you...tall person, you," Cindy tried to come up with a clever nickname for Dan and failed. "Have you guys been waiting long?" Our necks were starting to feel the burn.

"Not really. Alex wanted to come early and play in the arcade before you lovely ladies arrived," Dan looked even younger when he cracked a crooked smile and wrapped his long arm around Cindy's shoulders. She looked comfortable, which meant we didn't have to use the "my dad needs me home now" emergency escape plan to avoid a painfully awkward first date.

"Hey."

Cindy and I peeked behind the jolly white giant when we heard the sound of a less recognizable voice and found a beautiful brown boy who could play point guard alongside his tall center of a friend. I relaxed my neck vertebrae to come face to face with my future husband.

"This is Alex," Dan half-assed an introduction as he crouched over to whisper something under Cindy's curls.

"I'm Kaylah," I introduced myself with an uncomfortable, timid wave and turned around quickly when it was my turn to purchase a ticket. I took the chance to let out a long exhale when facing the cashier so that Alex, a six-foot brown angel with a fresh haircut, wouldn't catch my astonishment. He was *fine.*

"I'm hungry. You ate?" He approached me with assertiveness and familiarity after purchasing his ticket. Though to my ears the question sounded like a possible offer to buy me a movie snack, I soon realized Alex was being courteous in another way. "I was thinkin' about getting some nachos, but I don't wanna eat in front of you if you haven't eaten yet." I figured his mother had given him just as much money as my mother had given me for a movie ticket and food.

I grinned uncontrollably wide at his boyish courtesy and tried to flirt like any independent woman would, "No, I haven't eaten. But, I'm gonna get my own nachos *with* extra cheese, and I'm not sharing."

Then he smiled back at me, and I fell in love.

I examined the Polaroid pictures in my hands and realized our smiles had grown since that day, four years ago. They were literally bigger and so real that only something like our wedding could've ignited the pure joy captured by a Polaroid camera. I was looking forward to smiling through the rest of my life with Alex, but I quickly remembered that our happy ending was in danger of being crumpled like a paper ball and thrown into the trash when I went home to face another reality. Mom was the most hurt since my Steven incident, and the fact that I was once again the cause of more tears stung me with regret on my wedding day. Because my own mother failed to believe in my marriage, I realized I could expect the world to be even less forgiving. I could not expect my family to celebrate with me the way we celebrated the day my father came home on December 7, 2005. I could not expect my family, my friends, and my community to celebrate with me the way we celebrated the day I met Oprah on April 25, 2006. I could not expect anyone to celebrate December 19, 2008, with me the way I wanted to celebrate one of the best days of my life, so I decided not to share the good news with anyone.

CHAPTER ELEVEN

Winter blues toppled over my body like an avalanche as I spent the next two months losing control of my weight and popping a new zit in the mirror every morning. My hormones were at disturbing levels, and I had no way of describing my symptoms to the school physician other than telling her that I was very possibly experiencing PMS 24/7. One abnormal Pap smear, an ultra-sound, and two blood tests later, I was diagnosed with Polycystic Ovary Syndrome. All I knew about the syndrome before my diagnosis was that it was likely to cause diabetes and infertility in women my age. My doctor had poor bedside manners as she confirmed that the little information I had was correct and added that I was bound to see more unwanted changes occur in my body as time progressed. There was no cure and no understood cause for PCOS, only the common presumption that stress was the main culprit. I cried myself to sleep after getting my test results, knowing I had allowed school, my marriage, and my family to get so far under my skin that everything came together and literally made me sick.

My mother hadn't disowned me, but she showed no mercy over the phone, practically shoving divorce papers and a pen through the receiver. She refused to tell Nana because she thought the news would cause an unexpected heart attack for a woman her age. I agreed and reiterated that I was perfectly fine with not wearing my ring in public and keeping my marriage from everyone, especially Nana. However, Mom wasn't satisfied with my oath of secrecy, resorting to my father for help in hopes the ex-con could change my mind, and he only succeeded in pissing me off by reaching out to his mother when it was clear that I wasn't budging. My grandmother, who had probably experienced more pain than all of us combined when my father went to prison, couldn't bring me to my senses either. No one could understand that Alex wasn't my dad. He wasn't some kid from Riverdale who threw away a secure job at the sugar factory, a beautiful wife, a four-year-old and a two-month-old daughter for a fucking heroin fix. Alex didn't commit robbery after robbery, crime after crime, to support an addiction that he couldn't see was killing all of us even if I was lying on the floor trembling and foaming at the mouth myself. How dare my father try to tell me who not to love after he threw our love out in the trash like a dirty needle, and then snatched twelve years of our lives away just to come home and relapse. If the paramedics had gotten to his lifeless body ten minutes later, my father would've died the night of New Year's Eve, 2008; twelve days after my wedding. Alex fucked up *one* time. That didn't make him a fuck-up. That didn't make him my father.

I just wanted everyone to leave me alone. I didn't wear my ring because I dreaded the questions and the looks that followed when they heard the answers; and of course, I couldn't disrespect my mother any further. I was tired of justifying my love all the time, tired of explaining myself to people who didn't even deserve an explanation. I pretended I was single everywhere I went because the life of a single person was so much simpler. The only people in Boston who knew about my marriage were Flaca and Mishie, and that's how it would stay. The girls were wild, and I enjoyed learning how to smoke weed and drink Jack until I felt "nice" under their supervision. I was better in the presence of my Puerto Rican soul-sisters. They accepted me for who I was, and we laughed at all the pussies too afraid to love as hard as we loved. We had a shot for every person in our lives, especially our parents, who forgot what it felt like to be in love; and we never regretted an ounce of liquor, even when it ended up in the toilet the next morning. It was our optimism that would make the world a better place. Fuck what everybody else had to say.

I was coming to the end of my second year at Emerson and still hadn't made any friends other than my sisters. My marital status had very little to do with my dislike for Emerson College. I found every class painfully long and pointless and eventually decided that perhaps I had enrolled in the wrong program. When I shared my interest in changing majors with my professors, not one of them persuaded me to stay in Performing Arts, running my Hollywood dreams over with a bulldozer, reversing and going again. I knew the best thing for me to do was to leave the school altogether, but I refused to be that Brown sprinkle at Emerson who couldn't cut it and had to go back to the hood without a diploma.

I had completely stepped outside of my element at Emerson College and come to find everything and everyone in it repulsive. How could I attend one of the top Arts schools in the country and not come across one moment of inspiration in two years? How could not one opportunity spark enough interest for me to want to use my heart and produce greatness? I came from a small high school where everybody knew my name; where everybody knew how talented I was on stage and on paper; where people called me "Oprah Girl," and whether it was out of love or hate didn't matter. Either way, they knew I was great. Then I moved three-hundred miles away to a college where four-thousand more people made up the student body, and no one could see me. Why couldn't they see how great I was? Why couldn't they see who I was?

A piece of shit student coming out of 150 Boylston bumped into me so hard one day I thought it was deliberate. He hadn't even realized that the hot Dunkaccino in my hand completely exploded all over me, and only my already bleach-stained sweater saved me from second-degree burns. People rushed past, some glancing for a second and others snickering before continuing on to their over-priced morning classes. I turned around in the opposite direction of my improv class and headed back to my dorm. I cleaned up, collapsed onto my twin-sized bed and pressed my face into the pillow to suppress the howl wanting to escape my mouth. How could I expect anyone to see me if *I* couldn't see myself? As of recently, all I knew was that the only thing I had accomplished after two years in college was getting married to someone in prison, and that was too much information to share with anyone. There was no one around to congratulate me for it, no one around to tell me how proud they were that I married my first true love who was currently serving fifteen-years-to-life. I was suddenly sick to my stomach thinking, what good could come from this part of my life? On top of my imprisoned nuptials and restless family trying to convince me to file for divorce, I now had to deal with PCOS, a face full of craters, thirty extra pounds, and the possibility of never being able to conceive. I was the furthest thing from an Academy Award-winning actress. I was the furthest thing from a wife.

How could I have been so high at one point in my life and allowed myself to fall so low the next? I had known what a little bit of success tasted like, but it was quickly beginning to taste less sweet and as salty as the tears my lips bathed in. I started to think that maybe I had bit off more than I could chew. My accolades in high school made me feel invincible, like finally neither my neighborhood nor my brown skin could continue to define me. No dirt could stain my name; not even cheating on a biology quiz could throw me from my throne. I had never invested more than two minutes in understanding why I cheated on that pop quiz, and it would take two years in college for me to accept the one possibility that it was because I thought, no matter the outcome of my decision, I would get away with it. I would just cover up my mistake with another award, any award I could get to make people forget that I was just like them. Now I had no awards to distinguish myself from the others; instead, there were people around me who were more creative and achieving more in two years than I had my entire lifetime. I was back in elementary school, comparing myself to all the girls who were shorter, skinnier and prettier than me. I left Oprah Girl behind just to shrink back into that sad soul looking at me in the mirror to say acting was a waste of time, that I was the one most likely to *not* succeed, the one most likely to not find a solution.

I fought my depression at the Emerson gym for more than two months and dropped down from 196 lbs to 180 lbs when the school physician recommended an increase in physical activity and a healthy diet. She also started treating my PCOS with low-estrogen birth control pills, which put my periods back to a normal flow, so I didn't feel like *Carrie* at the prom anymore. The white-eyed monsters that matured around my jawline over-night were gradually downsizing their festering pools, but the scars they left behind would take a few more years to clear. I wasn't as comfortable with my appearance as I wanted to be for my return to New York, but I was happy just knowing I had survived the end of my sophomore year and wouldn't have to see another purple lion for the next three months. I had officially transferred into the Marketing Communications Program at Emerson College a few weeks before leaving for the summer vacation, hopeful that I'd find some form of creative inspiration when I returned in the fall.

I dreaded going home so badly that I wished for twenty-five-thousand dollars to magically appear out of thin air so I could actually stay at school over the summer instead. Flaca and Mishie kindly offered me the pull-out couch at their affordable housing apartment in Southie, but I had to decline because I was fully capable of living like Frank the Tank from *Old School* if I opted to stay with my sisters. The girls threw me a memorable going-away party instead, and Flaca surprised me with my first trip to a China Town sex shop as a parting gift. My husband and I were due for our first conjugal visit in August, so Flaca was thoughtful enough to plan an adventure at Sassy Sally's to find me some much-needed inspiration. I hadn't done anything with anyone since Steven, and now that I could do whatever I wanted with the man I married, I felt like a delayed learner in the taboo world of sex. Flaca, nicknamed for her boney frame, waved her excited, skinny arms in the air after we showed our IDs to an old man with a long, white beard sitting in a wheelchair. I followed behind her less enthusiastic, awkwardly taking in the colorful clutter that confused my eyeballs about which wall to explore first. There were countless gadgets and games and lacy panties with so many holes I couldn't understand why anyone would ever buy them. There were massage oils that peaked my interest until I found the fine cursive at the bottom of one bottle that read, "Tastes so good, you might swallow his dick whole." I dropped the bottle of pink liquid as if it suddenly bit me, quickly backing away. I was disappointed in myself for being in the middle of a sex shop and feeling like an asexual. The idea of walking into my first weekend visit with my husband and not performing satisfactorily made the cluttered walls appear to cave in on me, crotch-less panties and a rainbow of dildos all dangling in my face. I was catching hot flashes as my heart rate increased and tightened my chest. I squeezed my eyes closed to block out the blinding fluorescent lights and opened them only to look for the exit before I puked all over the old man's *Adventures of Buttman* VHS collection.

An abrasive tap on my shoulder kept me from the sweet salvation of fresh air as I turned around to find Flaca holding a huge, rubber dildo in each one of her tiny hands.

"How black is Alex? This black or this black?" She raised one shade at a time.

"I gotta go," the words fell out of my mouth at the disturbing sight.

"Oh, c'mon, Kay! This is supposed to be fun. Stop being a weirdo," she protested, flailing two dark penises in the air.

"You're the fuckin' weirdo!" I retaliated and threw up a fierce index finger to point the blame in the opposite direction, but couldn't help cracking a smile at her obscenity.

"Okay," Flaca sighed. "I doubt you can bring these on the visit anyway, so I'll put them back." There was disappointment in my sister's voice like we were in the middle of a candy store, and I just told her we couldn't take the king size Hershey's chocolate bars home with us. Flaca carelessly tossed the candy bars back into a bucket with the other flavors and instantly turned her frown upside-down when she spotted something else in the distance. "Can you handle some lingerie, you square?" Her Boston accent chimed in, so I wasn't that bothered by the insult.

"Yeah, that doesn't sound too bad." I relaxed my tone when I remembered that Flaca's boyfriend was also inside for something minor like car theft and it became more evident that this little escapade was just as much for her as it was for me.

I chose the most conservative boxed nightwear I could find, which was still completely sheer and out of my element, but I liked that it was white and covered my belly. Flaca picked a naughty garment I could've probably made in my dorm room using two belts and a stapler. I knew she was planning to save the pleather scraps in their cardboard box until the day her man came home, so I didn't judge her taste in lingerie out loud in case I hurt her feelings.

My sister put down forty bucks and some change for our new sleepwear before taking two pink plastic bags from the crippled old man. It was a relief to see her doing well after we had all been dropped from Bennigan's when the franchise went bankrupt a few months earlier. I had quickly migrated my hosting services to P.F. Chang's China Bistro next door. Flaca asked me for a hundred dollars one month to help her pay rent because she was unable to find employment. She was eventually hired as a sales associate at the T-Mobile store just a couple businesses down from where I worked. Mishie had a spiritual awakening that called her back to Roxbury Community College to finish up her associate's. While in school, she juggled a part-time gig teaching Hip Hop at a dance studio for children. I was going to miss my girls this summer but was glad to see that they were doing alright.

Flaca almost smacked me in the face with the Sassy Sally's bag she threw without warning and flashed one of her cheeky grins my way, "You're all set, sis."

I was back on the block for what seemed like an eternity. However, it was only about fifteen minutes before I found a lost one sitting on the doorstep of my new apartment who recognized my face and shined a mouth half-full of gold teeth, "Aayyee, Oprah Girl's home!"

"I don't believe we live together, so can you please take this shit somewhere else?"

My mother jumped at the opportunity to move when a "garden apartment" in the complex became available. Garden apartments were ground floor, two-to-four bedrooms with an attached 8x10 foot fenced-in, weeded space accessible by a rusty sliding door in the living room. My family had officially circulated every color in the building starting from before my birth with Nana and her mother's eighteenth floor-red side days in the late 1970s. My mother got pregnant at eighteen, motivating her and my father to save up for their own two-bedroom apartment on the sixth floor-blue side where Janessa would later join us. Dad got locked up, and my stepfather moved in a couple years after, eventually adding Richard "Nunu" Cruz to the family before we migrated to a three-bedroom on the fifteenth floor-green side. But hosting a Fourth of July barbecue or watching Nunu attempt to build a snowman in the backyard was my mother's idea of the American dream. So, when word got out that there was a vacant four-bedroom on the ground floor-blue side, she immediately put in an application. The landlord found it hard to deny an employed woman who was not only raised in the complex but grew up to raise three children there. It was frustrating to know that my mother thought a garden apartment on Riverdale Avenue was the best she could do. I often relieved this frustration on the lost ones who consistently sat outside on our doorstep rolling blunts and finishing bottles of Hennessy that they'd leave behind just to remind us that this American dream could only go so far.

"Tight, ma. I'll get out your way." The young man with bottom gold grills snickered as he licked the brown edge of a Dutch skin before folding it over to complete his blunt and placed it in the inside pocket of his black hoodie to save for later. I waited for him to get up and choose a direction to walk in, not caring whether or not he ever found his way out.

"Were they out there again?" My stepfather, Rich, stood in front of the open refrigerator door wearing a wife-beater tank and sweat pants when I walked in.

"Just one," I said, dragging in a Nike duffel bag and suitcase behind me.

"Welcome home."

Rich was against the move to the ground floor mainly because the lost ones were known to find refuge on strangers' doorsteps. The front of our door, specifically, was the ideal hang-out spot since we had the corner garden apartment that came attached to a concrete stoop and a steel railing I referred to as the "hood porch;" an attribute the other bottom apartments didn't have. During the summer days, the Indian kids from the ninth floor-green side liked to swing and sit on our railing, using it as a barricade in a game they invented and played for hours. I appreciated the summer days far more than the summer nights when out of nowhere, the lost ones crawled up on our doorstep like roaches feasting and multiplying by the minute.

The new apartment was across from the building's "community room," a space residents often reserved to celebrate baby showers or kids' birthday parties. Right outside the community room is where my seven-year-old brother would witness a man get murdered in cold blood just a couple months after our family settled in on the ground floor. Nunu had heard the shots all his life, but never knew what they could do until 4:30 on a Saturday afternoon. My baby brother had seen more than I had at twenty years old, which was a more heartbreaking reality when I remembered a line I wrote toward the end of my Oprah essay two years before— *The visible joy in my little brother's eyes overwhelms me with happiness because he doesn't understand the* night *of the world.* I was back home, and my family was going on a year at the garden apartment without lighting one barbecue or rolling a single snowball for fear of an unexpected bullet burning through our defenseless fence.

I appreciated Rich because I knew we were protected at least 90% of the time, whether he was around or not. My stepfather was respected and well-known on the block as, "Harlem," a nickname given to him in the '80s for no other reason than his ability to sell vials of crack cocaine as swiftly and efficiently as a dealer born and raised in crack-flourishing Harlem. However, Richard Cruz was a Puerto Rican born in the Bronx and raised with a Black man's soul in Yonkers, where he'd start a career at eighty-thousand dollars a year and also serve nine months in Valhalla on a drug charge all before ever seeing a high school diploma. Rich ended up back behind bars just two weeks following his release for minor involvement in a shooting, and what was worse than being locked up and broke for another thirty days, he frequently recalled, was seeing his mother cry. Rich was Carmen's only son, and her quiet, pain-stricken face was powerful enough for my stepfather to want a way out. Harlem left the streets but would be remembered from the Bronx to Beacon, New York as a good dude who bought groceries for crack addicts' kids and never sold base to pregnant women.

My stepfather was loved, and my mother thought because everyone on the block either grew up with Rich or grew up knowing his name we wouldn't have to deal with too many lost ones loitering on our hood porch. On the contrary, the lost ones would only feel more inclined to camp out in front of our door because they "knew" Harlem.

My stepfather's small talk often started with an update on the neighborhood's most recent newsworthy crimes. Apparently, investigators still had no leads on the February murder of one of his rapper friends who got shot four times in the back by a masked gunman in front of the infamous liquor store located just a few feet past *Alfonso's*. Naturally, there were no witnesses, even though the victim was said to be standing with a group of friends at approximately 7:30 p.m. before the shooting took place in the middle of an enormous housing complex lined with countless barred windows on both sides of the street.

"I heard it was a little nigga wearin' a mask. Pussy muthafucker," my stepfather expressed his grief, pressing buttons on the microwave to warm up a slice of lasagna Mom had made the night before.

"That sucks. I'm sorry," I said, removing my jacket and taking a seat at our small kitchen table. I wanted to say more, but I was bored by the story, like I had heard it more than once or twice, maybe the year before, or the year before that. Even so, I stayed to hear him talk because what I liked most about my stepfather was his ability to pretend like he wasn't aware of the latest drama taking place inside of his home. It was a relief to come home and not be hounded with brutally blunt questions like, "So, when are you getting a divorce?" that my mother had recently programmed herself to ask whenever we spoke. Instead, Rich normally followed the neighborhood scoop with updates on my little brother's progress in school and growing interest in football before moving on to ask me about the college life, a subject I found more depressing than murder.

"Transferred out of Performing Arts into Marketing Communications," I said, biting off a stubborn hangnail on the side of my thumb.

"You tryin' to get a job after school. I hear you. More money, more power," he chuckled to himself as he joined me at the kitchen table with a steaming plate of leftover lasagna. For over ten years, Rich had held down an Average Joe job as a maintenance man at a local boarding school for troubled teens. I could see the 5:00 a.m. wake-up time starting to take a toll on his droopy eyes. "But remember, money ain't everything. No one's gonna care about how much money you had when you die. All they gonna care about is the kind of person you were," he continued with a mouth full of food.

I pretended to be busy on my phone as he spoke, trying to recall which mobster movie I had heard his profound line of advice from. My stepfather and I rarely engaged in heart-to-hearts, mainly because I grew up rejecting his company since I was six years old. Although a toddler when my father left, I had a very clear understanding of who he was and that this other brown man wasn't him. My father was the brown man I saw every day until he got really sick and was only able to talk to me on the phone or see me in person once in a while. He wrote me letters on long sheets of yellow loose-leaf that I responded to with sloppy, incomplete sentences and colorful pictures I drew with Crayola crayons. I would hear the sound of my father's voice and begin to cry when I woke up to realize it was just a dream. This strange man's voice couldn't comfort me, and he rarely ever tried because he knew it. He kept to himself mostly, adopting an awkward, apathetic presence in our household that I would eventually grow up to feel responsible for. It took me over twelve years to come around and realize Rich had been the most consistent man in my life before I finally allowed myself to love him.

"Where's Mom?" I asked my stepfather only because I dreaded the idea of sticking to the subject of college life.

"At her second home, Shop Rite." He looked up from his plate at the decorative wall clock, a bargain purchase Mom was overly proud of. "I thought she'd be here by now."

Like she was telepathically summoned home by her husband, Mom barged in through the door less than a minute later carrying a large load of bright yellow plastic bags that I could always recognize as Shop Rite bags from a mile away.

Rich bounced up from his seat to help my mother with the groceries as she attempted to waddle herself in.

"I got it," he said, grabbing all the yellow bags with one hand.

"Yeah, you got it now after I made it all the way home," my mother hissed and caught her breath before turning a Chuckie doll smile my way. "Hi, stranger."

"Well, I tried callin' and you ain't answer. I figured you were out sneakin' around with Lusito again," Rich pronounced "Lusito" with a heavy American accent and chuckled at his own joke. Lusito was Mom's first (not-all-that-attractive) crush who everyone on the block knew as her one true love before he fell victim to the system and she fell for my father.

"Ew. Shut up," was Mom's normal response to the bad joke Rich often recited when she was taking longer than usual with one of her errands. Her face and tone expressed pure disgust every time my stepfather triggered the memory, which was exactly how I felt thinking back to my schoolgirl crush on Steven. But it was nearly impossible to picture Mom crushing on anyone, even Rich, though they had been married for almost ten years. My mother was far more affectionate with our cat than she was with my stepfather; so much so, that I took a vow in high school to always show my husband more love than what was displayed in my home. I was naïve for not considering the number of years a married couple invests into a relationship before kisses and cuddles become insufficient expressions of love. At the same time, I had to accept that my family was more different than any family I had ever watched on television. My parents were not a classic American couple, and we were not *The Brady Bunch*. My mother and Rich were raised on Riverdale, and it was quite possible that they had grown to know each other so well that love and loyalty were easily visible in a pan of homemade lasagna. But when I left for school, I found an outsider's perspective and started to believe that because the jungle raised my stepfather, looking over his shoulder came more natural than looking forward long enough to see a sprouted rose in the concrete. As for my mother, she was simultaneously too hardened by her past to remember that she was the rose and not the concrete.

I thought about what my marriage would look like after ten years until I remembered I'd still be waiting.

CHAPTER TWELVE

I joined the Retro Fitness two blocks from the complex and burned off ten more pounds on the Stairmaster before officially starting my summer job as a transfer hostess at the P.F. Chang's location in White Plains. I was desperate to get out of the apartment and make some money for my upcoming trailer visit with my husband. "Conjugal visits," I learned was just the standard term used by outsiders who had never actually participated in one. "Trailer visits" was the term passionately spoken among those who maintained a clean record and looked forward to the privilege offered by the Family Reunion Program in only a few New York State correctional facilities. Alex, excited for his first weekend with his family and me, gathered bits and pieces of information from other exemplary inmates that had trailer visit experience and tried his best to paint a picture for me.

"Well, it's not like a trailer in a trailer park," Alex explained over a collect call the morning of my first day at work.

"Okay, good. So, it's probably bigger, right?" I asked, as if I had any inkling of trailer sizes other than what I saw in *8 Mile*.

"Yeah, I guess. They're like little houses connected to each other and six guys get to go up with their families at once."

"Are we sharing a house with other families?!" My brain wasn't giving me enough time to digest his words. I was still too confused by the whole idea of actually getting to have an uninterrupted sleepover with my husband who was serving fifteen-years-to-life in prison.

"No. Hell no. There are six different houses for six different families. But one of the dudes I spoke to said the houses are attached like we're next door neighbors. I think. I don't know. We'll see." I could tell Alex was just as lost as I was, but I couldn't help hounding him for all the information he had.

"So, these houses come with more than one room in them, right? Just in case one of the guys has a really big family?"

"I'm sorry to break it to you, babe," his serious tone made my hands go cold and clammy just thinking about Alex, his mother, father, older brother, younger sister, and me all sprawled out on the floor together like orphans in a shelter.

"No one is allowed to bring their entire family tree like we're celebrating a Dominican baby shower up here. Third and fourth cousins and their doctors and mechanics gotta stay behind," my husband finally finished his thought. My sweaty palms dried up, and I laughed so hard at his dumb joke as the crowded Dominican baby showers I had frequented throughout my lifetime flashed before my eyes.

"You're an idiot," I shot back, unable to relax my grin.

"No offense," Alex said, sarcastically. I could hear him smiling through the phone. "Babe, listen... in two months, I'm gonna get to hold you in my arms without some damn CO watching me the whole time. That's all that really matters to me. I honestly can't wait to know what that feels like again," his words instantly eased my first-day-of-work jitters, and what I wanted more than anything was to kiss him before boarding the 5 bus to White Plains. I was forced to settle on blowing a kiss through the receiver, as usual.

"I can't wait, babe. I love you." I pressed the cellphone closer to my face, imagining his lips on my ear.

"I love you too, Kaylah."

Chills never failed to trickle up my spine and cover me in goosebumps whenever I heard my husband say my name. I didn't need a cute term of endearment to know he was speaking the truth. The sound of my name, and the way in which he delivered it was all the validation I needed to know that Alexander J. Mitchell was mine, and I was his.

I took the first available window seat I saw and settled in. It was another humid summer day in New York that left me more unhappy than usual with the black pants suit I had to wear for work like I was headed to a funeral at a chain restaurant. Luckily, I'd get to enjoy forty-five minutes on the air-conditioned 5 bus before reaching my destination.

I looked away from the window and down at my hands as we drifted farther from the shitty side of Westchester, heading north. I lightly brushed my fingertips over the smooth skin of the vacant ring finger on my left hand, remembering the way it sparkled the night before when I wore my wedding ring to bed. The only time I got to see the tiny stones glow around my finger was right before closing my eyes for the night, which prompted me to stay up longer than I should. I was officially married to the man of my dreams and still could only be married to him in my dreams. At the same time, I was growing accustomed to the idea of being a regular, single twenty-year-old girl in every aspect of life except my love life. Every morning, before even brushing my teeth, I first tucked my diamond ring in the secret compartment of a Winnie the Pooh jewelry box I had since I was seven. The sky-blue box, decorated with tiny Poohs happily eating honey, traveled back and forth from Boston with me so that wherever the sun came up, I was still single. I had checked the "single" box for each marital status question on the W-4 form at the new P.F. Chang's location and claimed no other dependents but myself. Whatever legal documents required my status and signature, whether for school or work or tax purposes, the "single" box was automatically marked without hesitation. I forced myself to understand that my union with Alex would only ever be accepted by God in an attempt to stop seeking the approval of others.

On my Facebook page, I had claimed "In a Relationship" since the beginning of time for the sole purpose of warding off any socially awkward boys that felt the need to use the popular networking site as a dating service. But, I certainly had no desire to make the sudden and shocking switch from "In a Relationship" to "Married." I was certain that it would only provoke a long list of "friends" stalking my page for a picture of the "lucky guy" before clicking "like" if they approved of the status change; or an eruption of incessant rings on Mom's cell that would have me out on the street faster than I could say, "I'm sorry." I avoided a public announcement at all costs for the sake of a semi-civil relationship with my mother and a normal life in the world. My inner "hood rat" often times thought to rebel against my own safety regulations by posting an obscene amount of Polaroid pictures of Alex and me taken over the years in a Facebook album titled, "Free Alex, Ya Dig?" However, it was no trouble putting her in check whenever I reminded myself that a relationship with Mark Zuckerberg was another one I didn't want to hinder.

As far as walking through the real world was concerned, I proudly declared *not* single every chance I got. About 80% of the male population at Emerson preferred the same sex while the other 20% was still trying to figure it out, so school was an automatic safe zone. If a guy found the courage to approach me while at the restaurant, I simply informed him that I was "taken" and left him a signature smile because I couldn't help being easily flattered. My mind stayed too busy painting pictures of my husband and what our trailer visits would look like when we got to hold each other every forty days. My colorful daydreams effortlessly filled page after blank page, leaving no space left over to entertain the idea of another guy. My imagination was too excited and too in love to spare more than a second adding the face of the burrito maker at Boloco who snuck his phone number into my paper bag. I was completely consumed by the mere thought of waking up next to my husband for the first time. In two months, I was going to know how peacefully he slept, how disastrous his hair looked in the morning, how sloppy he brushed his teeth, how long he took in the shower, how fast he devoured his favorite foods, how loud he laughed at his dad's bad jokes, how quietly he watched a movie, and how wide he smiled when he saw us all for the first time outside the visiting room. I was going to learn little things about my husband that a wife should know. For two beautiful days, we were going to live like a real married couple.

I almost forgot about the wedding gift I had gotten Alex a couple weeks before leaving Boston, and my level of excitement busted through the roof of the bus when I remembered he would finally see it for the first time in August. I never thought I'd find the courage to do it until I got married and courageously committed to forever with the love of my life. It was the ultimate surprise and made perfect sense in my eyes. The letters my husband wrote me every other week inspired the vision in my head. I wanted more than his name attached to me forever. I wanted a symbol to represent exactly how well we knew each other, and nothing conveyed the strength of our bond more than our handwritten letters. Alex's developmental cursive expressed both his rugged and delicate side, like I could see him and hear his voice in every sheet of loose-leaf I sat reading in my dorm room. "Love, Alex" is how he chose to sign off every time, which is what I chose to tattoo on my body, using his exact penmanship.

The artist, however, had her own opinions about my idea and shared an unwritten disclaimer before accepting the job.

"You know this is a jinx, right? You might want to rethink your decision."

She had the potential to be a nice lesbian, but her tone was grossly judgmental with a face to match. I had heard of the name-tattoo myth many times before and yet was still confident enough to walk into a tattoo parlor requesting Alex's name on my ass because I knew for a fact that a "jinx" didn't apply to our love and level of commitment. I stared her down, ready to take my business someplace else; but I knew I was more comfortable with a female artist (lesbian or not) and was afraid of not finding another with her pricing in Downtown Boston, so I decided to stay and fight.

"I'm a grown, married woman, and I don't need another person trying to tell me what to do, especially someone who just met me three minutes ago. If you won't do it, I'm more than happy to find someone who will." My heart was racing, my temper rising with every word, bringing me to the verge of tears. It wasn't what the heartless woman said that hurt my feelings so much, but how she said it that nearly made me change my mind, despite the tattoo idea putting a smile on my face all week long. My family had been stressing me out for months, telling me what they thought was in my best interest, and here a stranger was doing the same with a little extra judgment on the side. I was looking forward to doing something that could temporarily pull me up out of my funk and make my husband smile his incredible smile. I couldn't handle another objection in my life.

"Okay. You got it," the artist said, almost remorsefully, as she took Alex's letters from my hands. She sketched for several minutes, tracing his scrawl before executing my vision flawlessly on scrap paper and enclosing his signature in a simple, single-lined heart just as I asked. I squeezed my eyes tight, letting my mind run away from the piercing needle when Alex's face appeared. His jaw dropped in complete shock by the fact that I even thought to get a tattoo, let alone one of his name. He knew I wasn't someone who could easily consider the idea, especially because I could never think of anything worthy of the pain and worthy of staying a part of me forever; that was until I married him.

Forty-five minutes later, *Love, Alex* was permanently engraved in my skin, specifically on my left butt cheek—a spot only he would ever be allowed to see. The tattoo was perfectly sized and positioned conservatively enough so that the dark cursive would stay hidden even under a bathing suit. My husband had officially left his mark, and I couldn't wait to show him that it was on a place other than my heart.

I arrived to work fifteen minutes early and used the extra time to give myself one last look in the bathroom mirror at the Westchester Mall in White Plains. I had started wearing light makeup to decrease the appearance of my dark spots, which made me feel a lot more comfortable in public. Tinted moisturizer was the first baby step I took in learning how to apply makeup and hoped that my physician's theories didn't come to fruition so that I wouldn't have to use anything heavier to cover my face in the future. I darkened my eyelashes with a cheap stick of mascara from CVS, softly colored my cheekbones with the depleting pink blush I stole from Janessa while she was sleeping, and ruffled my hair that went limp in the New York summer heat after I spent an hour straightening it with the volumizing In-Styler that morning. Though I could button my size ten black slacks again, they still encouraged an unattractive display of *chichos* bulging through the camisole I wore under my black blazer. I buttoned the single button on my blazer hoping to hide the *chichos* better and appear slimmer in the all-black attire, making a mental note to start doing a couple sets of crunches each day. Buttoning the blazer didn't help cover my chest and even accentuated my cleavage a little more, which I couldn't decide if I liked or not. I checked the time on my Blackberry and quickly turned back to the mirror to stare at myself for another minute. I wasn't used to showing much skin and opted to pull the camisole up higher on my chest to avoid the risk of looking inappropriate on my first day at work. I stepped back once more to give my hair another flip and fluff before approving of the girl in the mirror. It was time to start her six-hour shift, whether she was ready or not.

I ran downstairs to the second floor of the luxury mall to find P.F. Chang's China Bistro with the same décor and ambiance as my store back in Boston. Though it all felt oddly familiar, my nervous smile made its natural elastic appearance while I stayed focused on lifting my camisole up from the top every so often when no one was looking. My training started with memorizing approximately sixty-five arbitrary table numbers, which surprisingly came as easy to me as memorizing the lines of a play. In fact, I had learned the tables the same way I learned lines, by producing my own song and singing it repeatedly in my head. I hummed an original tune comprised of mostly numbers while the young hostess trainer blabbed on about how important it was to get these tables down because the front desk was not only the heart of the restaurant, but everything the P.F. Chang's brand stood for; which, apparently, was a lot more than just really decent Mongolian beef. Once my passionate trainer friend was done reciting her melodramatic spiel from the employee handbook, I repeated back every table number in order on the first try and thanked her for the effective mentorship.

I was excited to practice some social techniques from Dale Carnegie's, *How to Win Friends and Influence People*, that I had just finished reading on the *Bolt* to New York. I made an effort to walk through my new store with good posture and introduce myself to anyone wearing a long-sleeve, black polyester top with a matching black, ankle-length apron. Lunch was off to a slow start, so I was successful in making eye contact and getting a strong handshake in with at least a dozen of my co-workers before walking away singing each person's name in my head. I focused on perfecting at least a half-confident strut when a middle-aged couple sitting at table fifty-four waved me down and broke my concentration to complain about waiting over ten minutes for Arnold Palmers they still hadn't seen. My sour-faced guests inspired me to assume a managerial position without hesitation as I rushed to the bar to save the day. A genuine smile of mine caught me off-guard when I thought about the possibility of achieving my mission to be the hostess with the mostest on my very first day, but decided to give myself at least an hour on the job before declaring victory. I approached the bar in haste to find the bartender reaching his designated area at the same time with the same level of energy. His mouth was moving as quickly as his feet, and it was obvious he had just returned from the back after sneaking a few bites of the chicken fried rice our cooks prepared for Chang's morning family meal. The blue-eyed bartender couldn't help smirking when he looked up to discover that I had caught him red-handed.

"You're the happiest person I've ever seen before twelve o'clock," his gloved hand covered his full mouth as he spoke.

I relaxed my grin when I remembered what my purpose at the bar was.

"Good morning. I have a couple guests waiting more than ten minutes for Arnold Palmers," I said, trying my best to avoid criticism in my tone and hold onto my smile just as Dale had taught me. The perplexed bartender furrowed his brows before swallowing the last bit of rice in his mouth and reached for the single white ticket waiting at the printer.

"Seven minutes," he retaliated, tossed the ticket in the trash and grabbed two clean pint glasses behind him to finally start making the drinks.

"Doesn't matter. They're unhappy," I didn't hesitate to respond, fighting the urge to share my honest opinion about the ridiculous delay for two half-lemonade-half-iced-teas at a dead hour. He was a snarky bartender I knew had the potential to mess up my good mood, so I chose not to say another word while waiting for table fifty-four's drinks.

He looked up after a long minute and slammed the freshly made Arnold Palmers on the well, causing me to flinch when a small drop of mixed juice caught the tip of my nose.

"Just give 'em one of those amazing smiles of yours, and I'm sure they'll forget how unhappy they were." The bartender made solid eye contact with me for the first time, long enough so that I could spot little specks of gray in his crystal blue eyes that practically danced against his skin as white as snow. He was one of those pale men that didn't tan well, having to deal with rosy cheeks and a flaky forehead for days after being in the sun. His small chest only exuded confidence under the black uniform because of his attention to posture. I leaned in to take the chilled glasses from the well and caught a glimpse of dark engravings peeking out from underneath his polyester collar. A large tattoo wrapped around the base of his white neck, leaving me curious to know what the rest of the artwork looked like and what it symbolized as I lifted the drinks off the bar. I then noticed my shameless co-worker sizing me up at the same time, his blue eyes resting on my breasts for a second too long. I immediately turned away to head back to table fifty-four, but not before receiving this testy, tasteless man's perfect wink. It was a classically cool wink. So classic, I could only imagine someone as cool as Paul Newman being able to pull it off. That was exactly who this guy reminded me of, despite the bad attitude and lacking a few inches in height.

I hated myself for somewhat liking the overly flirtatious gesture as soon as it had been delivered. I was appalled at the thought of this playboy using his moves just to hush me up and get me out of his hair—his neatly combed, light brown, almost blonde, hair. I tried to shake his face from my head before offering my signature smile to the unhappy couple just as I had planned to do, and not because the crude bartender had the nerve to suggest it. My dislike for him would only grow fiercer at the start of my break when I was in the mood to order egg-drop soup and reluctantly returned to the bar to pay for my lunch.

"Hey, boss. You should know we don't have to pay for egg-drop soup. You can just go to the back and grab a bowl...idiot." He threw the ticket in the trash after crunching it up into a small paper ball, then turned to snicker with his co-bartender who had just clocked in, *La nueva jefa. ¿Su nombre otra vez?* The bartender, as white as snow, directed his snarky question in Spanish at me, and I could only unhinge my jaw in response to the random sound of his flawlessly spoken lines. This guy just called me an idiot for ordering egg-drop soup, and instead of throwing myself over the bar top to sink my thumbs into his baby blue eyes, I just stared at him in awe.

"I'm Kaylah," I softly answered his question before finding myself again, "And you're the idiot. I didn't know if the soup was free at *this* location, so I put in the order like a responsible employee. Apparently, this store could use some more responsible employees," I shot back red-faced, but my curiosity got the best of me. "How'd you learn to speak Spanish so well?" He laughed at my sudden outburst, revealing a smile that had very possibly needed the assistance of braces once upon a time, charming nonetheless.

"Relax. We're all family here," he could see the steam leaving from my red ears and tried to justify his unwarranted insult before continuing, "And, my blood taught me. I'm Dominican." I could tell little Paul Newman's misleading features frequently caused people to assume he was some form of White at first glance, a judgment he thoroughly enjoyed proving wrong as soon as the moment presented itself.

¿De donde eres? He asked me another question in Spanish that I blanked on for the second time. I didn't want to talk about myself. He was probably the most annoying and interesting person I had ever met. I wanted to know more about him, about his perfect English, perfect Spanish, his

171

tattoo, and what his name was. I found my curiosity slowly starting to overpower the animosity I had clung onto from our first short conversation a few hours before.

"I'm Dominican, too. But I was born in Yonkers, and I'm not much of a Spanish speaker," I admitted shamefully.

"*Dominicana*? No Español? No bueno," he spoke in a forced American accent and mocked me without mercy. "But it's alright because you look like a light-skinned Indian chick anyway."

"Indian?" I exaggerated my confusion by looking over my shoulder as if he had to be referring to someone else in the room. "Me?" No one had ever mistaken me for Indian before, but I quickly found an appreciation for the presumption when I imagined myself playing the role of Jess in *Bend It Like Beckham*. Then unexpectedly, the bartender's random guess at my ethnicity brought a boulder down on my chest when I remembered I had once thought that my beautiful, dark-skinned husband could've been from somewhere south of the Himalaya Mountains, as well. A guilty conscience ignited a burning sensation in my cheeks and ears once I realized Alex hadn't crossed my mind since I walked into the restaurant. There was a sudden emptiness in my heart when I thought about how much I missed my sweet husband and regretted ever engaging in a conversation with the demeaning playboy behind the bar.

"Yes, you. Don't tell me you've never heard that before," he spoke confidently with a taunting smirk across his face before diverting from the conversation to greet a couple business men who placed their crisp suit jackets on the back of two wooden bar stools and pulled them out to settle in. I observed my first foe at Chang's as he handed the gentlemen lunch menus and welcomed them with impressive hospitality skills. He had an easy-going, very secure, borderline cocky way about him that made his caring and gracious delivery of words as baffling as his bloodline. His personality was like an onion with several foul and flavorful layers that I kind of enjoyed getting a little taste of. I forced myself to look away and take his distraction as an opportunity to escape, but the return of his snake-charming voice glued the rubber soles of my slip-resistant shoes to the floor.

"My name's Del Sol. Branden Del Sol. In case you cared to know, boss." Branden had dropped two freshly made Asian Pear Mojitos for his guys and waited for them to decide on appetizers while he re-introduced himself to me. I assumed he was a James Bond fan, but I didn't care about his favorite movies or his name anymore. My fifteen-minute break was nearly up, and I hadn't even poured my bowl of soup yet. I was prepared to exit the conversation and get back to work without eating anything.

"Nice to meet you, Branden," I rushed my words, skipped the handshake, and turned to leave.

"Wait. You came from another spot with free egg-drop soup, right? So, which location is missing their responsible and beautiful hostess with the mostest?"

I turned a full 180 in disbelief at both his forwardness and ability to read my mind. I tried to fight the flattery, but I knew his womanizing lines had defeated me when the corners of my lips curved into a smile and my brain shot an extra dose of dopamine through my veins.

"This hostess with the mostest is coming from Boston," I answered and instantly had the desire to punch myself in the face.

"Boston? School out there?"

"Yeah. Emerson College," my own words made me bite down on my tongue till it nearly bled. Please don't ask me what I'm studying, I prayed he would read my mind again.

"I knew you were a nerd. Nice to meet you, Kaylah."

I giggled nervously, following up with a deep inhale and long exhale like I was in the middle of a yoga class. The thought of him getting ready to ask more about school made me a lot less willing to stay at the bar, but he kept talking with a smile, and I kept listening with my own.

"Sorry for speaking so informally with you today; it's only because I feel like I've known you for years," Branden said, looking at me through squinted eyelids as if trying to remember my face from somewhere. "I hope you weren't actually offended." He winked again, and this time I had to straighten my mouth to keep from drooling. I accepted his apology with a simple nod before finally heading back to the front desk.

It happened so fast. It happened so fast. It happened so fast. One minute we were exchanging awkward texts and the next minute I had my tongue down his throat after knocking back three shots of Jack. I would forgive his reckless mouth by using my own reckless mouth two weeks later at Pat's, a bar across the street from Chang's that the crew escaped to every Wednesday night after their shift.

Earlier that day, Branden did another eye squint my way when I approached his bar to help with drink orders during the lunch rush. I waited for him to say something, but eventually snapped at his drawn-out silence, "Maybe you should get some glasses."

He pretended not to hear me and finally opened his mouth to speak, "Were you riding a bike down Riverdale this morning?"

I was about to drop a tray filled with Mai Tais when I heard the question and moved forward again to steady myself back on the well.

"Why?"

Branden gave a sly smirk, "Because I saw you."

I had started a morning work-out regimen that involved a two-mile bike ride to Gorton High School's track, a mile run at the track, and then a two-mile bike ride back home to get in shape for my upcoming wedding night. So, he did recognize me and had no need for glasses.

Branden was officially my work crush which immediately made me cringe at the thought of him catching me in work-out gear, all sweaty and without makeup. However, his next question squashed the petty anxiety about my morning appearance and ignited a whole new panic attack.

"Do you live on Riverdale?"

"Yes," I said, wishing I could chug a Mai Tai or two to replenish my painfully dry mouth.

"Would you look at that? I live on Highland. We should exchange numbers so we can text each other in case one of us runs out of sugar or something." The playboy who lived two blocks south of me then rubbed salt on my wounds with another perfect wink, leaving me as weak as the watered-down Mai Tais on the tray.

I was the first to admit to running out of sugar and needing saving that night.

"Hey." I stared at the one simple, empty word for several minutes before pressing "Send." I then immediately jumped up and ran away from the phone like it was about to detonate on my bed. I rushed into the bathroom to stare down regret in the mirror, feeling awful for even giving Branden my number in the first place. I heard the ring of a reply no more than a minute later.

"Hey, boss!"

"Wow. I'm so sorry. I meant to text my Uncle Billy." I really did have an uncle named Billy on my Dad's side, but we both knew he was the furthest person from my mind at eight o'clock on a Wednesday night.

"Aren't u glad u got me instead? Pick u up for Pat's at 9?" He was relentless.

Branden picked me up in a black 1994 Honda Civic that night and the following morning before work when I was too hungover to even ride the bus. We soon began carpooling whenever our shifts were scheduled around the same time, learning something new about each other every trip. It may have been half a bottle of Jack that made me realize it, but Branden and I definitely had strong chemistry. It was so fierce that a month would fly by and we'd officially be considered Chang's cutest couple, claiming exclusivity on July 15, 2009.

Branden knew about Alex; he just didn't know *everything* before he decided to call me his girlfriend.

"My boyfriend goes to Boston University," was just one of many lies to follow.

"Are you guys on good terms?" His blue eyes showed concern after engaging in countless heated, amazing make-out sessions for weeks. Branden was crushing on me just as hard as I was crushing on him, but he wasn't prepared to play homewrecker.

"No. It's been a rocky situation for a while," I lied again.

The truth wouldn't come out until after I drank too many shots of courage one Wednesday night that left me weak in

Branden's bed and wanting to feel cared for. He tried to stamp his lips on every part of my body, lifting my T-shirt up to brush against my soft belly before I pulled it back down self-consciously and distracted his mouth with mine. He took his wife-beater tank off, revealing the full artwork on his body for the first time. The tattoo was a play on his last name "Del Sol" meaning "of the sun." Engraved sunbeams pointed out from the base of his neck, over his collarbone, and down his hairy chest like a Native American tribal painting. In each sharply drawn ray was the name of one of his closest family members; his mother, Tirsa; his father, Joseph; his younger sister, Sylvia; his younger brother, David; and his youngest brother, Zachary. Branden was the product of divorced immigrant parents, leaving him to drop out of school and care for the family at fifteen years old. There was no need to add his name to the tribal art because his head was the center of all the sunbeams, symbolizing him as the first *son*, the first born, and the caretaker. It was the most powerful tattoo I ever had the pleasure of seeing and feeling on a person, and I liked him even more for it.

"Should I get a condom?" Branden breathed in-between gentle kisses. I nodded my head, barely taking a second to think about what I was doing. I didn't think about anything but the comfort of my boyfriend's bed and his ability to make me feel more safe in the hood than I had ever felt before. Branden handled me carefully like I was a porcelain doll he'd cry over if I cracked in half. He moved slowly as if he knew that my last sexual experience was six years ago and that I considered myself a born-again virgin, a born-again virgin who was losing her virginity for the second time with a man who wasn't her husband. It was the first night my ring finger stayed bare since my wedding day.

"It must've been a serious relationship for you to tat his name on your ass like that," Branden judged me when I turned over to face the wall after pretending to climax. He had no idea that my husband's name was just as important to me as every name carved on his chest was to him. A tear slid from the corner of my eye, crossed the bridge of my nose and landed on his pillow. I sobered up and suddenly wanted to die.

"I have to tell you something," I spoke to the wall. I could hear the rustle of sheets behind me as he tried to move closer to my choked whispers.

"Yeah?"

"Alex and me got married seven months ago. He's not in school. He's in prison for twelve more years."

Branden pulled my shoulder back to find my face soaked in tears.

"I'm sorry," my voice cracked when I looked up into his worried eyes, unable to see their blue centers in the darkness. He didn't say a word. He didn't ask questions or throw me out of his bed. He just rested his head on the pillow next to mine and wrapped his arm around my waist. His body felt like the warmth of the sun after months of cold rain and clouds.

CHAPTER THIRTEEN

I told my mother I was going camping for the weekend with some friends from Chang's. I told Branden I was going camping for the weekend with my Dad's family. I was actually planning to go on my first trailer at a maximum-security facility where I'd be forced to leave my cellphone in a highly secured locker for nearly forty-eight hours. I wouldn't even be able to request a time-out to open the locker and check for any missed calls or emergencies. I needed a story that not only explained my absence, but also explained why it was going to be almost impossible to reach me in my absence, and a camping trip in the middle of a dead zone was all the creativity my masochistic brain could muster.

The farther we drove from Yonkers and everyone I lied to, the easier it was to breathe. Busy highways turned into long, lonely pavements with views of green pastures, barns, cows, and horses every few miles. Life was quiet in the mountains past Albany where people didn't seem bothered by other people, and worries got tossed up in the clear sky to burn like stars, reminding us of the beauty in every struggle. I worried less and less the closer we got to Great Meadow Correctional Facility because I could feel my husband's excited spirit like it was my own. I gazed up at a cluster of white clouds where the sun fought to shine through, and I knew he could feel mine, too.

I put fifty bucks toward groceries when we stopped at the Wal-Mart a few miles out to help Judy buy everything she needed for her baby boy's first weekend with the family. I had fantasized once or twice about recreating the amazing lasagna I baked for my family's Easter dinner a few months before, but it was obvious that Judy had no intentions of ever leaving the stove; just like old times.

We rolled a cart toward the food aisles in a hurry, and my face flushed red when passing the restrooms as it usually did on every Wal-Mart visit following my embarrassing incident. However, I couldn't deny all the wisdom I had obtained since that day. Solo trips to see Alex became as frequent as my checkups at the OB/GYN, and I could officially consider myself just another savvy loved one riding the prison bus.

"I can't believe these a-holes won't allow black pepper. What's wrong with pepper?!" My mother-in-law barked at a wall of seasonings, her eyes madly scrolling up and down its organized shelves. In preparation for first-time trailer visitors, the Family Reunion Program mailed my in-laws a standard checklist of food items that were and were not allowed in. The permitted foods included only raw, hermetically sealed meats, hermetically sealed anything, double packaged bread, fresh produce, boxed foods, canned foods, and unopened bottles of seasoning. The prohibited items consisted of things like glass jars, fast food or home-cooked food, pressurized cans of whipped cream (Cool Whip was okay), plastic containers of milk, bottles of cooking oil over sixteen ounces, anything containing black pepper, anything containing chocolate liqueur, and anything else the correctional officer felt like adding to the list.

Luckily, it was fairly easy to avoid imprisoning ourselves at Wal-Mart for hours reading food labels because Judy was accustomed to buying raw meats, fresh fruits and vegetables to make a good old-fashioned home-cooked meal every night for the family.

"Wow, I'm gonna get to cook for my baby again, Kaylah. I missed that so much," Judy confessed warmly as she dazed out on a huge package of hermetically sealed chicken thighs and drumsticks. She was overwhelmed by the mere thought of preparing her world-famous buttermilk fried chicken, baked macaroni and cheese, sweet corn on the cob, and garlic mashed potatoes from scratch; a few favorites Alex hadn't tasted in over three years.

"He misses it too, Judy," I consoled her, knowing very well that she was missing a whole lot more than just spending all day in the kitchen for her youngest son. Judy's dark circles had become more visible through her rimless, rectangular glasses over the years. But her husband would carry enough blame on his shoulders for the both of them, seeking forgiveness at the bottom of wine bottles every night since Alex's arrest. Timmy was known to make the three-hour drive up for his wife who had a life-long fear of getting behind the wheel, but he rarely ever made it inside the prison's walls. My father-in-law usually settled on buying a six-pack at the nearest gas station instead and gulped it down in the parking lot before Judy wrapped up her visit over four hours later. The only reason Timmy agreed to the extended family visit was because Alex begged him to show in hopes of conducting a one-on-one intervention for his father. However, I was afraid little progress could be made, mainly because my husband was constantly too busy in his own head, blaming himself for both his incarceration and his father's alcoholism. Alex was also too much like Timmy in that he always denied feeling pain when someone or something hurt him and found a way to cope by acting like nothing ever happened just to keep moving.

We made it to the colossal stone wall in less than an hour, following signs to "FRP" where visits were processed in a small building separate from the regular waiting room. There were several other people waiting outside the locked door, other loved ones scheduled for a trailer just like Alex said there would be. Judy, Timmy, Alex's older brother, Junior, his younger sister, Britney, and I all helped carry our large load of groceries inside when a big-bellied White officer opened the door a few minutes after we parked around 11:00 a.m. We stood in line to present valid IDs and sign a few standard forms before sitting back to observe the other families sharing the intimate room with us, waiting to gain wisdom for our next trailer.

A middle-aged Latina with freshly dyed black hair that fell below her wide rear stood up first and began lifting several Wal-Mart bags of her own from the floor onto a wooden table top. We were surrounded by a sea of gray and blue plastic when I realized Wal-Mart was a prison family's savior and vice versa.

The woman's toddler jumped to his mother's rescue, but he could barely manage the weight of one bag, huffing and puffing tiny breaths before the long-haired Latina noticed and shooed him away. The latex-gloved correctional officer went fishing in the sea, pulling out every product so he could affirm none had been tampered with. He opened up two boxes of Goya crackers, a box of Froot-Loops, a box of Frosted Flakes, three family size bags of Lay's BBQ chips, and a package of double stuffed Oreo's; then, slid all his approvals to one side so the loved one could rearrange her groceries back into their plastic bags herself as he moved on to inspect others. After tearing apart the woman's whole weekend supply of food, the officer only spoke to deny her a container of cream cheese because of its peel-off foil top, which she opted to leave behind in the small refrigerator provided for such rejected items instead of throwing it away.

"That's interesting," I thought my cream cheese opinion out loud.

An elderly Black woman sitting in front of us overheard me and turned around to offer more enlightenment, "Yes, honey. They so paranoid we done opened up the top, put somethin' abnormal inside and glued it back on. Like we'd waste the Good Lord's time like that. Well, I guess some people do. Just make sure you get that hermetically sealed block of Philadelphia cream cheese whenever you feel the need to bring up cream cheese for your boy. It's the only one they'll let through. It's a shame it don't come in any other flavors but plain, though," the experienced FRP visitor whispered her top-secret information, barely taking a breath in-between words. She replied with a crooked grin before turning back around when we gave her our many thanks.

Mental note: No peel-off tops. Check.

After the Wal-Mart bags were cleared from the table, the busy Latina quickly plopped a black carry-on suitcase onto the table top to help accelerate the next thorough investigation. The officer unzipped the suitcase's front pockets first and dug his hands in each one, feeling around for anything of significance. He then unzipped the whole bag to massage his latex fingers through a lumpy pile of children's and women's clothing. He pulled out toothbrushes, shampoo bottles, Elmo's bath time bubbles, a bar of Dove soap, and a wheel of floss which was denied.

"The man let me have it the last time," the Latina spoke in a heavy accent.

"Well, then the man didn't know what he was doing the last time, sweetheart," Officer Grumbles carelessly stuffed the woman's belongings back into the carry-on and left her to reorganize everything again so it could close properly.

Mental note: No floss. Check.

We watched four more families get processed the same way, absorbing the secret life of trailer visits, learning what it takes to make an inconvenient situation as convenient as possible until it finally becomes second nature. We were the largest family left for last, and I noticed the faces of the other antsy loved ones fall flat when the Mitchells all stood up at the same time. Everyone in the room, including the correctional officer, had one common goal—hurry up and get out. Thankfully, the Mitchells had accepted Judgment Day like pros by the time it was our turn to approach the gloved man behind the wooden table. Timmy and Junior teamed up to collect every plastic bag off the floor and hastily displayed them before the bored officer; Judy then stepped in to remove our groceries from the bags while I focused on placing them back once the inspector had given the green light. Britney worked the end of the assembly line and cleared the long table of all our approved food, careful not to crack any eggs or crush the double packaged loaf of white bread. We were like synchronized swimmers in the lead for the Olympic gold medal. Miraculously, we weren't denied any goods and proceeded more confidently as we swiftly presented our duffel bags filled with clothes and toiletries for the weekend. After our speedy and thorough process was complete, the only things denied from all five family members were Judy's floss and my can of hair mousse, which hurt my feelings more than I thought it would. Then I remembered my husband's hair was almost as long as mine at this point and decided to borrow some of the hair products I was positive he hadn't left behind in his cell.

Mental note: No mousse. Check.

I retrieved an orange key from Judy to open our assigned locker where everyone's house/car keys and cellphones were being stored so that I could add my can of Tresemmé mousse to the items we wouldn't see for another two days. I spotted my Blackberry and rushed to turn it on once more before leaving it for good.

"Miss u already," Branden texted at 11:06 a.m.

"R u really camping?" Janessa texted at 11:47 a.m.

"What time are you coming back?" My mother's text came in at 12:11 p.m. as I held the phone in my hand, causing serious heart palpitations to beat through my chest.

"Your turn, Kay," Britney called me from the metal detector. Everyone had walked through and passed the last test before heading to the trailers. I was holding up the loved ones.

"Okay, coming. One second," I tried not to sound like I was in the middle of a nervous breakdown.

"Will be back around 12pm on Mon. Luv u," my thumbs pressed on the Blackberry's hard buttons faster than they ever had before. I shut the phone down and turned the key for the last time. Everything was going to be okay.

All six families and their groceries were loaded onto a dark blue, sixteen-seat prison van headed around the back of the facility to the magical world of trailers. We stopped twice on our tour of Great Meadow Correctional Facility. The first time was for another White officer to open the van doors, peer inside and count each one of us like cattle; the second time was when Officer Grumbles stepped out to unlock a tall wire gate that would lead us to our next and final stop.

The van finally pulled up to a green grass yard surrounded by three wooden porches, two doors to each porch that led to separate apartment-style houses for every scheduled family. The houses were painted a grayish-blue, each one marked with a bright white number from one to six. Our trailer was number one, which I spotted right away on the far-left side of the yard over everyone's bobbling head. The van made an annoying beeping sound when it reversed before coming to a stop, but it alerted all the men in green pants that Christmas had arrived on a beautiful Saturday afternoon in August. Five black and brown faces and one White sprinkle stepped out from their individual apartments to greet their loved ones, weary of getting too close to the van.

When I saw Alex, my eyes and tongue fell out of my face like Jim Carrey's did in *The Mask* once he saw Cameron Diaz at the Coco Bongo. My husband looked smokin' in a slick-back ponytail and a plain white T-shirt that I already made plans to take back home with me and never wash again. I had enough energy to tackle everyone moving off the van at a snail's pace in front of me and fly into my husband's arms, but waited patiently in the back seat when I remembered my manners. It was only a few more seconds before Alex flashed his life-changing, ear-to-ear grin my way, accelerating all my reserved energy to charge into his open arms, wrap my legs around his waist, and attack him with a kiss just the way Allie did to Noah in *The Notebook*. I had always wanted to jump into a man's arms like girls did in the movies, but the thought of being too heavy and injuring us both usually woke me up from my short-lived fantasy. It was easy to forget my annoying insecurities when my husband held me as if he had also been practicing in his dreams every night, with no sign of a struggle, and no desire to ever let me down. I couldn't believe it was him.

"Can *I* get a hug?" We heard Judy tease from behind us, prompting Alex to slowly help me down before throwing his arms around his mother and the rest of the smiling family. He immediately took the Wal-Mart bags out of Britney's hands after running his big fingers through her freshly flat-ironed hair to ruffle it out of place.

"Wow. It's been less than two minutes, and you're already a pain in my ass," sixteen-year-old Britney hissed at her older brother.

"Just wondering if they let you through with those clip-on weave things you like so much, Brit-Nerd," Alex clowned around with his little sister.

"Shut up, Alex," Britney shot back as my husband led us up the porch stairs of trailer 1 and into our weekend home.

The apartment was a dream. It was an average, small two-bedroom you'd find in a more rural neighborhood in need of a serious paint job and interior decorating; but under the circumstances, our trailer/apartment/house-thing was an absolute dream. It was fully furnished; equipped with a television, DVD player, radio, couch and loveseat in the living room; a small dining table, fridge, sink, and electric stove in the kitchen; a full bath and shower; a queen-size mattress and A.C. in both bedrooms.

"How did all of this stuff get here?" I said in complete awe, exploring the kitchen cabinets to find a full set of blue dinner plates, dessert plates, cereal bowls, coffee mugs, and drinking cups. There was also a microwave, toaster, silverware, pots, pans, baking utensils, spatulas, an egg beater and even a pair of oven mitts provided in our vacation home.

"Donations, mostly," a hyper Alex answered while rummaging through plastic bags and finding a place for each item. I was watching my husband put away the groceries. "It's not delivery, it's DiGiorno!" His eyes lit up like an overgrown child obsessed with pizza and TV commercials when he discovered the box of DiGiorno Supreme. "Ma, we gotta make this now. I skipped breakfast for this baby right here."

It was all too surreal. I had to lock myself in the bathroom for a minute just to cry and hopefully find truth in the mirror. Alex was on the other side of the door excited to bust open his first DiGiorno pie in his whole life. He was standing in the middle of a real kitchen helping his mother put away real groceries, and I couldn't relax long enough to enjoy the moment because I knew it was all bound to fly by like it never even happened. I had wanted this kind of simplicity with Alex since I was fifteen years old, and now it was mine for the length of a minute in the dream world.

"Babe, you okay?" Alex's knock startled me.

"Yeah, just a minute," I looked in the mirror and took a deep breath. Deep breaths always helped clear my tears.

"Are you pooping? Take your time. I want you to remember your first poop in the house with me," Alex shouted like an imbecile through the door.

"Go away, Alexander!" I snapped at his foolishness from inside the bathroom.

"That time of the month?"

"ALEXANDER!"

"Okay...I love you," he mumbled the words with a mouth full of some snack he couldn't resist taste-testing before the frozen pizza was ready to eat.

Tears started down my cheeks again when I remembered Branden confessing his love for me the night before. I said the words back to him but wasn't sure if it was the same love that came over me when I watched my husband put milk in the fridge. I loved Alex like I had never loved anyone in my life, and the only time doubt ever clouded that notion was when I thought about Branden. But neither Alex nor Branden deserved to stand around oblivious while my heart and brain played on a seesaw. It pained me to think about all the wrong I was doing. I always imagined growing up to help people, to inspire the masses, to change the world, and all I had accomplished at twenty years old was hurting those I loved the most.

"Baby, we're gonna go out and start a baseball game with the other families. You're on my team, so just wear an extra tampon or something when you're ready," Alex called through the bathroom door again.

"ALEX!"

"I love you so much. I'll be outside," he replied casually, unfazed by my outburst.

I washed my face for the second time and dried it on my black T-shirt when I realized there were no towels in the bare bathroom. I looked at my reflection once more to check for redness in my eyes and took a few more breaths before unlocking the door. The Mitchells had deserted the apartment, leaving behind an appetizing smell creeping out from the oven.

"Run, Forest! Run!" I heard Alex's enthusiasm through the screen door. The game sounded like it was off to a good start, but I used the pizza as an excuse to wait a few more minutes before heading out. Once the pizza pie and I were fresh and ready to go, I used our Great Value paper plates to deliver hot supreme slices to the wooden picnic table in front of trailer 1.

"And that's why I married you. You know the way to a man's heart, babe," Alex abandoned his outfielder position to take a huge bite of DiGiorno pizza for the first time. "Oh-em-gee. It's...so...fuckin'...good. Here," he spoke with a full mouth and handed me back his half-eaten slice, slow to catch a string of cheese at the corner of his lips. "They need me out there. Jump in whenever you want. I'll be back for this," Alex took one more savage bite from his pizza that I gripped in my hand before leaving me a greasy kiss on my forehead and running into the field like a big kid. "Oh, man! I love DiGiorno!" My husband had changed out of the awful green pants and into a comfortable pair of red basketball shorts I thought fit him slightly snug around his athletic rear but were a lot easier on the eyes.

The other Mitchells trickled over to the picnic table one by one to grab their slices in-between innings. It was a perfect summer day with smooth passing winds cooling the back of my neck where the sun had stayed resting for a while. Reality only threatened my dream when I found a White correctional officer staring down from the window of a tall tower, spying on our fun in the backyard. My eyes quickly came back to the baseball game and focused on the long-haired Latina's son wrapping his small body around the pitcher's green leg. I forgot about the spy when I remembered that it was Christmas, and I sat watching my favorite gift take a giant step forward to swing at the air with a plastic wiffle bat.

"Ha! You suck!" Britney fired from first base, a spot represented by one of the paper plates I had brought outside.

"Shut up, Brit! I needa concentrate!" Alex demanded, exaggerating a baseball player stance by poking his butt out and holding the bat high above his head.

"Batter's got a big butt!" Judy called out and finished in a fit of giggles.

"Ma! You're on *my* team!" Alex reminded his mother from home plate and completely missed the oncoming wiffle ball.

"Strike! You're out!" The pitcher in green pants called from his mound.

"This is pure treachery!" Alex reacted to the strike-out with a line influenced by his *Game of Thrones* readings.

Timmy and Junior were overcome with uncontrollable laughter as they made their way to the batting line. Britney snuck up behind her brother's neat ponytail and released his shoulder-length locks from his hair tie before throwing it to the ground.

"You got hair and ass like a chick!" my sister-in-law teased without mercy.

"You've always envied my beauty, Brit-Nerd," Alex boasted, focused on finding his fallen hair tie in the healthy green spears of grass. I wasn't really a fan of my husband's long hair until I saw it bounce freely in the sunlight and his stunning silhouette suddenly took on a resemblance to Jesus.

"You do kinda have a big butt, babe," I innocently admitted on the side, taking in his plump rear for the first time.

"Please, Kaylah. Not you, too!" My melodramatic husband pleaded and charged my way to shower me with happy kisses.

CHAPTER FOURTEEN

We sat on the floppy couches in a near food coma after eating Judy's traditional southern-style cuisine for dinner, trying hard not to fall unconscious during *Apocalypto*. Timmy had already succumbed to a Popeye snore on the loveseat while everyone else sat in fear of following his lead so early in the evening. Alex was excited to pop in the DVD and watch it with the family, but even my hyperactive husband could barely keep his eyes open. I sat cozily next to him, my arm locked with his and my legs limp over his lap. I studied the lines of his profile, watching his long, fluttering eyelashes fight to stay up. He sensed a smile creep onto my lips and turned his drowsy face to me.

"What's so funny?" Alex slurred slightly.

"You're actually full," I whispered my observation.

"There's a first time for everything," he gave up on trying to keep his eyes open while his lips moved. A few beats went by when I thought for sure I had lost Alex to a dream, until he finally came back to me. "Speaking of..." he spoke and peeked at me through one open eyelid before releasing my arm and stretching his hands to the ceiling. "Well, family. Day one was a success, if I do say so myself," Alex was even better at creating awkward moments than I was. "I'm pooped. Thank you all for coming. I love you. See you in the morning," he concluded with a forced yawn that made me really yawn, which then made me look like a player in his game plan. I shot him a glare when he took my hand and helped me to my bare feet.

"It's eight o'clock," Britney intentionally added to the sticky atmosphere, causing my brother-in-law to snicker while half asleep.

"Yeah, it's past your bedtime," Alex refused to let her win.

"Hush up, Brit. Love you too, baby. Love you, Kaylah. Good night," Judy tried to rescue Alex and me as we leaned down to give our mom a kiss on the cheek.

"Good night," I spoke with honest fatigue. My brain worked so long and hard to accept the day's events that I couldn't help but feel completely drained by the end.

We started toward one of the dark bedrooms and were a few steps away from freedom when Britney called out once more, "Keep it down in there, please. We're watching a movie."

I felt my entire body blow up in flames as I rushed into the room, wishing for an ocean to drown myself in after hearing my ruthless sister-in-law's last words. Alex didn't hesitate to grab one of his rolled sock balls from the bedroom floor and fire it out into the living room.

"Ow!" Britney blurted her final word of the day.

"I love that girl," Alex chuckled with more sincerity than sarcasm when he finally closed the door and locked it behind us. The yard's security lamps provided the only light in our room, creeping in through one window above the bed to make shadows on the bare walls. "Are you good?" My more than awake husband refocused his attention and checked in with me, knowing how uneasy I was about his family being in the house while we consummated our marriage eight months after our wedding day. A crashing sound of heavy rains in the Yucatan jungle vibrated the bedroom's thin walls and eased my nerves when I looked into Alex's eyes. I first found the trust I was searching for in his face before answering his question with a kiss. He broke away from my hungry lips to see me for a moment and returned with more passion as if he had affirmed I was real.

His hands covered me all at once, touching pressure points that increased my heart rate and destroyed every sleepy cell in my body. I was awake and excited and overwhelmed by the idea that one of my most frequent dreams was about to come true.

"Wait," Alex abruptly stopped kissing, and I wanted to cry like a newborn baby whose bottle had been pulled from her mouth. "Almost forgot," my husband flipped through what looked like a stack of blank CDs in the orange light coming in from outside. "Ne-Yo?" He turned back to me, showing off his signature grin while holding up a silver disc covered in handwritten scribbles that read, "Ne-Yo. In My Own Words."

"Yes," I said, catching his contagious smile. I also felt a sharp sting of gratitude when my husband didn't suggest Boyz II Men.

"Cool. I'm gonna put on the song I dedicated to you," Alex fussed with the CD player he had stolen from the living room and rearranged in our bedroom before the family's arrival that afternoon.

"You dedicated a song to me?"

"Yup, while I was making out with your yearbook picture in my cell yesterday," he admitted shamelessly.

"You're crazy," I said what I usually said when Alex made foolish, flattering comments.

"Crazy about you," my husband gave me his usual response and the familiar intro to "Stay" from Ne-Yo's debut album started playing on the small speaker he had also assembled in our bedroom for me.

"I love that song, babe. Thank you," I spoke sincerely, brushing my fingertips up his broad back and continuing where we left off.

"No. Thank *you*," Alex took my face in his hands to show his appreciation until it was my turn to pull back when I remembered something.

"On your stomach. Face in the pillow," my words surprised us both.

"Whoa! Babe, listen...I know you've heard stories about prison, but I promise I'm not into—"

"Oh, shut up and lie down, please," I cut off his obscenity, playfully shoving him away.

"You got it, boss," he snickered and cautiously made his way onto the bed. Alex's words hit me with a quick, minor heart attack when the first encounter with Branden flashed through my mind. My boyfriend had also once referred to me as "boss," but I found the resilience needed to abort that memory and focus on fighting for this memory with my husband. I kept my eyes on Alex as he lay face-down fully clothed while I went into my duffel bag in search of Flaca's wedding gift.

"Are you finally confessing to being one of those part-time dominatrix girls, babe?" Alex's imagination ran wild as he continued to breathe into the limp pillow.

"No, fool," I replied, pulling out my first lingerie outfit.

"I mean...if that's something you wanted to do, I guess I'd support—"

"Alexander!"

"Okay," he released a muffled chuckle.

I hadn't tried on my new sleepwear before the trailer visit, too afraid that the mirror would punk me out and force me to leave it behind. I quickly stripped out of my leggings and the oversized shirt I stole from Alex's room back home to slip into my white chiffon nighty that stopped right above my thighs. It was a frilly, overly sheer tank top accompanied by a matching frilly thong, both pieces hugging my body perfectly, albeit coming in a "one size fits most." I only accepted the form-fitting garment after reminding myself that I had lost over twenty pounds since my PCOS diagnosis and deserved to feel good on my wedding night.

"Okay. You can look now," I announced, standing before Alex at the end of the bed, trying hard not to cross my arms in front of my belly. He didn't hesitate to flip over and open his eyes after hearing the words. He absorbed me for a few beats as I stood awkwardly in front of him, relieved he couldn't see how red my face was turning in the dark. "Say something!" I demanded, nerves giving me away.

"You're beautiful," my husband's tone was the most serene it had been all day as his eyes scanned up and down my body. "You are so beautiful," he repeated, rising from his pillow and taking a closer seat at the edge of the bed to appreciate the view from a better angle. I then remembered I had even more to offer.

"Surprise number two," I spun around like a flirty cheerleader and presented my wedding gift to him.

"A tattoo?" The astonishment in his voice stretched my elastic lips to their full capacity.

"Yes. See what it says?"

"Love...Alex," he read it out loud and didn't say anything else. I took a concerned peek over my shoulder just in time to watch his soft lips land themselves on the tattoo like there was a magnetic attraction he couldn't resist. Alex's first kiss on my fleshy rear sent ferocious chills up my spine, covering me in a million little goosebumps. His large hands hugged the side of my hips and spun me back around so that I could watch him strip off his T-shirt and admire his fully-grown chest for the first time.

"You make me so happy. Thank you," a half-naked Alex wrapped his well-defined arms around my bottom and rested his curly head under my belly button as I stood towering over him. I ran my fingers through his healthy hair, hoping they nurtured him as much as his tight grip nurtured me. We spent several minutes in a silent embrace where I dazed off at the sight of my sparkling ring peeking from under his ringlets. I was finally getting the opportunity to digest Alexander J. Mitchell, my husband, my best friend, my soul-mate who would love me and cherish me for the rest of our lives. Alex's arms were around me. It had always been Alex. He broke my focus when he finally turned his head to slowly kiss my belly, pelvis and proceeded to sneak down lower until Ne-Yo's album started skipping on the second track, distracting us both at the same time.

"Ah, man. These lames can't take care of nothin'," my husband moved me gently and stood up to blow on the scratched CD like he used to do to all his malfunctioning video games when we were kids.

"Just put 'Stay' on repeat," I suggested, perfectly satisfied with embroidering the lyrics into my brain if it meant I'd think of this moment every time I heard the song.

"Say no more, baby girl," my husband turned his beautiful face back to me. "It might get hot in here. You want the window or the A.C.?" Alex asked me between quickened kisses under my ear, racing against the speed of my heartbeat.

"Neither. I wanna fog the window like Jack and Rose," I smiled like a giddy fifteen-year-old girl.

"You got all the good ideas tonight, babe," Alex replied, bringing his lips back up to meet mine. I wanted his compliment to inspire the dangerous initiative I took in the back of my mother's caravan over four years before and show him how much I had grown since then. I wanted to tell him about all the good ideas I had after extensively researching the stimulating parts of the penis just in preparation for our night. I wanted to show him how much I learned about the power combo of the glans, corona, and frenulum and shock the hell out of him with one of those tricks Flaca taught me using a fresh cucumber from my mini fridge. I wanted to dominate, but his kisses were too intoxicating, diluting my bloodstream by the second until I was only strong enough to help remove his boxers and lie down on my back. Alex's body completely overshadowed mine, making me feel tiny for the first time in my life. My husband was the first man I had been with who didn't match me in height and weight, which I realized played an important factor in how happy I was in bed. It was a relief to discover that when Alex took the wheel of my sex drive, it far surpassed any stalling experiences with Steven or Branden. I still hadn't taken my husband in, but I was positive he would fit me perfectly.

"Are you okay if I go down?" Alex pulled away from my lips, looking for air and permission.

"No," I answered after seriously contemplating for a few seconds. I didn't need hours of research to know that foreplay was essential to every lovemaking session; but for years, I had dreamt about what Alex's body would feel like and couldn't wait a minute longer to find out. "I wanna feel you," I confessed without the slightest bit of regret, thankful for the birth control pills my physician prescribed me to treat my PCOS.

"I wanna feel you, too," orange streaks of light from the window above our heads illuminated my husband's stunning face when he agreed. "Can I take this off for you?" He asked before kissing my hard nipple poking through the frilly tank top, sending a heat wave from my scalp down to my toenails. I was beginning to second guess the idea of leaving the window closed. I forced my lungs to take in a much-needed deep breath and concentrated on the repeating lyrics to "Stay" in hopes of bringing my heart rate back down.

"Okay," I agreed, completely under Alex's spell. I had planned to keep my security blanket on all night, but my husband's voice was powerful enough to wage war against my insecurities. My lingerie piece was already up over my head, and my thong had fallen somewhere by our intertwined feet. I was completely naked in front of a completely naked man for the first time in my life, and I embraced the moment like it was my regular nightly routine. I wished more than anything that it was; I wished that my husband could have me this way every night before he fell asleep and dreamt of having me again, especially when it was proven that no one but him could ever fill me so perfectly. Alex's body felt so right that tears flooded my eyes, thinking of the wrong in allowing someone else to try me on for size. Guilt snatched my euphoric climax immediately after I sobered up from the natural high and gained back control of my limbs.

"Babe, you alright? Did I hurt you?" Alex panicked on top of me, preparing to leave me until I pulled him back in and wrapped my legs tighter around his waist.

"Don't go," I pleaded as if his body was the only thing keeping mine from falling apart. "I'm sorry," a part of me was ready to admit my broken promises. "I love you so much. That's all," but the other part of me remembered my husband didn't want to know about them. I wiped my tears and pretended to be a strong wife, praying the façade would become a reality when I made it back home.

"I love you. I love you. I love you," Alex said for every teardrop he kissed off my face. We explored each other's bodies for hours after my eyes dried, learning our marks and lines, strengths and weaknesses, experiences and inexperiences. I looked up at one point to find the window blurred in fog and swiped it blissfully just like Rose had, finally coming to some understanding of how Jack made her feel. My time with Alex was defined by the dewy strokes across the window, telling the story of a night nothing short of amazing, and yet too rushed to be fully appreciated. The orange lights glowed through my handprint reminding me that no matter how long we avoided sleep to christen the sheets, this was not our bed and we were not at home. Becoming one with Alex brought the kind of clarity I only heard about on TV or read in books. I never actually thought I could attain it until my wedding night. My bliss suddenly turned to frustration as I lay my head on his fine chest hairs, dreading the thought of having to leave his side. I had given Ne-Yo's voice a rest to hear my husband tell his favorite childhood tales of the times before he got lost in the jungle. I listened to his bedtime stories, and the sound of his relaxed heartbeat dragging behind mine, imagining what life would have looked like had he never gone out that night.

Summer in New York always gave the wild permission to grow wilder, especially after the sun fell down behind the Palisades and its leftover heat made it easier to camouflage like a chameleon. My husband had transformed so much in the night that it was getting harder to remember what he looked like in the day. He searched for his skin in the company of other lost ones, but they too were just black and brown boys who found comfort in knowing that no one could see them in the dark.

Living in the city of villages, our geographical knowledge of Yonkers never went further than Whites owned everything east of the Saw Mill River Parkway; Latinos owned South Broadway, New Main Street, Palisade, and Nepperhan; Blacks owned Riverdale, School Street, Elm Street, Ashburton, Warburton, and Locust Hill. Our minds were just as small and segregated as the city that raised us. So when someone said, "I'ma be where the Mexicans be at," it was natural to assume they were hanging out on a deteriorating curbside off Nepperhan Avenue, which is where Alex and the lost ones sought refuge that night. In celebration of another successful season with his Blue Devils and the end of classes, seventeen-year-old Alex smoked a fat blunt and chugged from a bottle of Hennessy before discovering just enough courage to walk down the street where the Mexicans be at, coming out of bars even more drunk than him. Alex was gonna catch a real twisted one slippin' and dip out after cuz his momz was gonna start bitchin' if he got back to the crib at the crack o' dawn again.

My future husband chose to rob a drunk Mexican because that was all the courage he could find at the bottom of a bottle and at the end of a blunt he shared with the lost ones. However, the mission was flawed once the target selection in their real-life video game proved more than sober and functional enough to put up a fight for his wallet, forcing Alex to prove functional enough to fight back only after looking up at the piercing eyes of all the lost ones around him. My future husband sent a flying fist at the Mexican's jaw to show off everything the jungle had taught him, and when the Mexican still would not forfeit, the lost ones joined together to form a single mass of dark shadows below the dying lamp posts. Alex's panicked shadow quickly peeled itself off from the black blob and ran away in search of camouflage before the Mexican warrior was inhaled, limbs vanishing under rags left on the bloody concrete. Blue and red lights brightened my future husband's dark skin just as he was aching to run into his bedroom and camouflage beneath the cold sheets, but the young lost one would only feel the cold clasp of handcuffs that night. Alex would never know how long the blob ate and which shadow served the final blow. Three days later, all he knew was that the Mexican's name was Jose Velasquez, he was Peruvian, and he was dead.

"Babe, you listening?" Alex checked to see if I had fallen asleep during the recap of his fifth birthday party at his Aunt Carmen's place, which I pretended to hear for the first time.

"Did they use a breathalyzer before they interrogated you?"

"Way to kill the mood, babe," Alex always tried to avoid the subject.

"Did they?"

"No. Why?" He spoke firmly.

"Why wouldn't they? Not only were you drunk *and* high during the act, but you were drunk *and* high during that interrogation. Why would they question someone who isn't in their right state of mind?" It was a clarity that wouldn't be tapped into until I fell in love with my husband for the second time, and for the second time concluded I couldn't live without him. I wanted to fight.

"What do you mean 'why'? Because they don't give a shit."

"The person who provided liquor to *children* should be locked up, too. But I guess that's all just too much paperwork," an unexpected anger started pulling me out of the miraculous scene of lying in bed next to my incarcerated husband, but I couldn't help it.

"You good? It's a little too late for cold feet," Alex used humor as usual to lighten a subject matter that made him uncomfortable.

"How long were you in the room for?" I ignored his efforts.

"C'mon, Kaylah. Not now. I'm tired." Though it had just hit 4:00 a.m., I knew sleep was the furthest thing from Alex's mind.

"Please?"

"Like six, seven hours."

"Long enough to get the story they were looking for."

"Where's this coming from? You tryna be a lawyer now?"

"Maybe. I bet your D.A. didn't mention how long they questioned you without running a breathalyzer test or calling your mom. You sat there by yourself like a little punk and didn't request a lawyer. You have rights, Alex."

"You think I knew shit like that? You think I knew what the fuck was going on?" Alex moved to bump me off his chest.

"How'd you get the hate crime?" I tried to relax, planning to go as far as he'd let me.

"Kaylah," his tone was serious and slightly intimidating, but I couldn't drop it. It astounded me to know that the love of my life was one of the last people to see Jose Velasquez, a man who was the love of someone else's life. I needed to torture myself with the details.

"I'm your wife, Alexander. I married you without asking any of these questions because I know you, and I love you. But, I can't live without the answers for the rest of my life. How'd you get the hate crime?"

Alex inhaled deeply and released a long breath before lifting an arm over his eyes, either trying to block out visions of that night or hold back tears.

"I told him I went to rob a Mexican around Nepperhan." I listened closely to my husband, imagining a detective from the east side of the Saw Mill using a notepad to catch the unfiltered words falling from a Black teenager's mouth, not knowing that it was the way we spoke, the way we specified on a daily basis, with or without the influence of drugs and alcohol. I fantasized about going back in time just to walk into the interrogation room and tell the detective that even my Nana had once nicknamed Alex *El Indio* because he looked like an Indian.

I also heard something else in his vernacular and didn't hesitate to voice my concerns, "Don't talk like you acted alone, Alexander." His devotion to the jungle's number one rule of "no snitching" was frustrating and painful to witness as his wife, someone he was supposed to feel comfortable saying anything to. No matter how many questions I asked, I didn't deserve to be treated like an interrogator out to get him. Nonetheless, as his wife, I made it a point to remind him of the facts I actually did know before his mind tricked him into believing the cover up story and the guilt left him dead in a cell. "So, you *guys* never shouted any racial slurs, called him out for being an immigrant, or waved the American flag in his face before you killed him, right?" I continued, feeling my temper rise.

"Calm the fuck down. We ain't do nothin' like that, and he was very much alive when I left. I ain't know I was leaving him to die. I was broke and bored, and now I'm here. Go to sleep," Alex turned his back to me. He was Troy from *Fences*, getting locked up after unintentionally killing someone during a robbery. I was Rose, painfully loving him despite all his disturbing flaws.

"You could've fought that hate crime," I stated something Alex already knew. "Shouldn't the lawyer have looked into all your damn ethnicities, at least? *You* don't even know what the fuck you are."

Judy was part Black, part Trinidadian. Timmy, on the other hand, was the product of a rape and grew up hearing that his father was *most likely* a Puerto Rican passing through. Timmy's mother was as Black as the Harlem streets; his hair as coarse as her past, but his skin was as white as the correctional officer snoring up in the tower over our trailer. The first time I saw Alex, I found it impossible to guess where he was from, which made sense once I met his mixed parents and learned he was just as confused as I was. My husband was his brown mother in male form, yet resemblance wasn't enough to truly understand how to identify himself.

I didn't have to be Alex's wife to call bullshit on him targeting a specific race. If the undeserving, innocent Jose Velasquez was white, black, brown, green, or yellow that night, he still would have been attacked because the actual motive to rob took precedence over the color of his skin. That was another sad fact Alex's D.A. didn't bother to explore. It hurt me to know I had once connected with forty-nine students on the *Oprah Winfrey Show* to fight for the expulsion of hate from the world and married a man convicted of a hate crime almost three years later. Though the irony consumed me, I found solace in knowing the charge was invalid, and my husband's jungle vernacular was more at fault than he was. He spoke in colors, the way we all did.

"Kaylah, I played a part in a man's death. My goddamn ancestry isn't gonna change that. I'ma do this bid and I'ma go home," Alex's voice cracked into the pillow before falling silent, and I sat up quickly to see if his confession had broken him down. The side of his still face stayed hidden under long, frizzy locks. I looked down at his chiseled upper arm displaying his first and last tattoo of the fading words *Judy, I Love You, Ma*. His arm had outgrown the four-year-old tattoo. I wanted to have sympathy for him, but the more my thoughts roamed, the higher the fire in my chest flared.

"I bet if you said you were gonna rob a Black guy up on Nepperhan there would be no hate crime on your record," I grumbled as I lay back down. My husband tortured me with silence, provoking me to fill the space and torture him with more words, "Why'd you get charged as an adult?" I asked the wall, our backs facing one another.

I suddenly pictured myself dumping Emerson and applying for law school like Hilary Swank did for her brother in *Conviction*. However, there was no chance for an exoneration in Alex's case, especially when we both believed he deserved to go to prison; and although my husband also believed he deserved to stay, I knew in my heart that he didn't. There wouldn't be a parole hearing for another twelve years; the last of his teens and all of his twenties would be spent "rehabilitating" behind bars. So, since I couldn't physically bring him home any faster, I would spend most of that rehabilitation time dreaming about debunking at least one charge, the one that bothered me more than murder in the second degree; the one that truly went against everything I stood for and believed in. I found myself in the worst predicament of my life, seeking World Peace while fighting for my convicted murderer husband to have some chance at a normal life when he came home. Lord knows, my father wasn't expecting freedom to look so much like prison.

OPRAH GIRL

"I don't know," Alex admitted, emotionless, after I thought he had fallen asleep. It was an honest answer that made me want to throw my fist at the wall. He was a kid! A stupid ass kid who had just celebrated his seventeenth birthday at New Roc City two months before. I wanted to know how a child whose face lit up at the sight of an arcade could be treated like a fully-grown man and sent away for the rest of his life? I knew my curiosity was dangerous. I knew I was one question away from dwelling on all that could not be changed and creating my own hell on Earth. And still, I had to know.

"Why'd you cop out?" I was thankful for the wall because the look on his face probably had the power to keep me up without so much as a wink of sleep for the remainder of his bid. His guilty plea was never up for discussion until I decided to corner him on our wedding night.

"I was scared," my husband confessed without hesitation, saving me from the wrath of more dreadful silence.

Alex voluntarily added himself to the long list of statistics that kept the crooked system alive. I would go to sleep on the first night in bed with my husband, angry with no one but him.

CHAPTER FIFTEEN

I actually found great pleasure in being back home for the winter break after my first horrific semester as a Marketing major went exactly as expected. I was one group project away from throwing a tomato at a PowerPoint presentation while shouting, "Hadooouuuken!" like Ryu during his fireball move in *Street Fighter* with hopes of getting excused from all future group assignments (or the class, indefinitely). I couldn't even sit and appreciate being bored in a single classroom because I was always busy grouping up for the next marketing extravaganza, providing a little bit of colored perspective to another pale cluster of almost-ambitious humans with embarrassing time management skills. The only thing I felt like marketing more and more each day was my Dominican roots. Emerson enlightened my soul with the art of public relations, daring me to stroll down its ridiculously clean sidewalks wearing the Dominican flag for a cape while blasting Anthony Santos on a boombox like I was a walking Washington Heights apartment window. Dominicans in New York were as commonplace as yellow taxis, while the Emerson campus looked like a severe drought had wiped the place clean of salami and plantains, leaving me behind as the sole Dominican survivor.

I was reluctant to admit that Branden also played a big part in my increased level of D.R. pride. My initial shock during our first encounter died quickly when I realized the white-faced, blue-eyed twenty-six-year-old lived and breathed for his country. He helped me embrace the island of our origin with less uncertainty and more confidence. My double broken Spanish usually left me feeling more offensive to my culture rather than of my culture, so I restricted myself to only bringing out the basics in emergency cases like guiding South American tourists through the P.F. Chang's menu. Then Branden came around to remind me that Dominican was in my blood and I was, without a doubt, *Dominicana*. I even learned how to enjoy tasteless *aguacate* right out of its coarse skin, eventually falling so in love with the odd texture and nutritional benefits that it became a required side for every meal, including cereal.

When it came to music, (aside from the *Moulin Rouge* and *West Side Story* soundtracks) Hip Hop and R&B were the only genres found on my iPod. I was particularly a big Eminem fan until more out-of-the-blue retro sounds of the Dominican *campos* gradually replaced "The Eminem Show" on my earbuds. The heart attack inducing group that was Aventura started taking up a lot more gigabytes on my hand-held devices, bringing thoughts back to high school days when girls went nuts for the latest tracks by the kings of *bachata* as I sat clueless, unable to understand their devotion to "my" music. I caught onto *bachata* lyrics faster than I thought I would after Branden took it upon himself to download all the essentials onto my laptop; starting with the legendary Juan Luis Guerra, who I had always known to be my first cousin twice removed because Nana (a.k.a. Maria Luisa Guerra) never let a day pass without reminding us. Branden reacted the way most people did when I shared the fun-fact, his eyebrows spiking and blue eyes bulging. But, I never thought much of the relation until absorbing the lyrics of "Burbujas de Amor" for the first time. *Bachata*, I discovered, was every heart's song, expressing all of the human body's vulnerabilities at once without shame or apology. Eventually, I couldn't remember not knowing about its magic.

"There's pure talent running through your veins, babe," Branden dropped a poetic line on my first Wednesday night home. We sat in his parked car on Highland playing a game of most interesting facts after opting to pass on Pat's and just talk. Infatuation had occupied most of our time during the summer, permitting us to drink and suck face, thus forgetting that part where we actually had to get to know each other. Our lips, however, spent the fall season apart, forcing us to catch up and start figuring one another out through Skype. My laptop routinely rang in the late afternoon, and I connected within seconds, excited to give Branden his daily dose of the Emerson Chronicles that usually left us both on screen crying through rib-cracking laughter, and at the same time, inspiring him to go back to school after every conversation. We learned enough to make us miss one another more each day, so it felt good to let my guard down in person without hiding behind awesome make-out sessions.

"Ha! I thought you might like that one," I replied, watching the traffic light turn red for the eighth time.

"No, not because of the *bachata god*. I would've said that even if you hadn't told me about him. There's just something about you," Branden looked over at me while I absorbed the red light. "The slam poetry is by far my favorite part about you, and I'm a little upset you didn't tell me sooner. But whatever, you're fuckin' amazing, babe," my boyfriend

210

continued throwing compliments over to the passenger's side. He was a beautiful man for thinking of me so highly even after I told him about Alex. I clearly gave Branden the false impression that my marriage was in shambles, a problem he thought could be easily resolved by asking me one question, "Do you want to be with me or not?" I answered it. I just failed to add that I also wanted to be with Alex.

"Thank you," I responded warmly to his praise, unable to recall the last time someone spoke to me that way. "But you're the only talented one here. Learning how to speak perfect English from a rap album is pretty impressive. I hope it's on your resume," I returned a sincere compliment. Branden's beautiful migration story blew me away when he admitted that Nas's earth-shattering "Illmatic" album helped him conquer the English language at eleven years old. He also confessed to never repeating the "N-word" again after it became dangerously clear that a boy as white as him only said the word if he was looking for trouble. Nonetheless, it came as no surprise when my boyfriend showed so much interest in my poetry.

"I didn't do anything. It was all Nas. He's the man," Branden displayed a rare modest side when talking about his favorite rapper. "Like I said, there's pure talent in *your* veins, so let's hear it," he demanded with his charming smile, only half-expecting me to take the dare. I flinched at his request, unprepared to feel so hurt when the thought of not having put pen to paper in over two years dug into my chest.

"My favorite homemade sandwich is turkey, Swiss, and mayo on toasted wheat," I offered an underwhelming interesting fact to stray away from the subject of writing.

"That's nice, I'll keep it in mind. Now spit something," Branden said, unimpressed.

"I haven't really written anything recently," the words were rocks tumbling out of my mouth. I wanted to make it sound like I was still writing, but couldn't bring myself to completely lie.

"So, perform your favorite," Branden pushed enthusiastically, too intrigued to give up. I wrote my favorite poem at seventeen years old in honor of the Yonkers Puerto Rican/Hispanic Day Parade. As the parade's 2006 Youth Godmother, I performed an original piece for a charity event in a ballroom full of Yonkers' public figures, media and my family. It was the first time my father saw me perform anything, which added to the most nerve-wracking moment of my entire life. Yonkers lay buried under violent crimes only six months into the year of 2006, setting the foundation of my four-minute piece for the annual cultural event. What used to be my proudest creation, however, now filled me with aching remorse whenever I remembered having referenced Alex's case for the sake of a rhyme and the basis of my overall theme. I never mentioned his name, but because he was involved in the most high-profile case of the early summer, my imagery was clearly understood by every government official in the room who was reminded of how happy they were to get another "predator" off the streets. I had attempted to gear more toward the discussion of gang violence and assumed because Alex's case wasn't gang-related it wouldn't overshadow the message, but I wouldn't realize how erroneous in my thinking I was until after the words fell out of my mouth and everyone caught them. I married Alex over two years later, and every time the poem even crossed my mind, I felt like I was exploiting my husband all over again, causing people to hate him all over again. I wanted to avoid officially being the worst wife in the world and changed the subject again.

"Kiss me," I blurted randomly, trying harder to distract Branden by reaching over to the driver's seat and puckering up.

"What? Nuh-uh. I want a poem," he rejected my efforts, turning his face to the window.

"I can't remember it off the top of my head," I lied. Though written three years ago, I loved the poem and would probably never forget the words for as long as I lived.

"Try. You're a writer. Your words are like your babies. You can't forget them."

I hated him for understanding the person I wanted to be, the person who actually considered herself a writer or some kind of creative influencer. I used to be her.

"Don't you come dropping similes on me, Mr. Del Sol. You have no idea who you're dealing with here," I teased him, getting sucked back into his magnetic twinkling eyeballs.

"Show me, Ms. Pantaleón," his perfect enunciation made me fall in love with the sound of my last name that most people enjoyed shortening to "Pants" because they couldn't resist cracking the unoriginal joke. I was also really into the sound of his certainty when he spoke in demands, coming off protective rather than arrogant. But I wanted to keep stalling, thinking of ways to close the curtain on this highly anticipated performance inside his car. There was no use in digging up another poem when I knew my memory had the most solid grasp on my favorite baby. Though it was getting late and I should've just said "good night" before insisting on walking the two blocks home, it was hard to let go of such good company.

"Okay, I'll try," I finally gave in, planning to speed up the flow to make it a little less painful.

"Yes!" Branden clapped his hands together in celebration. His genuine excitement made me even more uneasy. The last time I slammed a poem was at a crowded open mic on the

Emerson campus during freshman year. It was the slow clap and awkward silence following my first performance at school that proved my official induction into the world as an alien, something too foreign for anyone's comprehension. The blue ceiling lights suddenly blinded me and soaked my forehead in sweat as I made it off the stage to the sound of a lifeless room. I hadn't attended an open mic or created any new material since.

"Please don't laugh," I pleaded before sharing a disclaimer. "I move my hands a lot and tend to turn into someone else if it's done right and I'm feeling it."

Slam poetry's energy was different from any art form I had taken on in the past. I discovered it after watching an old YouTube video of an underground poet named, Oveous Maximus, winning over the tough Apollo audience solely by rhyming a story about his mother. I was left drooling over the poet's talent and style, immediately searching for "more videos like this" before finding my own way to emulate it. I had always written poems free handedly, paying little attention to techniques and proper format; just using my love for the sound of words playing with other words and falling off the tongue. The deregulated essence of slamming suited me perfectly, especially once I realized it was a fulfilling combination of both acting and writing.

"That's what all good performers do, right? C'mon, I'm excited," Branden egged me on, turning in his seat to get comfortable.

"Okay, okay," I faced forward, concentrating on the traffic light again to avoid his eyes and hopefully find distraction from the inevitable guilt that would ensue. "It's called *Little Latina*," I took a deep breath and silently apologized to my husband.

"Imagine this...a young, intelligent mind
No older than six. She's got bold black hair,
Caramel-colored complexion,
Big brown eyes that command her father's attention,
'Papi...one day,
Can I be President?'
Silence,
For fear of frightening the
Innocence.
So, Papi stays quiet.
Her question runs through his mind
Like his blood runs through her veins,
And the pause pains his heart.
Why's it so hard to start?
Hesitation...
As he thinks back to the smothering
Indignation,
Yes, in *this* nation
That practices the right to
Life, liberty, and the pursuit of
Happiness.
Who knew he would have to pursue
For so long?
But like any Latino,
He stood strong, accepted his place
In society, living like the 'PRs' lived
In *West Side Story*.
But, it was no movie back then.
It's no fairytale now, and Papi thinks,
How much harder it must be for the
Latin lady
Standing before me, to grow up in the

Free land of prosperity, land of all imaginable
Possibilities. Ironically, Little Latina opens
Her present,
Opens it wide and she falls right in it,
And just like her Papi, she feels it,
Not only in the form of the word
'Spic,'
Not just in the criticisms for
Blamelessly being born Hispanic,
And not in the failure to understand
I'm also intelligent,
But in every word, in every thought and gesture
Of ignorance
That feeds into the stereotypes and eventually
Leads into the use of
Guns and knives on each other.
Can't comprehend the concept of
Beating on your own brother.
I'm feeling safer without having to read the paper,
Without having to dry my eye for that guy
Whose life was taken
'Cause he was mistaken for a
Mexican."

I wanted to stop there when the thought of talking in bed with Alex on our wedding night interrupted me. I wanted to stop there when I remembered our one year anniversary was coming up in four days. I only continued when I looked over at Branden's mesmerized face and knew for sure he was more impressed than he anticipated. I took another breath and found the next line.

"Does it have to be an inevitability?
Every form of brutality pervades my daily existence,
And I hear a voice in the distance,
'It's no dream, Kay. You're really in this! This is
Your reality, it's no fabricated story!'
But why? When given the beautiful blessing of
Life, we choose to spend it all in a never-ending fight?
And forget to thank Him, Amen, I'm alive!
Instead, we linger in the seventh circle of the
Inferno, staying stuck in this state of
Undying, undeniable, and seemingly unsurpassable
Hate."

I could feel tears burning my eye sockets, threatening to unveil the guilt eating at my heart and soul with every word. My poem brought to light everyday truths in Southwest Yonkers that had cornered the love of my life and locked him away. There was no opportunity more perfect, no platform more public I could have used to also help him, to shine a light on a faulty system; a system more corrupt than the people it claimed to serve and protect. Instead, I only reinforced public perception by agreeing with the idea that Alexander Mitchell had committed a hate crime and deserved fifteen-years-to-life in prison for it. I was just like everyone else, not knowing the whole story and pretending to.

"Is that it? That was—" Branden chimed in awkwardly when my dramatic pause went a second too long. I refocused on the green light ahead and proceeded with the rest of my poem before he could finish his thought.

"That's why Papi stays silent.
How could she ever be

217

President when at times, her own race won't allow
Her to progress, to ever pursue that
Happiness?
But those big brown eyes scream,
'Papi, save me!
Tell me, I can
Stand in front of a crowd of all races, all religions,
Perceptions, perspectives, personalities,
Ethnicities, eccentricities,
That flag and this flag, this color and that color!
Tell me, I can have a thought worth thinking,
I can speak my mind, and all these people will listen.
Tell me, not only with this exterior, but with my
Interior,
I can make a difference,
And break this awful silence.'
He stares into the eyes of a new generation,
And there is no more contemplation.
There is no need for hesitation. The answer is easy.
Though his little Latina only knows what she sees,
She can't help but believe
Because when her papi says it,
She'll never forget it,
'Si, mamita
You can!
You can!
You can!'"

The traffic light switched to yellow when I concluded my
first performance in the passenger seat of a1994 Honda Civic.
My attention finally returned to Branden, finding him
speechless as he held onto an exaggerated jaw-drop.

"Liked it?" I casually broke the silence with a weak smile.

"Liked it? That was...I'm so...How old were you when you wrote that?" The inability to gather his thoughts was flattering and made my smile widen a little more.

"Seventeen. June 2006," my pride slowly started coming back to me when I answered. I wanted to tell him I had since dedicated the poem to Jose Velasquez, but that subject was bound to drown me in tears and expose just how much I really missed my husband.

"*Before* Obama. That's blowing my mind right now. You are the female Obama," Branden mentioned another one of his all-time favorite people in the world, and the comparison left my ego so inflated that I surprised myself when I went fishing for more praise.

"I was on *Oprah*, too. There's another fun-fact for you."

"Oprah? How the hell...Who *are* you?" My boyfriend whispered melodramatically and again repositioned himself to get a better look at my face.

"Definitely not the female Obama," I let out a small laugh and remained lighthearted enough to trick myself into believing that I was at least a good person.

I was many things, but mostly a traitor in more ways than one.

CHAPTER SIXTEEN

I struggled to slip on a long-sleeved, black spandex dress with a hemline that ended too many inches above my knees. The mummifying garment showcased my hipless apple figure and maybe even helped accentuate the appearance of my scoliosis a little bit, but there was no time to waste ransacking Janessa's closet for a new outfit. I rushed my foot into a pair of sheer black pantyhose, hoping they would somehow make the dress look better on me. The Chang's crew was celebrating their holiday party at a place other than Pat's, forcing me to at least try dressing up in something other than jeans and a sweatshirt.

"So, who is he?" My mother appeared out of nowhere like Michael Myers, making me jump fiercely enough for a hangnail to hook onto the pantyhose and start a small run.

"Shit," I caught my breath and left the nylons at my knees as I waddled over to my vanity in search of a remedy. "I thought you were sleeping already. It's almost ten o'clock," I found a bottle of clear nail polish and dabbed a couple drops on the tear to keep it from growing.

"No, I'm right here. So, who is he?" My mother sounded creepier than usual, or my nerves were playing tricks on me. I honestly didn't want to engage in this conversation and give her the satisfaction of fessing up about Branden, who grew more impatient by the day waiting to meet my family. Her cold presence was hard to ignore as I blew on the wet spot above my knee, deciding I had no choice but to humor her.

"Who is who?" I cringed at the thought of where this was going.

"Oh, stop it, Kaylah. You've been staying out all night and sneaking back in at six o'clock in the morning for the past twelve days. I'm not stupid," she listed her accusations with a hint of enjoyment in her voice. My mother normally exaggerated when she wanted to prove a point. I had arrived from Boston only five days ago, so I maintained my innocence on all counts and refused to confess. I didn't know how I ended up with the doomed bedroom directly across from my mother and stepfather, while Janessa and Nunu enjoyed prime real estate in the garden apartment's west wing, but it was completely unfair.

"I have a lot of friends at Chang's, Ma. I'm just trying to have a good vacation," I stated my rebuttal just as the pantyhose reached my belly button. I stretched my tight dress down as far as it would go and proceeded to dig painstakingly through the bottom of my closet for my most comfortable wedge heels. I was annoyed with myself for slipping on the delicate pantyhose before hunting the shoes down.

"And when are you getting a divorce?"

"Ma, please," I called out from inside the closet. She added to my frustration effortlessly.

"What, Kaylah? You're clearly having a good time. What do you need him for?" I took another one of my mother's bold questions rhetorically and left her words floating alone in the air. I knew the subject was bound to come up again during my break, so I officially made up my mind on a solution to the soul-sucking problem but hadn't figured out a way to execute it yet. I stood up after finding my black patent leather wedges and shoved my feet in without bothering to dust them off first, positive no one would notice their mistreated appearance at night.

"Hello?" Mom called for my attention, rolling her eyes and neck with severe attitude the way I once saw a female lost one do after she got caught stealing a Sunny D from the bodega.

My top drawer nearly flew off the hinges when I opened it to retrieve a heavy booklet and slammed it down on the dresser in front of her.

"Hi," I replied sarcastically, failing to match her nasty attitude and turned my attention to the mirror. She finally stepped out from her idle spot at the doorway to examine the packet I presented.

"You got them?" Her voice softened, and shoulders relaxed, letting her long, boney fingers feel through the thick sheets of paper to affirm their authenticity. I hoped the monstrous packet would nip her with a paper cut.

"When?" My mother couldn't digest the moment fast enough.

"Yesterday," I answered without hesitation, hastily brushing my eyelashes with a rusted stick of mascara.

"Have they been signed?" My mother's brain went hazy as she gave the pages a closer inspection, her eyes actively searching for signatures on lines marked "plaintiff" and "defendant."

"Yeah, he met me real quick at the courthouse yesterday and then went back for commissary," I spoke in a sarcastic monotone while coloring in my overgrown eyebrows.

"Don't get nasty. When are you gonna sign them?" I loathed every word leaving her mouth, but the friendlier tone reminded me of the person I used to like talking to.

"Not sure. After Christmas, some time," I remained indifferent, locking eyes with the eyes in the mirror, finding something else to fix.

"Well, get it done before you go back to school, so you can go back a free woman. Congratulations," she spoke casually, like I just handed her a list of all my predictable negative STD results. "Let me know when it's final," my mother placed the booklet back on the dresser and paused to wait for my reply.

"Mm-hm," was all I could say to set her free.

"Have a good time. Momma loves you," she brought back one of her favorite sayings that I hadn't heard all year. My mother stood in the doorway for a few more beats to take in the sight of me powdering my cheeks pink before she finally walked out.

The eyes in the mirror swelled up the instant her presence left my room. I continued mindlessly circling the soft bristles around my cheekbones even as the tears slid victoriously down my face. I had surrendered on the night of my one year anniversary.

The DJ played my favorite Aventura track, "La Novelita," keeping me twirling away on the dance floor in Branden's arms for the fifth song in a row. I was a sweaty mess, and Branden was no longer the same height as I stood with my two-inch heels on. But my body was so captivated by the guitar's enchanting rhythm that I had no energy left over for worries. He taught me *bachata's* one-two-three-step rule in his bedroom before we left, and I was unstoppable when I finally applied my private lesson in real life at a packed club that Saturday night. I was inspired by two Jack-and-Cokes, good music, and my handsome boyfriend who thoroughly enjoyed dancing with no one but me in the excited midst of professional award-winning *bachata*-dancing couples.

"YOU GOT IT!" Branden shouted over the booming speakers and into my ear when he spun me around, my two feet meeting his two feet successfully after the full 360 was complete. The *bachata* turn was definitely taking the longest for me to get down, so the moment I felt my body come back around to sync with his body and the guitar strings, pure joy lit up my face even more under the club's psychedelic lights.

"AAAAHHH!" I took in my proud moment on the dance floor, my happy feet still keeping up with the one-two-three-step. "I DID IT!" I roared confirmation over the blasting music. I saw Branden's muted chuckle across from me as he kept one of his hands protecting my hip and the other protecting my right hand in the air, leading the way swiftly and magically like we were Olympic figure skaters going for the gold.

"IT'S THE SONG! IT HELPED ME MAKE THE TURN!" I was getting too ambitious with attempting conversation in the middle of the thundering Spanish club.

"THE WHAT?" I predicted Branden's reply.

"THIS IS MY FAVORITE SONG! THAT'S HOW I MADE THE TURN!" I roared again, slowly and directly in his ear, hoping he caught every word without losing an eardrum.

"REALLY? I WAS JUST ABOUT TO DEDICATE IT TO YOU!"

"ME?" The grin on my face was out of my control. It was hard to relax my cheeks after taking in every one of Branden's words. "SO WE HAVE A SONG?"

"*TU ERES LA MAMI DE MI VIDA!*" He shouted the lyrics along with Aventura, announcing that I was the girl of his life to anyone who could miraculously hear him. I heard him, and that's all that mattered.

"I LOVE YOU!" It wasn't the first time I said the words, but it was definitely my first time shouting them at a deafening volume surrounded by a crowd of happy dancing people, and it felt good.

"I LOVE YOU!" He had no trouble catching those three words and re-gifting them with a grin on his face almost matching mine.

There was something about screaming "I love you" to the top of my lungs in public that made me feel very much alive. Branden reminded me of everything I loved all at once. He reminded me of how I loved writing short stories and reading them to my class; obsessively organizing my poems in plastic covers before snapping them into my poem binder; the look of a new journal's fresh, untouched pages; performing new material; performing old material; performing; writing; the stage; the audience; Shakespeare; Mr. Vicari; memorizing lines; transforming; the movie theater; the Dominican Republic; reading scripts; words; making people happy; people; my dad; daydreaming; dreaming; Riverdale; trailer visits; letters from Alex; phone calls from Alex; Alex. Branden reminded me of how great and how selfish I was at the same time, but I wouldn't let him go on the dance floor or in my life. Instead, I had to let go of the one person I always loved in order to get back to everything I always loved. I wanted to blame my mother and everyone opposing my marriage for Branden's easy entrance into my life, for distracting me from fully loving my husband the way he deserved. But, I was the only one to blame. I married Alex with the pure intention of proving his fears wrong without once stopping to think that there could be a man out here who cares about me as much as I care about him and we could be happy, and I wanted to be happy.

We were headed back home around 4:00 a.m. when I pulled the hefty packet from the huge black purse I found in Janessa's room and smoothed out the crinkled corners before presenting them at a red light.

"What's this?" Branden asked a sleepy question before reading until his droopy eyes took the words in and awoke instantly. "Yeah?" He looked up at me for confirmation.

"Merry Christmas, Del Sol," exhaustion consumed my whole body, and I could only manage to offer him a small smile.

He took a minute to gather his thoughts, and we both waited for a word to come out of his sagging mouth.

"Thank you? That's weird to say, right? I honestly don't know what to fuckin' say," the energy in Branden's voice was back as he clutched the papers in his hands with no intention of moving, even when the green light appeared.

"Yeah, 'thank you' is weird. You don't have to say anything. I know you didn't ask for this drama, but I'm happy you stuck around. So, thank *you*," I said the words not really able to believe they had come from my mouth, but somehow knew they were sincerely spoken as I leaned over to confirm them with a kiss on his lips. "I'll be seeing him before I head back to Boston so he can sign," I explained, looking down at my nails to choose the longest one to chew on.

"Does he know?" Branden asked, genuinely concerned.

"Yes," I lied.

"Is he okay? It must be hard in there," Branden reminded me of that too. It was hard in there, especially hard once he found out his wife was leaving him for another man.

"He's upset, but he understands," I shared a wishful thought.

"You should come back to my place and celebrate," Branden leaned over for another kiss just as the traffic light turned from yellow to red again.

"If we ever make it there," I snickered and pecked him once more, taking the disheveled booklet from his hands and placing it carefully back into Janessa's purse.

"Right. I'll go on the next one," Branden said, leaving my lips and repositioning himself behind the wheel.

"I'm sorry, you should take me home. I forgot I promised Janessa we'd go out for breakfast tomorrow...I mean, in a few hours," I lied again. My sister had turned sixteen in September and fully embraced her hanging out privileges, adopting a more definite social life than mine in Boston and New York combined. I'd be lucky if I saw her for breakfast, lunch, or dinner that Sunday. I just didn't want to sleep in his bed knowing my one year anniversary happened a few hours before. I had some nerve trying to live righteously after giving both my mother and my boyfriend the same early Christmas present on and around December 19th. Showing my mother the divorce papers wasn't something I planned to do until she came into my room and broke me down for the last time. I then passed them over to Branden out of frustration in hopes he could make me feel better about my decision, and I still didn't know if he had.

"Damn, okay. Raincheck. Are you coming over for Christmas Eve? Or am I going—"

"No, I'll stop by," I rejected his inconspicuous self-invitation to my place for the holidays. My mother wasn't about to hit the jackpot twice with divorce papers and an introduction to my new boyfriend all in the same week. I had no idea when I would be ready, even though I reassured Branden that it would be soon.

"Okay..." his voice trailed off into a sigh as he pulled up to my apartment building.

"I love you," I rushed the words and a peck on his lips to avoid any more discussion about meeting my family. I was also practically sleep walking and wanted to hit my futon as soon as possible.

"I love you, too," Branden replied, but I was already out the door.

I turned the key in the lock as slowly and quietly as possible, careful not to let my keychains rattle too much before gently pushing the heavy block of steel open. I snuck into what we call "good hood heat," instantly warming up from the bitter early morning cold and finding Janessa fully dressed at the refrigerator drinking from a giant jug of Mott's apple juice.

She took her last gulp and let out an abrasive, thirst-quenched sigh before greeting me, "I figured it was you because a burglar wouldn't take twenty-seven minutes to get the door open." My sister was a shameless exaggerator like her mother. She put the jug away and pulled the hair tie from its usual place around her wrist to secure her long, heavy curls in a floppy bun. She had also just gotten back from an eventful Saturday night.

"Also, a burglar wouldn't come around here, so there's that," I shot back, removing my peacoat and wedges.

"Touché, sis. Touché," she agreed while digging through the wooden cabinets for an early morning snack before heading to bed.

"How you been, stranger?" I walked into the kitchen with one big toe poking out of my shredded pantyhose to pour a glass of water from the faucet.

"Don't you 'stranger' me—is that my dress?" Janessa did a double take, twisting her neck away from the cabinets to stare me down.

"Relax. You know you couldn't fit one of your tities in this thing," I spoke to my little, over-developed sister in the lovingly offensive manner we both preferred.

"That's not the point, hoe," she didn't hesitate a comeback while sprinkling two packets of maple and brown sugar flavored Quaker Instant Oatmeal into a bowl. "Where were you and your man-boobs tonight? Does Alex know you're out here trickin'?"

I shot her a glare that I hadn't realized revealed my sins until she stopped fidgeting with the microwave and dropped her perfectly plump bottom lip.

"No? Really?"

"I'm not..." I tried to deny the truth in her crass jest, but there was no point.

Though almost five years younger, I could easily say Janessa was my first best friend. She was the kind of sister who never snuck into my room to read my journal because she knew every detailed entry before it was written. A secret with her was as safe as keeping it in a bottle chained to a half-ton anchor at the bottom of the ocean. If I was Batman, she was my Alfred.

Needless to say, Janessa was the first to know of my wedding plans and the first to give her blessings. Mom used to sit my little sister in my bedroom as a watchdog whenever Alex was over, but Janessa would always get pleasantly distracted from the job by a game of Scattergories or a Jason flick from our *Friday the 13th* DVD collection. Janessa saw me with Alex, and she saw me without Alex. If anyone understood how I felt about my husband, it was my little sister.

"Say it ain't so, Joe!" An avid sports fan like Nana, Janessa referenced the 1920 Black Sox Scandal whenever coming across some devastating news.

"Ssshh!" I hushed her at five in the morning while everyone was still sleeping. "I don't know. It's rough," I stuck my face in my glass of water to avoid making eye contact with eyes that looked just like mine.

"Ooooh, you thought being married to a man doing fifteen-plus was gonna be *easy*. Gotcha," Janessa harshly whispered her favorite smart-ass tone and blew on a spoonful of hot oatmeal. She took the bite and didn't wait to finish chewing before talking again, "At least he didn't knock you up yet."

Though my little sister was happy to hear of my decision to get married, she had one request before the ring went on my finger—no kids. I had a difficult time coping with Dad's incarceration, but Janessa was only two months old when he went away and never got the chance to build the connection with our father that I had. No matter how many letters he wrote or how many times he called, she wouldn't really know who he was or care to. It was a trauma that inevitably strained their relationship and dictated her perception in the world. Even though we grew up to realize an absent father was the hood way of life and we fit right in, it didn't mean we had to continue the cycle. My sister held onto the strong belief that no child deserved to experience what we did for twelve years, especially if there was a choice. Alex and I had already agreed not to get pregnant until he came home for the same reasons and more, but hearing my little sister voice her concerns helped solidify the decision.

"You're annoying. I just think I could be happier," I admitted, pathetically.

"Or Mom thinks you could be happier. Sucker," she slammed me after taking another full scoop of oatmeal like a starved foster child and glanced over at the dining table. "Really, Kaylah? Is that my kangaroo purse? I needed it last night, shit face." She chewed and charged toward the table with a bowl in one hand while using her free hand to inspect the oversized bag. "I need you to start acting like you have a vagina and buy your own dresses and pur—" She paused abruptly and startled my heart when I remembered my papers were in there.

"It's that serious?" She put her bowl of oatmeal down to take the uncontested divorce booklet in both hands.

"I think so," I stayed in the kitchen gulping the rest of my water, almost drowning.

"But, it's Alex. You've always loved Alex," she said the words as if a vivid memory of Alex and me shot through her mind like a shooting star, too fast to know if it ever happened.

"Yes, I have," I gave Janessa my first definite answer of the morning and turned the sink knob all the way left to clean my glass and let the loud rush of water wash away my thoughts. "But, love is not enough, sometimes," I couldn't recognize the sound of my voice under the crashing water.

"Bullshit," my sister replied. She was a hopeless romantic like me.

CHAPTER SEVENTEEN

I watched Alex as he sat stiffly at the dining table and zoned out on the "defendant" line in the open booklet. His long locks were gone, so the tension in his neck was completely visible.

"Alex, I told you I was bringing the papers. Please don't make this any harder," I spoke from the living room couch a few feet away, fighting sleep. It was my first trailer visit alone, and the exhaustion from the grueling trip was severe enough to leave me comatose for a week. Not having a driver license started taking a toll on me, but it was a relief to know that once the divorce was final there would be no reason to attempt mission impossible every forty days.

In order to make this trip, I had to connect with another prison wife whose FRP visit was scheduled on the same freezing cold dates in January as ours. Her name was, Trish. She was the wife of Alex's best friend, Derek, who I was particularly fond of because he had helped Alex enroll in college courses by-mail at Great Meadow and made an impressive cheesecake from scratch for the Mitchells and me when he and his family were neighbors on the last trailer visit in November.

Though I appreciated Trish and Derek's kindness, I almost cancelled this weekend because the thought of boarding a bus from NYC to Albany, sleeping over Trish's apartment, grocery shopping the next morning before the trailer, having the most depressing trailer in trailer history, and boarding another bus headed to Boston all in the blistering January cold was stressful enough to cause a brain aneurysm. Even so, I was determined to get Alex's signature before going back to school and hoped to lessen the blow by having him sign on our last trailer visit instead of our last regular five-hour visit where we wouldn't be allowed to give each other a proper good bye.

"This is really what you want?" He finally broke the silence after a good ten minutes.

"For the millionth time, I *have* to, or I gotta drop out of school," I lied. Before the visit, I sent Alex a lengthy letter explaining that I was forced to file for divorce because my grandparents were unwilling to help me pay off forty-thousand dollars in loans if I didn't leave him. It was a weak story and may have only worked because Alex never got the chance to meet my father's family. I didn't want to make the situation worse for him by admitting I had fallen for another man and broken all my vows seven months into our marriage. If I mentioned Branden, Alex would only fight to prove that our differences were more than reconcilable.

"I'm never getting married again," Alex claimed stoically, finally allowing the pen point to touch down and glide across the bottom line.

"Don't say that. There are plenty of Saunders chicks dying for you to come home," I replied to his dramatic conclusion, trying to make light of the moment.

Alex turned around in his chair to meet my eyes with a violent glare I never thought could possibly come from a face that made me smile in my sleep.

"You're a bitch," he spoke as if it was the only thing he knew to be true. The words not only caught me by surprise but instantaneously turned the man I had loved since I was fifteen into a complete stranger.

"Excuse me?"

"You're a bitch to come up here on a TRAILER VISIT, not a REGULAR VISIT and make me sign some goddamn divorce papers like I'm a fuckin' free one year trial. We got MARRIED, Kaylah. You don't just try marriage out to see how it goes. So no, I'm not getting MARRIED again. I chose to spend the rest of my life with YOU, not some fuckin' chick from Saunders. I love YOU. You STILL can't see that, and that's the only reason these muthafuckin' papers are in my face right now." Alex barely took a breath in-between his obscenities and concluded his tantrum by throwing the packet to the floor, making me jump at the sound of its heavy pages hitting the hard tiles.

"I'm sorry. I—"

"What are you sorry for, Kaylah? For coming all this way to end our marriage? Or for promising me you could handle this? I told you this shit wasn't gonna be easy. I TOLD YOU, and you still made me believe you were strong enough. You made me believe it could work. My God, I'm so fuckin' stupid," he directed his last words up at the ceiling before resting his chin on two clenched fists, his elbows grounded on the table.

I didn't even know I was crying until I felt a warm, salty tear alert my lips. Alex clearly suspected there was more to the story than I led on, but couldn't bring himself to accuse me for fear of hurting more. I wanted to wrap my arms around him and protect him from all the pain in the world, but there was no way to because at that moment, I was his only pain in the world.

"It's alright. I'm just gonna keep doing what I do. I'm gonna stay focused on my programs and classes, and I'm gonna make my first board, and I'm gonna be home real soon. Everything is gonna be alright," he declared his affirmations aloud, making his way to the bedroom and closing the door behind him.

The New York winter air gnawed at my face as I rushed up the steep hill on Vark Street to seek refuge in my boyfriend's cozy room. At the top of the hill were several moving dark shadows that I mentally prepared to approach without a word and without a glance. My nerves flared when one of the shadows acknowledged mine.

"God bless you, mami," the voice calling to me sounded hoarse and rusted, in need of oil. I kept moving because that's what I learned to do when I was outnumbered by lost ones.

"Oh, she don't like talkin'," another shadow observed mine. I had made it past their black blob and was halfway to my destination when I heard another.

"Wrong way, Kaylah."

I turned around only when the shadow called my name to find a small orange burst of light go dark in the night sky to join the thunder. I could see the gun from where I stood frozen, preparing to fire again.

"Kaylah."

Alex's pretty face waited for me on the other side of my eyelids and the fear of being in danger, even in dreams, overwhelmed me with an urgent craving for his forgiveness and the need to tell him exactly how much he's meant to me since I was a little girl.

"I love you," I started there, waiting for the rest of my thoughts to catch up.

"I love you, too," his dimple came out for the first time since I arrived at the trailer. "Get up, I wanna show you something." Alex helped me up from the couch where I had fallen asleep after baking him my specialty lasagna. I was fighting to stay awake when I came across *The Color Purple* on *AMC*, recalling what a great actress Oprah was, how I once shook her hand, and how much I missed being called "Oprah Girl." My dreams had started off pleasant until someone warned me I was going the wrong way.

"Thanks for the slammin' lasagna, and I'm sorry for calling you a 'bitch.' That's not my style. Here, put this on," Alex complimented my cooking, apologized for being really mean, and handed over my coat all before I could wipe the sleepy crust out of my eyes.

"You're forgiven, but why are we going outside? It's so cold," I whined, reluctant to follow his instructions.

"Won't take long," he assured me in a bland, hasty tone and walked ahead through the door, out onto the porch.

It was a colder night than I even anticipated, my sleepy cells turning to ice and shattering into little pieces. I thought to go back inside to add on more layers, but Alex was already waiting for me at a frozen picnic table dusted lightly with snow flurries. I walked through the deserted yard enclosed by a massive concrete wall lit with orange lamps and couldn't help peeking up at the tower to see if we were being watched in the night. We were.

"Sit down and look," Alex commanded in his green state prison coat and dropped his wool-covered head back to look up at the sky. I sat down next to him, hesitant to get too close because I couldn't quite figure out his mood.

"Come here," he pulled me over until I was perfectly tucked under his arm and his warm embrace instantly calmed my nerves. "You don't get stars like this in Yonkers or Boston, so I thought you might appreciate the view while you're here."

I stargazed with Alex for the first time since we met five years ago, trying to keep my teeth from chattering so that I could absorb the night sky in upstate New York the way he wanted. It really was an amazing view, and once the stars twinkled in our brown eyes the entire journey up to see him was suddenly worth every exhausting second.

"It's so clear and beautiful," I managed a few words of observation between shivers to prove I was a good sport.

"Yup, because there's beauty in every ugly place," Alex remained unfazed by the freezing temperature while making unusual conversation, but it wasn't hard to see where he was going with it. Along with the brilliant starry night, I appreciated having his body right next to mine and dreaded never feeling it again after I left. He puffed a few more white breaths into the cold before sharing his thoughts, "I wake up every morning in an ugly place, babe, and I regret that. I regret being there that night. I regret not saving that man. I regret disappointing my family. I regret disappointing you. I regret asking you to do this bid with me because that was just another selfish act on my part," Alex's subdued rambling pulled my chin down from the sky to search for his eyes. It was obvious he had locked himself in the bedroom that afternoon to cool off and organize his thoughts. Yet, my unprepared heart was starting to ache more with every prepared word leaving his mouth. "I've been in this ugly place for almost three years, and you've been the only beautiful part about it, but you don't belong here."

The water falling down my face made the winter air even more unbearable. I arrived mentally stable enough to get a divorce until the idea of divorce fully registered, and my husband started officially breaking up with me. Alex was breaking up with me again.

"What are you saying, babe?" My chapped lips trembled more than before.

"I'm gonna let you go," he didn't hesitate to answer and removed his glove to wipe the tears from my face with warm fingers.

"You're breaking up with me?" My voice suddenly cracked into my fifteen-year-old self while I drowned in the rapid waterfall. What did I expect? For him to divorce me, but stay with me, while I stayed with Branden? Yes.

"Didn't you just divorce me? I think that hurts way more," Alex flashed one of his precious grins and leaned in to catch the drops trickling down my cheeks using his kisses. One kiss. Two kiss. Three. "You're gonna be okay. I'm gonna be okay. Let's go inside."

We kept each other warm underneath cold, white sheets for the rest of that night and the following. I had less than twelve hours left with my husband, and all I wanted was a clear head to fully appreciate him. I wanted to stop thinking about text messages and phone calls coming in from Branden, my mother, and whoever else I may have lied to about my phone "acting funny," and how I had to go get it fixed once I made it back to school. I wanted to stop thinking about knowing Branden's body better than I knew my husband's, and the possibility of loving one man more than the other. I wanted to stop thinking about my future and God's inevitable retaliation against every one of my lies and broken promises. I wanted to stop thinking about the idea of never being loved this way again.

"I'm gonna miss you," Alex breathed heavily into my ear after reaching a state of bliss that only promised to last for a few more hasty heartbeats. My crowded brain wouldn't even allow me to enjoy that much. I still assured my husband that my climax had followed right behind his so to avoid letting bitterness outweigh in a bittersweet moment. At that point, I was honestly convinced that I could live the rest of my life without ever having another orgasm just as long as I could experience a few minutes being a normal wife in a normal marriage.

"I miss you right now," I answered wholeheartedly, looking away from his eyes before they erupted a new wave of turmoil in mine. He kissed my forehead before leaving my bare-naked body and settled in beside me to face the ceiling.

"So, what's up with junior year, second semester? What's next for the great Kaylah Pantaleón?" Alex enjoyed forcing a Spanish accent that made him sound like Zorro whenever he pronounced my name. I always loved watching my husband step from behind the hardcore prison façade and remember that it was okay to be his goofy self. Alex knew I had many more tears to spare and his random post-coital question was just a desperate attempt at keeping me calm. It took me a few seconds to explore my swollen brain and squeeze out something I looked forward to at Emerson.

"Emerson has an LA Program that sends students to California for one semester. It's not easy to get in, so I gotta start working on the application now to make it for fall 2010," I replied with a little more energy in my voice than I expected to hear. The idea of making the cut bumped my spirits up thanks to Alex's genius plan. There was still hope for finding a solution just how I always dreamt I would. I knew I would most likely find it in California.

"You got that. From the hood to Boston to LA. Proud of you, baby girl. You're gonna do big things. Just don't turn

Hollywood on me, please. Leave all the fake ass and tities over there," Alex stated his stipulations in all seriousness and closed his eyes.

"Promise," I consented, a smile curving my lips as I watched him.

"Thank you," his eyelids rested as he spoke.

"You? What's next for the great Alexander J. Mitchell?"

"Oh, you know, same old, same old. I got some co-star auditions lined up for a couple ABC pilots in February. I really gotta invest in new headshots after I'm done with that mandatory substance abuse program. And my commercial agent is still waiting to hear back about the DiGiorno Pizza national spot, so keep your fingers crossed. I'm down to eat pizza on set all day. Besides that, staying outta trouble, reading books, taking classes, just livin' the dream," Alex delivered his thorough agenda without missing a beat as though he could see it all taking place behind his closed eyelids.

"You're worried about *me* turning Hollywood?" His fictitious itinerary stretched my cheeks to my ears, feeling refreshed by an imagination I helped color in.

"No, don't worry. You already know I'll be wearing you on my arm at the Oscars," he assured me confidently.

"So, you're thinking about being an actor now?"

"Yeah, babe. My football career is shot. I can't play baseball for shit. What else is there to do?" Alex opened his eyes and turned on his side to watch my body shake in laughter under the sheets. He let me enjoy the moment for a few more seconds before continuing, "Promise you'll keep taking care of yourself too, please. I found an article on PCOS in some *Cosmopolitan* magazine and that shit really is no joke." His voice dropped a note, forcing me to catch a breath, gradually reduce the size of my smile and turn to face him. He was worried about me.

"You read *Cosmopolitan*?" I couldn't resist teasing my husband and smirking across from him.

"I was looking for my horoscope," he admitted shamelessly, making my smile grow wide again.

"I've been keeping up with my work-outs. I could be a little more disciplined with my diet, but don't worry. I'll be alright. I promise."

"Good, 'cause I still want you to be my baby mama," Alex said, turning to let a yawn float up to the ceiling. He guarded his dreams with humor to avoid fully believing in them. Alex was terrified of life's next disappointment.

"Then I will be," I replied, wanting to keep the dream alive.

"Can I tell you something, Kaylah?" Alex's question immediately followed my last word as if he hadn't heard what I said. I tried to read his mind when we locked eyes, and I prophesized that he would beg me not to file for divorce. I needed him to fight for me more.

"Anything," I dove deep into his brown eyes glowing under the ray of orange yard lamps, seeing him for the first time at Cross County again with no facial scruff and a worry-free smile. He would ask me to be his "wifey" four days later.

"I gotta fart. This is a courtesy warning," Alex took on the voice of an FBI agent before erupting like a bag of popcorn during its first few seconds in the microwave. I flipped over to hug the cold wall next to me, guarding my nose and mouth before convulsing into a fit of laughter.

"Gaahh! Alexander!" I shouted a muffled cry from under my fingers.

"What? I had a lot of cheese this weekend. Don't act like you don't wanna bust one real quick. I haven't heard you fart since I met you. You're a fuckin' weirdo," Alex casually shared his opinion on my lack of flatulence as I thought back to every time I ran into the bathroom and turned the sink water on to relieve myself just so he wouldn't hear me. "If you can't fart with the one you love, then it's just not meant to be," my husband continued with his unique relationship advice that he probably found in the pages of *Cosmopolitan*. I had held in so much gas during our trailers I was practically filled with enough air to float me back to Boston, but I refused to let my self-conscious tendencies dictate our destiny.

"In that case," I accepted the dare and presented evidence of our everlasting union that came in the form of deflating airy balloon sounds. Alex and I both exploded laughs into our hands the moment he heard me fart for the first time, and I was overwhelmed by a sudden sense of relief in more ways than one.

"That's my girl!" Alex congratulated me with his signature grin and initiated a high-five.

"Shower?" I couldn't help making the suggestion after we came down from our happy seizures.

"Yup."

Our naked bodies raced each other to the bathroom to share a hot shower. We were going to last forever.

CHAPTER EIGHTEEN

I gave Branden a highly concentrated weed brownie the size of a quarter sold to me by my roommate with a certified medical marijuana license to treat her insomnia, Lyme disease, rheumatoid arthritis, and very possibly none of the above. My boyfriend had just arrived in LA the day before to celebrate Thanksgiving with me after finding out I couldn't afford to fly back home for the holiday. He was working overtime at P.F. Chang's to pay off his first semester back at Mercy College, so I was completely surprised and grateful to hear that I wouldn't be spending Thanksgiving alone.

"If consumed entirely in one sitting, you will be dysfunctional for up to thirty-six hours," Branden read the small font printed on the back of our miniature chocolate brownie.

"I can't," I panicked at the thought of consuming even a crumb, afraid of catching an actual high after Flaca and Mishie determined I needed more practice hitting the blunt because I never inhaled the right way.

"Oh, c'mon. When in Rome, babe. Edibles are a guaranteed high," Branden dumped peer pressure all over me, clearly excited to try a Californian brownie his first time in LA. "And if we get the munchies, we'll have plenty of your delicious food left over to eat."

"Oh, shoot. The potatoes!" I jumped when Branden reminded me of my redskin potatoes boiling on the stove in preparation for a mashed potatoes recipe I looked up online before his arrival. I was throwing together my first Thanksgiving meal for two, consisting of a small baked chicken, mini sweet corn cobs from the frozen food aisle at Von's, canned cranberry sauce, cheesy mashed potatoes, and paper plates. I even purchased a pumpkin spiced scented candle to set in the center of my small dining table to bring the romantic ambiance together. My main goal was to make up for the incident back in July when I completely forgot about our one year anniversary, which Branden celebrated with a surprise candlelit dinner in his apartment while his family was away in the Dominican Republic. What added fuel to the fire was my unintentional facial reaction when I took the first bite of his homemade chicken alfredo.

"It's...good," were the only words I could muster after nearly choking on noodles a little too al dente swimming with chunks of chalky chicken in a flavorless, white sauce. I managed a few more bites while trying to distract him with incessant chatter about my marketing internship in the city, but I had always been too expressive for my own good, and he caught on quickly. Branden wouldn't speak his mind until later that night in bed when he confessed to thinking that I didn't care enough, justifying his accusation with examples like, "You haven't even posted any pictures of us on Facebook," and, "You still haven't gotten rid of that disgusting tattoo." I reminded him that I wasn't the type to flaunt my relationship on social media like everybody else in the world, but the truth was, posting a picture for the public would make it all too real. I could feel Branden growing distant the next few days following our anniversary, and I buried my face in my pillow, wanting to suffocate myself the night I arranged to get a butterfly tattooed over Alex's name in a desperate attempt to keep my boyfriend from leaving me. The lesbian tattoo artist from Boston had been right all along.

"Ready?" Branden reminded me that we were preparing for takeoff.

"Alright, but I want less than half!" I agreed to the brownie challenge while straining the potatoes, just a few steps away from completing Thanksgiving dinner.

"You got it," he approved, taking a huge butter knife to neatly and unevenly slice down the tiny treat before passing over my portion.

"Gross. I'm eating chocolate weed," I commented through an open mouth, adjusting my jaw to the sticky chomps.

"Says here it could take about forty-five minutes to kick in. Do you mind if I use Word on your laptop while we wait? Gotta get some ideas down for my poli-sci paper," Branden asked while chewing on the brownie like it was a delicious stick of gum.

"Sure. I need a little more time with these potatoes, anyway. The laptop should be on my bed," I replied from inside my head, too focused on perfecting my first side of mashed potatoes from scratch.

"Thanks, babe," Branden walked off to the bedroom I shared with Claudine, my pot-loving roommate who drove back home to San Diego for the holiday.

For four pricey months, Emerson set me up with room and board in a beautiful one-bedroom condo at the Oakwood Apartments, a gated luxury complex located in Burbank. I still hadn't made any real friends at school so I never chose a roommate. But thank you, Jesus, I wasn't paired with a musical theater major who would've sung me out the door in the first week. Claudine was cool for the most part. I only had to lay down the law when she wrongly assumed I wouldn't mind her smoking a blunt at all hours of the night in our bedroom while I slept. She made up for her pothead ways by having a car, which I quickly learned was as necessary in LA as having a beating heart. I lucked out with a ride to class whenever it was one that my roommate and I were both scheduled for, but was forced to rely on incomprehensible public transportation any other time. Fortunately, I got my hands on a beautiful metallic-blue bike when I started working as a casting intern at CBS. My employment came right around the time Charlie Sheen was losing his shit, so they were giving *Two and a Half Men* memorabilia out like candy. My California Cruiser was sexy; however, it was also tramp-stamped with the bright yellow *Two and a Half Men* logo across its body, so I was left promoting the show all over the valley. I still greatly appreciated a free bike, as well as the up close and personal view of the majestic Warner Bros. Studio I had the honor of pedaling past every day, five days a week.

After I watched my passion for acting go from bright to sporadic flicks of dim light like a Riverdale lamp post, I started imagining life behind the scenes, hoping to find a career path that wouldn't keep me too far from the dream and my solution. Spending twenty minutes a day getting acquainted with a hormonal copy machine and developing the aching back of an eighty-year-old after sitting for too long were sure signs that the office life was not for me. On the other hand, I did enjoy watching nervous actors coming and going all day (especially the famous ones), listening to my casting directors throw golden critiques around during the gritty decision-making process, and the occasional trips to Warner Bros. Studio to check out our talent on the set of shows like *Big Bang Theory* and *Mike and Molly*. After over two years at Emerson, I was finally getting my groove back, dreaming of all that could be if I just stuck to the original plan. Sunny California boosted my confidence and my grades, and replanted the Hollywood seed that Nana was the first to fertilize.

"What the fuck is this?" Branden came charging from the bedroom with my laptop in hand.

"What?" I frantically looked up from the bowl of half-mashed potatoes.

"This!" Branden placed my Apple computer down a little more aggressively than necessary to show me a typed twelve-font document beginning with the words, "Hey, my beautiful husband!" My heart landed on my stomach when I realized Branden had come across one of my many saved letters to Alex.

"And this!" He clicked out of one document to present another starting off with the line, "My fly guy!" I was done.

There were probably a hundred more where that came from. I never really sent Alex a typed letter because I believed it took away from the intimacy of receiving a personal, handwritten letter from his wife. What I did do, was type my letter onto a Word document first. That allowed me to organize my thoughts before transferring each sentence onto loose-leaf paper by hand with the reduced appearance of grammatical errors, scribbles and cross-outs. Every letter to Alex usually took about two hours to complete; one hour to type up and one hour to copy down in cursive before folding it neatly and sealing it in an envelope for sendoff. It may have been a minor case of OCD, but I didn't mind my husband having a collection of flawless letters handwritten by me.

"Oh, it's for my book," was the first line to dribble out of my mouth, and I noticed my improv classes may actually come in handy.

"What? What book?" Branden's white face went completely pink at this point, nostrils flaring.

"I had an idea to publish a compilation of fictional letters between pen pal lovers, a woman in the world and a man in prison. Clearly, inspired by true events. Some letters are original, and others not so much...for an urban love story kind of thing. Dope, right?" I kept my composure while the words ran like rambunctious children in a playground, skipping carelessly off my tongue. I hadn't even thought about writing a poem since senior year of high school, let alone a novel. I honestly couldn't repeat any part of my fabrication if he asked me to, and I really hoped he didn't ask me to.

"Dope? Look at these fuckin' dates. This one was typed LAST WEEK!" Branden's flaming face shriveled with confusion as he clenched my laptop and shoved the screen toward me so I could get a good look at the letter I wrote to "My first true love," wishing him a happy six years since we met and begging him to call or write because I hadn't heard from him since our last trailer. Alex proved determined to give me what I asked for, to let me go, to divorce me, but not having him in my life was making me sick, and I was terrified at the thought of losing him forever. He had to know I didn't care if I was the best thing about prison, that it was my job to be, and I wanted back in. I copied the letter onto decorative parchment paper with an old, medieval appeal, symbolizing that my love for him had started way before our time. I wrote that in the "P.S." and mailed it out well before November 20th. I was still waiting for a reply.

"Well, yeah, like I said...some are real and some are not. Obviously, the most recent ones are fictional. Relax. I should've mentioned the project to you sooner. My bad," my nonchalant attitude desperately fought to block my heart from leaving my body as his eyebrows fell down into place and he unflared his wide nostrils. I went back to mashing potatoes like any pathological liar would.

"But, his name. You use his name. Alex. This is hilarious," Branden talked to himself, almost in a whisper as he squinted at the screen lighting his rapidly moving blue eyes. I needed him to stop reading.

"Huh? Put the computer away so we can eat, please." I casually tried distracting him by placing plates of food on the table. After finally setting my laptop on the kitchen counter and releasing a few snickers into his neck, Branden started toward me and then abruptly stopped to cower in what appeared to be excruciating pain. I dropped the bowl of corn onto the candlelit table and crouched fearfully beside him in time to meet a loud, terrifying howl that dragged out of his gaping mouth before he collapsed onto the carpeted floor.

"Oh, my God, baby. What's wrong?"

"Alex. Alex. What kind of name is that? It sounds like an alien's name," he looked up at me, tears in his eyes. "A girl alien!" Wild laughter erupted from Branden's wide open mouth, literally spitting in my face before rolling over onto his back. I was confused until the sight of his relentless state of euphoria made me smile, then smile bigger, then grin from ear-to-ear and possibly beyond my ears. I was completely convinced my face would stay stretched like a rubber mask for the rest of my life. But I could care less about my face or anything else as I joined my boyfriend on the floor, choosing ceiling fans for our next topic of discussion. I don't remember much after that. I just remember we were happy for the moment, and I was thankful.

Water fell from my face blurring the black ink on the sheets of loose-leaf Alex sent me a week after Branden left. I rushed to the laptop to write a letter back to my husband.

I took Nana's long, boney fingers in my hand and together we held over one-hundred years of experience in the deep lines of our palms. Her seventy-nine years showed a courage like David fighting two Goliaths and a strength like the Virgin Mary having twins, each named Jesus. My twenty-two years came up dusty, sitting around collecting so much debris it was hard to see anything beyond the present.

Branden sat across from the hospital bed, holding her other hand, and I wanted him to go. I wanted him to leave because he couldn't possibly understand my pain and therefore, couldn't hold her with the same level of love and admiration that I did. Mostly, I wanted him to leave the room so that I could confess all my sins to her. I hadn't gone to confession in over three years, and I wanted to believe that if I confessed everything before her and the Lord, that He would have mercy on me and bring her back to life.

"Can you give us a minute?" I directed my question to Branden without taking my eyes off of Nana.

"Sure," he said to me before topping the back of her limp hand with a kiss and carefully placing it at her side. *Adios, Doña Maria.* His farewell pinched my heart when I thought of all the other times he had left her with those words, and she immediately responded gleefully *¡Adios, Blanquito!* But, there was no reply for the little White boy that day. She loved Branden because he made me happy; the same reason she had loved Alex.

"Okay, Nana...good stuff first," I started after Branden closed the door behind him, warming her cold fingers with

both of my hands. "As you know, I have a degree now and still
no marketing job...but that's probably because I really don't
want one. So...your *Artista* is thinking about finally getting
back to acting... I don't know how yet, but I have more time
now to figure it out. I lost ten more pounds... The doctor says
I'm at a healthy weight and my PCOS should be okay as long
as I keep exercising and taking the birth control pills. Yeah,
yeah, I'll still give you great-grandchildren...Don't worry. Dad
is doing a lot better... He left the program and has a really
good job as a maintenance man in the city. I'm proud of
him...Gramma Brooklyn is, too. Even Janessa is starting to
talk to him more...that's nice, right? Party City is having a
crazy sale on Halloween decorations, so we can get some for
your birthday party. I don't think I'm dressing up this
year...Don't be mad. But you have to get better so you can
cook...We need those *pastelitos*, Nana. Make mine with extra
raisins, please. I can't believe you're turning eighty
already...That SlimFast is keeping you young just like you say.
I can't write anymore, Nana...I look at the screen, and I get
scared. Yeah...same with my journals. What if I'm not good
enough anymore? I worry so much about my future. I think
I'm gonna be a waitress for the rest of my life...I stopped
dreaming big. I need to do something to help you and
Mom...We can't stay on Riverdale forever. I know...I have to
pray more. I'm sorry for choosing Emerson, Nana. I know
you didn't want me to leave to Boston, no matter how much
you love Big Papi. I wish I could get those four years back to
stay with you. Please forgive me. I'm not even thinking about
California anymore. I'm never leaving again...so, please wake
up. Nana...I got married to Alex. *El Indio*. Remember? ...But
he's in prison right now...I was scared to tell you. Alex is a
really good person...you remember. Yeah...like Mom and Dad.

I'm sorry...I know you didn't want that. Don't be mad at Mom. She told me to get the divorce. We signed the papers...but I threw them out after I showed Mom the signatures. I'm still married. No...Branden doesn't know. You're the only one who knows...Oh, Janessa and Yanel, too...but that's it. I still see Alex...I see him a lot, especially ever since I got my license and the car. The only reason I wanted to learn how to drive was so I could see Alex more...Oh, of course...to pick you up from Shop Rite, too. We spend a weekend together every forty days...it's so beautiful. You wouldn't believe everything we can do. I even cook for him...no, I haven't made your *moro* yet...maybe I'll try next time. There's a backyard where we can play baseball and basketball and look at the stars...we watch movies...and we laugh. Oh, my God...we laugh so much. But the only way to see him is if I lie about where I am. I look Mom in her face, and I just lie, lie, lie...I'm so tired and sad. Did I tell you Branden was the one to teach me how to drive? He was really patient with me...He loves me, Nana. And I love him, but I don't act like it. I asked for a GPS for Christmas...and I think he's going to buy it for me. I just want a GPS so I can use it when I go see Alex upstate...Isn't that horrible? I know...I lie so much. I can't do it anymore...my heart hurts. And I know Branden is starting to get suspicious...so is Alex. Tell me what to do. I love Alex, Nana. But he's not here to help me through this, and he's not here to hold your hand...so right now, I think I'm starting to hate him. I hate him for leaving me alone. I'm sorry for everything, Nana. Please open your eyes. I'll be good...I'll leave them both. I'll stop lying to everybody. I won't go to California. I'll start writing again...and acting, too. Remember? 'I can hit the ball...I can catch the ball...and I can throw the ball better than anyone. I am great…Why can't they see?'"

My confession wouldn't wake her up, but only make her go sooner in the same hospital where Mom, Janessa, and I were born. She left us on October 24, 2011; Trujillo's birthday and one week before our favorite holiday.

CHAPTER NINETEEN

Two months later, Nana's cat died, and Mom had a heart attack. My sins had killed off my grandmother and then went after everyone else. I had never experienced a heartbreak more damaging than the one that nearly sent me to my own grave after seeing my fragile mother in a hospital bed with the same long, boney fingers as Nana's. Branden was there to catch my fall again, proving once more that he was the best man for me.

By the summer of 2012, my family had officially moved out of the building...and across the street. At that point, I had very little hope left of seeing Hollywood again, settling on the greater probability of never leaving Riverdale, and finding it easier to adopt the hood mentality, "it is what it is." The thought didn't faze me anymore once I decided to never make the same mistake that I had with Nana. My mother needed me, and I planned to stay as close as possible, even if that meant one day renting out my own apartment on the block; so, I did. My mother, Rich, Nunu, and Janessa moved across the street into a three-bedroom apartment with no color code, and I took a one-bedroom on the sixth floor-green side in the building that raised me. Though directly across the street, I couldn't deny the significant difference between the two sides. The new side was largely populated by senior citizens and equipped with a more efficient security system, resulting in very minimal criminal activity. The halls were cleaner, and apartments came with modern hardwood floors I had always dreamt of walking on barefooted. Unfortunately, my P.F. Chang's paystubs were documented proof that I could only afford rent reduced to four-hundred dollars monthly for an apartment with scratched tile floors in a low-income complex on the old side. It was safe to say the new side was a noticeable upgrade from the "garden apartment." At least, my door was bulletproof.

Though continuing the generational Riverdale life cycle, there were some major changes I made after Nana died; the first one being my hair. I attempted to find another form of freedom by cutting off my curls into a Halle Berry-esque hairdo after officially dropping back down to my lowest weight since the second-grade of 150 lbs. The look required a few weeks to adapt to, until the day came when I started appreciating features I hadn't bothered to take notice of when hiding behind curls; like a long, elegant neck and a pronounced jawline. I also had to applaud myself for cutting my own umbilical cord off from P.F. Chang's where I was promoted to a waitress position and constantly comforted by my boyfriend's face behind the bar. My new-found independence would ship me outside of Westchester County to a restaurant called, Tommy Bahama, in NYC where, although crowded and polluted, I could take a breath of fresh air. But first, I had to have the time of my life with Yanel in the Dominican Republic.

I was not old enough to appreciate my beautiful country on my last visit. I made up for lost time when my best friend introduced me to her vibrant *campo*, a vintage village of handcrafted blue, pink, and green houses where we were always in the midst of *una bachatica*, and one cold Presidente away from throwing the *campo* party of the century. By the time my adventure came around, I had more than enough practice on the dance floor and would find the good life at every hazy, colorful nightclub we hopped to next, never once spotting a body sitting off to the side. I was surprised with how many men came up requesting a dance with me, but never hesitated to accept just so I could keep moving to the hypnotic rhythms of *tamboras* and *guitaras* all night.

"It's that haircut, girl. No one cuts their hair that short in D.R. The guys must love it, though!" Yanel strained her voice over *merengue típico* exploding from the speakers to explain the frequent attention coming my way inside and outside the club that I never experienced in New York, and definitely not in Boston. I also knew that my recent weight loss helped boost my self-esteem over the last few months, and could feel my confidence accompany me out on the dance floor every time. My funky haircut was a headliner in her own right, but my self-confidence was what kept one dance partner attracted to me long after the music stopped and the club cleared out. I found infatuation with Joel on the last four days of my trip, only ever kissing him once at the club and one other time at the river where he spotted my (now very visible) tattoo peeking out of my bathing suit bottom and inquired about its meaning. I hated being reminded of the disaster on my ass. The tattoo artist on Yonkers Avenue had not only branded me for life with a smudged butterfly, but also turned my delicate, fine-lined heart into a black, jumbo sharpie-lined heart, finished off with a tribal slash down the middle where Alex's name used to be. I had never seen a more random and pointless tattoo, and never imagined I would find it on my left butt cheek. It was completely my fault for walking into the parlor wallowing in a state of depression and giving no other instructions but, "I don't care. Do whatever. I like butterflies." I had no right to complain.

Unfortunately, as nice as Joel was to look at, my severe lack of Spanish speaking prevented us from engaging in a fluid conversation and instead, left him putting a puzzle of words together just to guess what I could possibly be trying to say. When it came to our game of "Guess That Tattoo," I did my best to explain that once upon a time, my "ex-boyfriend's" name was on my butt and I had to get it covered. Although I felt like I was in the middle of an SNL skit, my novela was eventually and successfully relayed. However, I had apparently exhausted the words *amor* and *pena* during the brutal few minutes of my performance, and Joel would find it coincidentally appropriate to nickname me *AmoryPena* from that point forward. Love & Shame. My entire life had been summed up on one hot day in D.R.

A few weeks after my trip, Branden discovered a picture of Joel and I cuddled up at the club, and I confessed to having a few drinks and kissing him. I hadn't realized what I was saying until all the words escaping my mouth pinched his eardrums hard enough to set off the sensor in his laser beam eyes and fry my face off.

"You did what?"

"I'm sorry. It didn't mean anything," I said coolly, as if his rising temper was uncalled for.

"So why is his picture still in your phone?" He was tight-lipped while holding my iPhone up to help refresh my memory.

"I haven't gotten around to looking through my pics! Babe, seriously...you're blowing this out of proportion," I snatched my phone back, and he told me to get out of his house.

I spent the following days losing any sense of independence or confidence I may have had by calling and texting him enough to qualify for a restraining order. I baked chocolate chip cookies from scratch and left them at his door, and even resorted to standing out on Highland in the dead of night to throw pebbles at his bedroom window, begging him to talk to me. There was only one thing left to do, and I did it the way I usually did things—without very much thought. I asked Branden to move into apartment C-615 on the sixth floor-green side. I had made another desperate attempt to keep him because rejection felt too much like suffocating.

He moved in fairly soon after I cried myself numb and convinced him I was ready to live together. It happened gradually, just one drawer at a time. He appreciated my renovations; the wall-to-wall cream carpet to hide the original, chipping tiles; the earthy, peanut butter brown color painted on the living room walls; and the white crown molding additions to the living room and bedroom. If my first apartment had to be on Riverdale, I was going to make sure it looked closer to a MiMA luxury apartment in Tribeca. In fact, when Branden suggested we purchase blinds for the large windows in our living room, I immediately shot him down because I had left them bare on purpose.

"It looks more like a NYC condo without blinds," I said, dazing out in front of my tall, broad, barred windows, looking at a view of the red side from six stories high. I couldn't remember where or when, but I knew for sure I had heard Oprah once share that while growing up she had always associated wealth with trees. She would then practically have Central Park for a backyard one day, a bazillion square feet of land covered in freshly cut green grass, roses, fruits, veggies, and trees, lots and lots of trees. Aside from having more than two-hundred dollars in my bank account, I began to associate wealth with windows. I liked big, sun-welcoming windows and even pictured my dream bedroom having a glass ceiling so that I could fall asleep while stargazing. My blindless Riverdale windows would have to do for now.

Branden and I christened the sheets on our first official night living together, and I was drunk with appreciation for having someone to hold and care for the way he cared for me. Now that I had everything I needed, I was grateful, but I wasn't satisfied. Branden removed himself from my body, and the sight of his naked, slim frame walking to our bathroom left me feeling like a slimy roach in our bed, living a small and purposeless life. I didn't know what was happening, whether this bubbling repulsion was caused by him or me. I turned away from the bright doorway, and my eyes met with a happy Winnie the Pooh eating honey on top of my dresser. The box kept my life's deepest secret as I thought about how perfect Branden was; hardworking, protective, motivating, affectionate, intelligent, and free. We had gone as far as discussing baby names for our future kids, reaching the final decisions of Braylin for a girl, and Brayden for a boy. As if they were running amuck and just starting to potty train, our kids' names were often brought up in regular conversation when we were on good terms. He was just waiting for me to show some consistency before getting down on one knee. I really wanted to be the one for him.

When Branden returned, my eyes left the jewelry box and I rose from our bed with a steamy, relaxing shower in mind to cleanse me of this strange, icky feeling. Then, I realized the bubbling sensation could have been just that as soon as my bare butt peeled off the sheets and the unmistakable sound of a fiber-rich day freed itself from my body, stopping all sense of reality in what was by far the most embarrassing moment alone with Branden in three years.

"AH! Excuse me!" My naked body shook with nerves and giggles, desperately wishing for him to join in.

"That was disturbing. Please don't ever do it again," my boyfriend requested after his eyebrows went into electric shock and finally came back down to complete his face. It was the first time Branden ever heard me pass gas since we started dating in 2009, but the fact that he also never did so in my presence was a hint at his opinions on flatulence.

"Relax. It's natural!" My giggles faded, and I was instantly offended.

"So, do it in the bathroom! It's not ladylike," Branden used our six-year age gap to speak to me like my elder, reminding me of my manners.

"Oh, farts are not ladylike? You know what *is* ladylike? My PERIOD! But you can't ever stand to talk about that either," I found a kink in his personality and latched onto it. Branden always kept his distance from me one week a month and cringed whenever hearing things like, "I'm on my period," or God forbid, "My flow is heavier than usual." He was not the type to buy me a box of tampons or rub my belly to soothe the excruciating cramps. Clearly, his idea of the perfect woman didn't fart nor bleed.

"Why are you being random? And why do we ever have to discuss your monthly thing? That's YOUR business!" We argued back and forth in the nude like newlywed Neanderthals in their first cave.

"It's YOUR business, too. I CAN'T WAIT for the morning you wake up to find blood all over the sheets. I PROMISE it will happen!" I was beginning to feel suppressed anger from other irrelevant subjects affect my tone, and I couldn't control it.

"Wow. That's disgusting," he decreased his volume and somehow sounded even more demeaning while finally crouching over to pull up a pair of tighty-whities.

"Yeah, and I'm gonna make YOU wash the BLOODY sheets covered in all the BLOOD OOZING out of my BLOODY VAGINA filled with SO MUCH BLOOD. You fuckin' WEIRDO!" I concluded my tantrum and rushed bare-assed to the bathroom to start my shower.

Branden slept back at his mom's that night, and we made up the following day with Chang's take-out and uninspiring sex. We survived the next few weeks as a cranky married couple bored with the holidays until he left to D.C. for his first semester at George Washington University. Branden applied for the transfer from Mercy College after deciding to seriously pursue a career in politics. I was proud of him for realizing his potential and detaching himself from the family he practically raised. He worked long hours to allocate as much money as he could out of pocket, but would inevitably seek federal loans to cover his first semester away from home. Although relieved to walk into my apartment and not find Branden flossing his teeth on the couch, a big part of me wanted to reward him for his relentless work ethic and prove just how much I appreciated him. I decided to help rekindle our chemistry by boarding a bus to D.C. for a surprise visit on Valentine's Day.

My boyfriend loved me for taking my thoughtful side out of hiding and spoiled me with kisses and margaritas at a local Mexican restaurant to celebrate Love. However, my efforts were forgotten in an instant when he returned from the restroom to find my head tossed back in joyful laughter next to a guy who came to introduce himself and crack a few jokes. Branden's face was expressive enough to wipe the smile from mine without saying a word before I timidly wished the stranger a good night. We left the bar in a daunting silence, his short legs moving hastily ahead of mine. He had accepted the fact a long time ago that I was a naturally friendly person and couldn't help talking to people who showed an interest in talking to me. I didn't feel like I had done anything wrong, so this time there would be no apology leaving my mouth. I tried to brush the incident off by skipping up to him and holding his hand, but he shoved it away instinctively as if I was cursed.

"I'm not the man for you," Branden stated matter-of-factly, holding a breath and keeping his eyes on the long sidewalks ahead.

"What? Because I was laughing at a stupid joke? You're acting like he got my digits and I tongued him good night," I skipped up in front of Branden to force eye contact, determined to make him see how irrational he was being.

"It's the *way* you laughed. You haven't looked that happy with me in a long time," Branden confessed his issue, and I could see him running a slide show of all my frowning moments in his head.

"I don't even remember what he was talking about! You're losing your shit over a sixty-second convo!"

"I'm losing my shit over someone who insists on not thinking about my feelings. I'm done," Branden turned away from me and sped up his pace even more.

"Would I be here if I didn't think about you, Branden?" I caught up, looking like a stray puppy running behind him.

"Yeah, this was *another* great comeback of yours. But why do you have to keep making comebacks? Why can't you just stay on track with me?" He finally took a break from his 5k to meet my eyes and wait for a reply. His exhaustion matched mine. We were both tired of trying to make it work, feeling like our relationship was more grueling than our restaurant jobs. I wanted to fight his point for the sake of having the last word, but I didn't know how to answer. In his crystal blue eyes, I suddenly saw an *idea* of what I wanted. I was in love with the idea of having someone to call at the push of a button, someone to wake up next to, someone to cook dinner for me, someone to go to the movies with, someone to eat take-out and watch movies at home with, someone to hold me, support me, inspire me, and be with me. Branden was perfect, but he was right; he wasn't the man for me.

"I'm trying," I answered, and had no tears left to support my claim. My phone rang before he could open his mouth for the next argument, and I glanced at the screen for a second, sent it to voicemail and tucked it back in my pocket.

"Who was that?"

"I didn't recognize the number," I lied and shrugged my shoulders.

"It was Alex, wasn't it?"

"What? No." I lied again. "Why would you say that?"

A year or so ago, prison facilities had entered the twenty-first century and opened collect calling up to cellphones for the first time after limiting connections to landlines only. I added thirty dollars a month on the prison phone service (roughly ten thirty-minute conversations) so Alex could reach me directly instead of relying on his mother or someone else in the Mitchell household to initiate a three-way call. I was excited to know that I could finally look forward to Alex's phone calls working around my schedule as oppose to his family's. But I had been distancing myself from the luxury in recent months, rarely answering the phone so I could focus on being a better girlfriend to Branden, or figuring out what the hell I wanted. I spent the last three years sneaking off to trailers, disappearing for two days at a time, creating outlandish stories to cover my tracks just to come back to the real world and act like nothing ever happened. With the exceptions of Yanel and Janessa, my friends, family, employers, co-workers, and any new people that entered my life only ever knew about Branden. I was only married when I took my ring out of the Winnie the Pooh box and put it on my finger before I snuck off to see Alex. I was two people living two different lives, stuck in one body, and the lies were beginning to tear it apart and expose the two sides.

The abrasive ring came in again, vibrating both my pocket and my frantic heart at the same time. I saw the "845" area code and rushed to turn it off completely when Branden swiped my iPhone, nearly taking my hand along with it.

"Hello?" He greeted the operator who informed him of "a collect call from 'Alex,' an inmate at Eastern Correctional Facility. To accept this call, please dial '3' now." Branden glared at me and shook his head in utter disappointment before pressing '3.' I looked for a nearby bus to step in front of.

"Alex?" Branden dug his finger in my open wound when he turned the speaker on.

"Uh, yeah. Who's this? Where's Kaylah?"

I turned around, unable to watch Branden talk into my phone because I felt close to tackling him to the ground to get it back.

"This is Branden. Kaylah's boyfriend of three years. Has she told you about me? I know you guys used to be married, but you calling at 9:30 at night is a little concerning."

Alex took a few seconds to absorb Branden's merciless blows. I wanted to walk and walk and cry and cry until my legs gave out and my eyes turned to dust. I didn't want to be standing in front of my boyfriend and my husband at the same time, but I knew I deserved to be. This moment was inevitable, so I accepted the real-life nightmare and turned around to stare down the monster situation I created.

"Uh. Yeah...yeah, she's talked about you. Sorry to bother. I got accepted to Bard College a few months back at this new spot I'm at. I just wanted to give her the good news. Is she around?"

Tears poured down my face when Alex stopped talking. I didn't understand why or how he could stay so composed after hearing what Branden had just said, and especially after I had been ignoring his calls for so long. I wiped my thankful tears, keeping in mind I was still an awful human being when I reached for the phone.

"Oh. That's awesome, bro. Um... good luck with that. She's right here," Branden almost sounded disappointed as he passed Alex over and avoided looking at my face. I took it off speaker.

"Hello?"

"Are you okay?" Alex's voice had no emotion.

"Yes. I'm good. Congra—"

He had only waited to hear if I was okay before hanging up on me.

I arranged to get on a five-hour bus ride back to New York the next morning, a day earlier than planned. Branden talked the entire way to the bus terminal, trying to convince me that he had overreacted and wasn't ready to let me go. I responded with sad, tired eyes and a guilty shake of my head, knowing I should've let go a long time ago.

"I'll always love you, though," I assured Branden as he waited in the bus line with me.

"C'mon. Give it some thought, at least," he pleaded, tossing my duffel bag in the luggage compartment.

"Okay," I agreed just to lessen his grief before I boarded the *Greyhound.*

"Thank you. I love you." Branden took me by the shoulders and locked lips with me for the last time.

"I love you, and I'm sorry," I came back from the kiss, hoping he would never know everything I was truly sorry for.

Less than a week later, I came home from work to find more than a dozen sandwiches—turkey, Swiss cheese, and mayo on toasted wheat—packed in plastic baggies and strategically spread out on my bed to display the shape of a heart. In the center of the exhibition was a note that read: "Made you a snack. Love always and forever, Branden." My ex-boyfriend had traveled five hours to New York to only build his sandwich heart and leave my extra apartment key on top of my car tire before boarding a bus back to D.C. the same day. It would forever be the sweetest thing anyone did for me, or for the person I wanted to be. I sat on the bed and picked one of my favorite sandwiches to bite into, wishing I was the kind of girl who deserved this much love.

I was eating my dinner when my cell buzzed at 10:00 p.m., and I jumped at the sight of the "845" area code I hadn't seen glow across my screen since the Valentine's Day from hell. I answered, listening to the operator announce, "Eastern Correctional Facility," an honor prison that Alex's clean record had recently qualified for. I took a few seconds before pressing '3,' trying to gulp down the piece of sandwich in my mouth without choking.

"Hello?"

"Hey," he sounded tired or bored, but his voice still made me smile.

"I'm glad you called. How's school? Congratulations. That's an amazing opportunity."

"Thanks. It's good. Haven't gotten anything lower than a B+ so far. How's Branden?"

I deserved the pinch in my chest that accompanied his question and prepared myself for more bruises.

"I fucked up, Alex. I'm so sorry. We're done. I promise. How didn't you blow up on the phone that night?" Though grateful for Alex's composure, I was still also very confused by it.

"I already thought somethin' was up, but I guess I was in denial. Didn't think Kaylah Pantaleón was capable of something like that. But hey, look where I'm at," he took a second to let his words sink in before continuing. "So, yeah...I guess I wasn't surprised to hear his girly ass voice after you tried to divorce me, covered up the tattoo, and ignored my calls. Oh, and you sent me fifty dollars a month outta guilt. You're a bad cheater," he released a long exhale like that all hurt him to say, more than he expected it to. I had been called a bad cheater before, but I held onto the moment to appreciate his words because it had to mean I was never a cheater to begin with. I was a good person who fucked up really bad.

"You didn't tell him we were still married."

"I wanted to. He sounded like a lame ass frat boy whose heart I really wanted to break. But for all I know, he could've been the type of dude to lay his hands on you if he heard some shit like that, and I couldn't live with myself if I let you get hurt, no matter how much I hated you."

"You hated me?" The emotion was predictable, but the idea of Alex falling out of love with me was a lot to digest.

"Hell yeah. And then I remembered who you were and knew for a fact you woulda never played those games if I was home," he spoke confidently.

"I'm sorry."

"I know. We'll be alright."

"You're not leaving me?" I couldn't wrap my brain around this conversation that moved in a completely opposite direction from my expectations. I was still waiting for the part where he said we were done and hung up on me.

"I thought about it, but I know I won't find another woman who can make lasagna like you." I hadn't felt my grin stretch so wide since I took a picture with Oprah.

I absorbed all of my husband's words and scanned my bed covered in sandwiches, feeling like I was getting a Valentine's Day do-over. Though I still yearned for a chocolate rose more than anything, I was surrounded by the kind of love that made me want to dream again.

CHAPTER TWENTY

I spent the next two years getting into the best shape of my life doing CrossFit and finding a way back into acting so I could keep my promise to Nana. I signed up for Central Casting NYC, the go-to service for background actors, and quickly landed a gig on some TV show called, *Orange is the New Black*. My first day on set took place at an old, abandoned building surrounded by tall fences crowned with barbed wire in upstate, NY in the spring of 2013. Rumor had it that the location was once a children's asylum, which gave me the creeps to think about after finding children's artwork painted on the white concrete walls in different parts of the building. It looked like something out of *Nightmare on Elm Street*. I wouldn't realize the *Netflix* original series was a dramedy based on someone's life in prison until the eyes of a flamboyant wardrobe supervisor scanned me once from head to toe before piling my two arms with khaki scrubs, a gray sweatsuit ("just in case"), a gray long john shirt, white tube socks, and black Frankenstein boots. God sure did have a sense of humor.

The hasty stylist emphasized the "S" sound whenever he spoke. "Nails, please," he requested to see my nails to confirm they were polish-free after already burying me under the costumes. I managed to rescue one hand from under my garments for approval. "And the other," he used a flimsy pointer finger to double tap at the air, commanding my other hand to show itself for thorough inspection. I adjusted my arms and clothes to abide by his wishes, already convinced background work was a tough gig. "Okay. Let me know if something doesn't quite fit. And pleasssssee don't lose my hangers," he cracked a split-second smile before flicking his wrist to shoo me away and sized up the next inmate.

I was called week after week for season one of *OITNB*. My boyish haircut made me the ideal prison candidate when the makeup was stripped off my face, and my hair was deprived of mousse. I passed most of the time using my iPhone to search for auditions in the city, sleeping, and eating from an unfair display of every artery-clogging snack in the world they called "crafty," short for "craft services." It didn't take me very long to understand life's motto for background actors: hurry up and wait. We were a huge mix of different colored women who rushed to meet a 6:00 a.m. call time about three times a week to sit idle in "holding" (the background actor's waiting room) anywhere between thirty minutes and two hours before production decided to "use" us. Unless a scene in the "prison auditorium" or "prison cafeteria" called for all colors to participate, we were usually called just one color at a time.

"Okay, I need one more Spanish Harlem girl...who can I use?" The White, rubbery, non-athletic production assistant looked like someone I once saw at Emerson as he took the pencil from behind his ear and poked his chin with the eraser in seemingly deep thought. No one ever actually answered the question, knowing very well a P.A. always chose which face he or she thought fit the scene best. But, if a background actor wanted to increase her chances of getting picked and being seen on TV, she locked eyes with the P.A. to signal, "you can use me." Most girls kept their faces down in books or glued to their phones, perfectly content with getting paid eighty-five dollars to sit around doing nothing. I had to admit I wanted to get used, and I wanted to learn, so my eyes stayed alert and waited for the P.A. to connect every chance I got.

On set was where the magic happened. Locations for our prison scenes alternated between upstate New York and Kaufman Astoria Studios in Queens. Our shoots were mostly scheduled at Kaufman where the prison cafeteria, recreation room, visiting room, and commissary store were set. It was an uncanny feeling to sit as a background actor in a makeshift visiting room when I had frequented real prison visiting rooms my whole life. If anyone could act like an inmate with a few years in, it was me.

Cafeteria scenes were the most feared because they always involved having at least eighty people on set at one time, crushing crew and talent's dreams of getting out before ten o'clock at night. But the open space in the cafeteria's set design was where I first appreciated expensive camera equipment, learned camera crew lingo like "wide shot" and "turning around" and "martini," and sat next to stars pretending to eat cold scrambled eggs and chocolate pudding. I filled a space at the Spanish Harlem table across from the Black girls one day. The Brown girl next to me had a long, auburn ponytail with blonde highlighted bangs and plumpy lips that reminded me of Janessa's when she smiled. She was the first to make polite conversation at the table, breaking the awkward silence among timid inmates afraid of making noise between takes. Her name was Dascha Polanco, a Dominican from Brooklyn I wouldn't even know was a main character in the show until the director called, "Action!" and the camera angled directly on her face to capture her slow, sensual bite into an orange wedge while she locked eyes with a sexy correctional officer who happened to be another main character. I would also later discover that the sexy correctional officer graduated from Emerson College in real life, and I wanted to punch myself in the face for transferring out of Performing Arts.

"New orange wedge!" A P.A. called out into the cafeteria after the director's "Cut!" and a frantic woman from the props department came hustling in with a fresh, juicy slice of orange. They were going for another take.

Laura Prepon and Taylor Schilling were cool to gawk at, but they never bothered acknowledging background actors, which I figured stars learned to do after many years of experience on set. Dascha, on the other hand, was just getting her feet wet and still normal enough to make eye contact and spark conversations with the little people, even me. She learned my name, and we mostly chatted about fitness and how much we loved working out while standing in front of crafty eating fresh homemade brownies. By the second season, I had agreed to do a topless scene in the bathroom, which I was relieved to discover a fully dressed Dascha was also a part of. She cheered me on in-between takes, making me feel better about my random decision to strip for the first time in my two-minute acting career. "Show them muscles, baby!" I could hear her shout after every "Cut!" from inside the stall where her character was supposed to be struggling with constipation. Dascha was a young, sweet, funny, *thick*, sexy Brown girl who looked like me. Every time I saw her, I saw my dream; a reminder that it was possible.

There was inspiration everywhere I turned on the set of *Orange is the New Black*. It was my first glimpse at life in front of the camera, and my passion started piecing itself back together each time I got to witness magic. When actually watching the show at home, my fever spiked a few more degrees every time I caught a second of my face on the TV screen. I was pretty sure which blurred head was mine, too.

My experience on the show even went as far as helping me remember how much I missed talking to God. In one of my last episodes, I sat close to Danielle Brooks for our final flood scene in season two where we were all bunched together on mattresses in the recreation room. I tried to control my star-struck tendency to stare and kept my head down most of the time, but I could still make out something she had whispered only to herself, "Last scene of the day. God is good."

I appreciated Danielle's quiet humility so much, I wished I could have looked up and given her a big hug to say, "Thank you!" That would've held the scene up another fifteen minutes, so I silently agreed with her instead, and took my own moment to thank Him for putting me exactly where I needed to be.

I went on to experiment with other shows, and I quickly realized *OITNB* had been the best background gig in town. No other show provided as many days of work per week or involved a full twelve hours of sitting and eating crafty in comfy prison scrubs. I still jumped around different sets, growing and learning, but most of my time was inevitably spent working at Tommy Bahama and going to see Alex. My husband was a full-blown college student made possible by B.P.I., Bard Prison Initiative. The program provided faculty from Bard College in New York to instruct their liberal arts courses at Eastern Correctional Facility so inmates could have the opportunity to receive a diploma while incarcerated. Inmates who were granted an associate's degree after two years would have to reapply for the bachelor's program if they decided to continue their education. Alex had just completed his first two-year program for the associate's degree and walked at graduation in January 2015, planning to apply for the bachelor's as soon as possible.

I bought my scholarly husband a fitted, long-sleeved, wine-colored Ralph Lauren Polo to wear under his cap and gown with those ugly, mandatory green pants. But not even the pants could convince me I was sitting in a prison auditorium when my husband walked across the stage in his silky black cap and gown, showing off his heart-stopping grin while the cap's tassel bounced just as happily from side to side. I stood up and roared his name along with all the Mitchells a few rows from the stage, our voices stretching his smile to its full capacity. The entire ceremony was mesmerizing and more inspiring than I ever imagined. Key speakers included inmates who left me choking back sobs as they shared stories just like Alex's about a time when they were young and lost, but grew up to find freedom and their identities in education. Cardinal Dolan lit up the stage with his natural jovial spirit and powerful commencement speech, doing God's work by reminding each man in a real cap and gown that he was not defined by his circumstances, but by the heart that the Lord blessed him with. My husband was following his heart when he applied to Bard College, determined to prove that he was meant for so much more and belonged at home with me, finding a solution to better the environment that raised us. My faith in him was reinforced the day of the graduation, and I felt more confident than ever that he was going to be okay with or without me.

I decided I would also follow my heart and leave to Los Angeles in the next six months. My mother's health was in good condition, as long as she didn't find out I was still married, so I continued to keep it from her until I saved up enough money and made the official move across the country.

I tried to get in as many trailer visits with Alex as I could before I left, and continued creating outrageous master plans in order to sneak off on my fatal adventures, despite being twenty-six years old and living on my own. I also had to start brainstorming a way to tell my husband I was leaving. It was something I thought I could easily say while watching him enjoy a home-cooked meal made by me, but the words only clung onto my tongue more fiercely. I needed guidance in all aspects of my life and sought refuge at church, confessing the same sins every week about how all I do is lie to my mother and everyone in my life that has no clue I'm married to a man in prison for murder, who I said I divorced but never really did and who I once cheated on with a man for three years and the man I cheated on him with never found out I was still married, and now I'm moving to California and I think I might really divorce my husband this time unless he still wants to be with me then okay, we can make it work and I'm sorry, but I also have to tell you about this one time I cheated on my biology quiz in high school. The priest and I were on a first-name basis by week three, and I was always surprised when he didn't hit me with fifty-thousand Hail Marys each time we met. Reconnecting to church made me tolerate myself a little more, but I still walked out of every mass in tears, begging for the strength to tell my mother the truth.

Stress started keeping me up at night, making me dysfunctional throughout the day. On one particular drive up for a trailer visit at Eastern Correctional, I had even fallen asleep at the wheel. One minute, I was worrying about Mom calling Mishie to confirm I was really staying with her in Boston for the weekend, and the next, I woke up in the middle of a Nascar donut at the entrance of a different exit that my 1993 Toyota Corolla had steered itself into after I lost consciousness. I was in pure shock when I opened my eyes to find myself in mid-spin, and the first words to leave my mouth were, "God is here! God is here! God is here!" The words exploded from my face before any thought could process as if someone else had said them for me. I had never known that kind of fear in my life but somehow knew that I was protected no matter what. I escaped wildly out of the seatbelt to check for the damages. The car came to a stop without crashing or even bumping into the exit's metal railing that was inches away. The dark marks on the pavement were evidence of a full rotation, but all my car took was a bunch of dead grass and weeds stuck in the rims of its two tires on the driver's side. I was safe, my car was safe, and there was no one on the road to witness the miracle with me.

Only a near-death experience could prepare me for what came next. The correctional officer had just finished processing my food and belongings with five other families when the FRP director walked into the waiting room to pull me aside and hand me a large manila envelope.

"This is confidential material that you and your husband need to discuss when you're ready," Ms. Bellis, a middle-aged Black woman with a toad-like voice, rubbed my back in a consoling manner that only stressed me out more.

"What is it?"

"It's not for me to say, but you can open it now and talk it over with your husband when you see him in a few. Maybe you wanna step into the restroom for some privacy," she kept speaking in a froggy tone that pitied me, and it made me want to curse her out for everything that had gone wrong in my life. Here she was, a stranger, giving me one more thing to worry about.

I needed to know what the manila envelope contained before I had a panic attack at Eastern Correctional and my visit was terminated. I walked into the restroom without hesitating another second to pull out a white sheet of paper. My husband had been tested positive for genital herpes.

The world stopped and started again two seconds later. I slipped the sheet of paper back inside its envelope and didn't say anything when I returned to the waiting room. There was nothing I could do but wait to see my husband.

Alex was the first one in green pants to appear out in the yard when the prison van pulled up filled with six families, and I checked for any sign that he might already know. I moved slower off the van than I ever had at any other trailer visit. His face beamed with pure joy when it saw mine, and I knew that I would have to tell him myself.

"What's wrong, baby girl?" His smile withered when it became obvious that my mood did not match his.

"We have to talk," I avoided his big eyes, gripping the envelope in my hand as we walked to trailer 4.

"What's that, Kaylah? Are you divorcing me again?" Alex eyeballed the envelope containing the worst news since my grandmother died. I followed him into the apartment, dropped the bags, sat on the couch and waited for him to open it. I dropped my head in my hands and just waited.

"Wow," was the first word, followed by more of the same thing while he tried to process. "Wow. Wow. Wow."

I kept my head in my hands, thinking of something to say, but the only thing that came to mind was *I'm sorry*, which had never helped me out before.

"This can't fuckin' be happening, bro. This can't be real. Why would they tell you before me?" Alex spoke to himself until he remembered I was in the room. "You never checked yourself with that dude?" I looked up to find his face just as distorted as the day I asked him for a divorce, but this time I thought I might be escorted out in handcuffs after he told a correctional officer I committed a crime.

"I didn't think to. He told me he was clean, and I trusted him. I've never even had any symptoms. Why does it automatically have to be me?" My head started to clear up and allowed myself to think of other possibilities.

"Oh, so now I'm gay all of a sudden?"

"I don't know. I don't know what you do 24/7. You coulda fucked a female officer, too. But if you've done anything, please just be honest," I pleaded, feeling the tingling attack of tears getting closer.

"Oh, my God, and I'm over here waiting for YOU to say, 'I'm sorry,' at a time when you really need to be FUCKIN' SAYIN' IT!" He slammed a hammer fist on the wooden coffee table, making me jump, and the papers fly to the floor.

"Did you do anything, Alexander?" He had lost a lot of his pride when going to prison, so anything else that could possibly threaten his character he was going to deny. I was afraid of the answer, afraid of loving him less, but I had to know.

"You're fuckin' crazy. I can't even stand to look at you right now. You *disgust* me. I shoulda left your dirty ass a long time ago," his words came through clenched teeth to burn through my soul. This anger was different from the day I presented him with divorce papers. That day had still seemed to be in his control. What came over Alex now was pure maliciousness that had been brewing since the night Branden pressed '3' and answered his phone call. My husband had brushed off my sins like they meant nothing, in hopes they would never come back to remind him of where he was and how he had no control over anything. It was the way he chose to cope while stuck behind bars, denying feeling any kind of pain just to keep moving. But Alex was hurting the whole time, and my broken promises would return to light a fire inside of him. He was ready to hurt me back.

"What?" I looked up from the tiny diamonds on my ring losing their luster with every one of his words. I sat in utter disbelief, the attack of the tears charging as I hugged my body, suddenly feeling cold and alone.

"You heard me. You really gonna sit here and act like I don't deserve to be pissed the FUCK OFF! You gave me herpes...Kaylah, out of all fuckin' people, a Riverdale HOE."

"I was in ONE fuckin' relationship you PIECE OF SHIT! And LIKE I SAID, I've never had any symptoms! IT'S NOT ME!" I choked through a waterfall, but I couldn't let him tarnish my name more than I had already done myself. He knew exactly how to hurt me.

"Well, if it's not you, and it's not me, I'ma call up Ms. Bellis and figure out where the FUCK THIS CAME FROM! And WHY THE FUCK they would tell you before tellin' me?! This shit doesn't make any fuckin' sense," Alex cursed to himself, stomping his big boots toward the emergency phone. "Is there anything else I should know before I call this lady?" He picked up the outdated phone in the living room, letting its curly cord dangle in the air before pressing any buttons.

"I kissed a guy in D.R.," I said without a second thought or glance in his direction, not knowing if I could have infected him in that way. I just didn't want there to be anything else left to hide.

"Of course you did," Alex dialed the real world, and a correctional officer answered. He attempted a more professional tone over the phone and requested to see Ms.

Bellis immediately in regards to the "information my wife just gave me." We waited in silence that felt like it would strangle me to death before the FRP director arrived. This was the punishment I had known was coming all along. God had spared my life on the highway to instead stamp me with a symbol that would remind me of every mistake for as long as I lived.

Five minutes later, a hasty hand gave an abrupt, urgent knock on the door that knocked on my heart in the same manner. Alex jumped to answer it after snatching the document and envelope from the floor and clenching them in one hand. Ms. Bellis walked in, followed by a husky middle-aged White woman wearing glasses, dressed in a white coat and pants. The woman in white opened her mouth first.

"Mr. Mitchell, I'm nurse Stevens. I handle all the clinical files for you guys in the facility, and there are a lot, a lot of files, Mr. Mitchell, and I am so, so, so sorry that I mixed yours up with someone else's. I don't know how it happened, but I can assure you it will never happen again. Please, please forgive me."

For the first time, I saw someone who could possibly be more sorry than me. The relief hugged every cell in my body and released all the water I had left to cry and cry, even more so when Ms. Bellis tried to console me again with a pitiful backrub.

"My apologies, Mrs. Mitchell. I hate that I was the messenger," the FRP director whispered her froggy voice into my ear, looking to reconcile.

"This is a serious mistake you made," Alex spoke to the nurse, barely moving his lips.

"We all make mistakes, Mr. Mitchell. I am truly sorry for mine," she said, taking the erroneous information from my husband's hand. I couldn't hear anything else after that. I bowed my head and continued sobbing on the couch, thanking God for saving me twice in one day. She made a mistake.

Alex closed the door and let a heavy sigh seep through his tight lips before turning to look at me; my head down, my hands and wedding ring seeking warmth between my thighs. His big boots slowly walked over to where I sat shivering on the couch, and he settled in beside me, stretching an arm up and over my head to embrace my shoulders.

"I'm so sorry," my husband kissed the side of my head.

"I'm moving to California."

The Hudson Line on the Metro-North had derailed while I was working one of my last shifts at Tommy Bahama. What would have been a thirty-minute ride back to Yonkers, instantly turned into an hour and some change as I headed toward the 4 train at Grand Central Terminal. It would be close to midnight by the time I arrived at Woodlawn train station in the Bronx, having to then hop on the Bee-Line bus to take me all the way home. I instinctively thought to call Branden for a ride to Riverdale from Woodlawn. Then, I remembered we were no longer together, and that I didn't deserve any of his favors. I called my stepfather instead, and he met me an hour later at the train station.

Rich had been hanging out with some friends on a Friday night and was just about to go back to his side of the street when my call came in. He always jumped at the opportunity to help me out.

"Thank you!" I greeted him when I jumped in the 2008 Dodge Avenger he shared with my mother.

"All good. It's a nice night to be out and about. How was work?" He sounded genuinely cheerful as he pulled away from the curb.

"Eh, I'm making money. That's all that matters," I answered, keeping the thought of being three-thousand dollars short of my California savings goal in the far back of my head.

"That's good. Next month, right?"

"Yeah, first week in June," I said with conviction, determined not to let my date change for the third time.

"Wow, right around the corner."

"Yup. I'm excited," I lied. I was terrified. I had no place to live, no car, no job, and less than five-thousand dollars in my savings account. I didn't know what I was doing. All I knew was that I had to go.

"I'm excited for you. Your mom, you already know, she's scared to lose her baby. But I think she's also kinda relieved, to be honest. She thought you might've been messin' with Alex again. I told her if you flyin' across the country, you ain't got no strings attached here. You know, anything to keep her blood pressure down." He talked with a shoulder lean to the left and drove with only his right hand on top of the steering wheel, keeping his eyes on the road. It hadn't even crossed my mind that Mom could start suspecting something now, but it made sense because my trailer visits and weak stories had doubled since breaking up with Branden. I was glad to be leaving, so she didn't have to worry anymore.

"Yeah, she's nuts. Please take care of her. She's always stressing for no reason." I kept my eyes on the window.

"I know. I know. And I definitely will," he took a few beats, probably filling his head with memories of his wife, good and bad, since the day they met. "So, acting, huh? That's what you lookin' to do out there?"

"Yup, that's the plan."

"Yeah, you always loved entertaining a crowd. But writing? You know that used to be your thing, too." Sometimes, I forgot how long my stepfather had been around.

"I don't know, we'll see. I'm hoping to find some inspiration to do everything I want while I'm there," I spoke truthfully, imagining opportunities that would make my dreams come true in the first thirty days. I worried about how much longer I would be imagining.

"Well, I'm always rooting for you. You always been a go-getter. Proud of you."

My reply to his warm praise hit the tip of my tongue, but couldn't make it out when something caught my eye up ahead. I wrinkled my face, trying to get a clearer view so that I could confirm my eyes had only been playing tricks on me. Then, I heard Rich speak again, and I knew that my eyes weren't deceiving me and that my stepfather was shaken up by the same distant vision.

"What the fuck?" He couldn't gather his thoughts in time, speeding up faster and faster until I thought for sure he was about to end my mother's life right before my eyes. My heart dropped when the car finally stopped on top of the sidewalk, my eyelids slowly unfolding to find her still standing only a few inches away from the grille. Rich put the car in park and ferociously removed his seatbelt to jump out, forgetting about me or anything but the sight before him.

"WHAT THE FUCK IS THIS, RAYSA?!" He approached my mother with an overpowering stance that made me think he was seconds away from plummeting her to the ground. I cautiously stepped out of the crooked car parked on the sidewalk.

"Aye, back the FUCK UP. You almost just killed her you crazy muthafucker," the stranger standing next to my mother spoke to Rich first, stepping in front of her for protection. Mom was in a state of shock, silently gripping a camo jacket around her shoulders that I knew didn't belong to her.

"MIND YOUR FUCKIN' BUSINESS, LUSITO!" Rich stepped closer to the stranger, antagonizing him with his broad chest and significant height difference.

"RELAX. I took her out for somethin' to eat. Relax, my nigga." The stranger was a skinny, light-skinned Latino with a long head and dark eyes that looked in my direction when I closed the car door. "Aayyyee, Baby Kaylah. How are you, mama?" The stranger knew my name, but I had never seen him before. I had only heard of him, like a folktale come to life.

"ARE Y'ALL FUCKIN'?" Rich looked over Lusito's shoulder, clearly directing his question to my mother. My stepfather snatched Lusito's eyes away from me, and they turned more violent.

"Like I said, we went out to eat, my nigga. Ain't nothin' goin' on."

"I'M NOT YOUR FUCKIN' NIGGA, YOU BITCH ASS MUTHAFUCKER! COME HERE, RAYSA!" Rich shoved Lusito to the side like he was made out of cardboard and grabbed a fierce hold of my mother's shoulder, making her shriek with fear.

"DON'T FUCKIN' TOUCH HER!" Lusito pointed a small, black gun at my stepfather, stopping everyone dead in their tracks. South Broadway was a ghost town at 1:00 a.m., leaving my mother and me as the only witnesses.

"LUSITO, NO!" Mom screamed, facing me from the other side of the arm holding the gun, seeing the same two men glare at each other that I saw.

"You hurt her, I'll kill you," Lusito's voice lowered in volume, speaking to no one else but Rich.

"Put the gun down, bitch. And leave my fuckin' wife alone."

Lusito didn't say a word. Instead, the sound of the safety clicking off spoke more than enough for him. I was in a bubble, not even able to hear my mother screaming for help at the top of her lungs in a neighborhood nobody cared about. The world was the kind of silent no one ever knew until they died. I suddenly loved and appreciated every flaw in my body and every day I had known pain since being born because it all prepared me for that moment. I loved everyone in my life, and I wanted to tell them all how sorry I was for everything I had done, but I finally got the chance to show them instead by coming out of my bubble and stepping in front of my stepfather before the trigger was pulled, before I could hear a bullet rule the world one last time. All I could hear was my name after that. My name. My name. My name. Over and over again. It was like I died and went to heaven.

"Kaylah!" Alex's pretty face waited for me on the other side of my eyelids. He was more beautiful than ever before, even with big, brown eyes watered with worry. Didn't he know? There was no need to worry anymore. We were free. We were together. Did I not tell him? That everything was okay?

My bad dream came a week after my mother confessed to having an affair with her first true love, a man before my stepfather, before my father, who also left her behind after falling victim to the system. They would hold hands again twenty-seven years later when she was married with three children. My mother told me her story while she cried and cried. Talking on and on about how sorry she was and how she made a mistake, and how she loved Rich so much and that it would never happen again. But she had to tell me and get it off her chest before it killed her. Then I told her it was okay, that she was human, that I loved her, and that I was still married. What I didn't say was, "I'm sorry."

Alex shook me out of the dream on our last trailer before I flew to California, the first trailer my mother knew of. She knew where I was and who I was with for the first time in seven years. There was no need to worry about anything else for as long as I lived. I wrapped my arms around Alex's neck and kissed his perfect lips, appreciating my husband with a clear head and a pure heart for the first time since I was fifteen, and most likely the last.

I boarded my flight to LAX three days later with one suitcase and one carry-on where my Winnie the Pooh jewelry box was tucked safely inside. I had no idea what waited for me three-thousand miles away from home, or if I would ever be back. All I knew was that I was whole, I was free, and that God loved me.

Kaylah Pantaleón, a Dominican-American native of Yonkers, New York has had a passion for writing from an early age. She developed a true love for the written word at the tender age of four, when she began to devotedly write letters to her imprisoned father. As a child of divorce and an incarcerated father, she has used her first-hand experiences to pen rich, authentic award-winning tales. Her writing acknowledgements include the 2006 Sarah Lawrence Fulbright Summer Scholarship for Writing Award; the 2007 Harvard Radcliffe Book Award; the 2007 Latino Caucus Scholarship Award for Best Essay; the 2007 American Association of University Women Writers Award; the 2008 New York's Most Influential Latina Award; and the most notable being the 2006 Oprah's National High School Essay Contest Finalist awarded by media titan, Oprah Winfrey. Now a graduate of Emerson College and a resident of Sherman Oaks, California, Kaylah, a budding actress and author, invites readers into her world to share her trials and triumphs since appearing on *The Oprah Winfrey Show*. Oprah Girl is Kaylah's debut book. Follow her on Instagram @kaylahpantaleon.

CPSIA information can be obtained
at www.ICGtesting.com
Printed in the USA
FFOW04n1533030417
34112FF